# VIKINGS™

## UPRISING



MGM TITAN COMICS

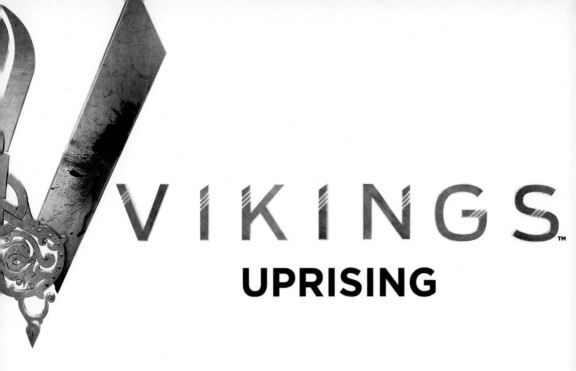

# VIKINGS™

# UPRISING

**WRITER**
## CAVAN SCOTT

**ART**
## DANIEL INDRO

**COLORS**
## KEVIN ENHART

**LETTERS**
## JIM CAMPBELL

**EDITOR**
## NEIL D. EDWARDS

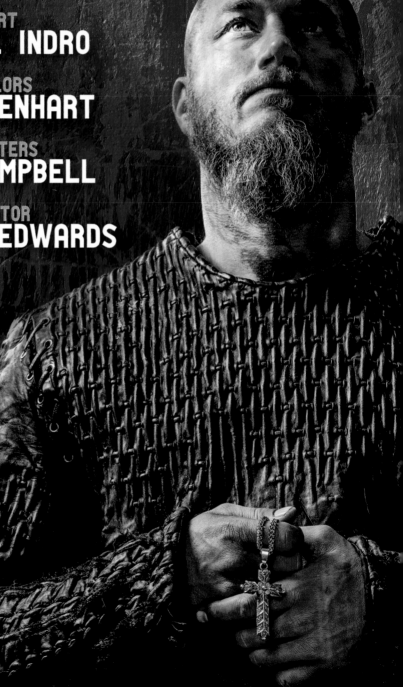

**TITAN COMICS**

Senior Editor **Martin Eden**

Senior Production Controller **Jackie Flook**
Production Controller **Peter James**

Production Supervisor **Maria Pearson**
Art Director **Oz Browne**

Head of Rights **Jenny Boyce**

Publishing Manager **Darryl Tothill**

Publishing Director **Chris Teather**

Operations Director **Leigh Baulch**

Executive Director **Vivian Cheung**
Publisher **Nick Landau**

**WWW.TITAN-COMICS.COM**

**Become a fan on Facebook.com/comicstitan**
**Follow us on Twitter@ComicsTitan**

For more information on Rights, contact Jenny Boyce at jenny.boyce@titanemail.com

ISBN: 9781785858598



ver artist: Claudia Caranfa. End page artist: Simon Myers. Back cover artist: Chris Wahl.

CIP catalogue record for this title is available from the British Library.

10 9 8 7 6 5 4 3 2 1

Printed in China.

MGM

**This story takes place during Season 4 Part 1, episode 10 of the *Vikings* TV show.**

# THE PANTHEON OF CHARACTERS

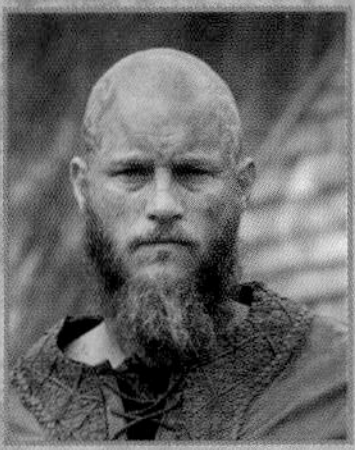

## RAGNAR LOTHBROK

Risen from being a simple farmer to a Viking raider and king, Ragnar has become a living legend. But recent events have taken their toll on him, leaving him a broken man – not least the killing of his advisor Athelstan, his addiction to a herbal medicine thanks to the slave girl Yidu, and his murder of her.

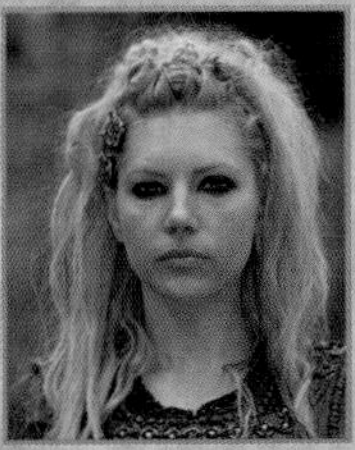

## LAGERTHA

Once the tempestuous wife of Ragnar, the two became estranged, during which time she was made Earl of Hedeby and remains a powerful shield maiden. She joined Ragnar on his forays to England and the raid on Paris, but after recent events is skeptical that her former husband is the man he once was.

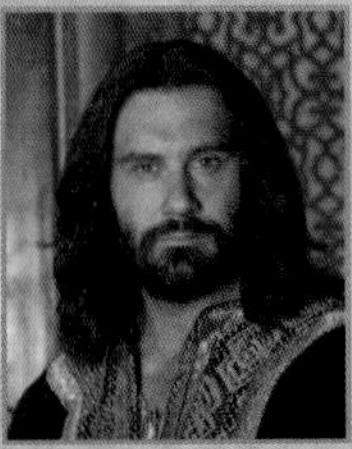

## ROLLO

Ragnar's brother; he is a powerful warrior, but has a troubled relationship with Ragnar, his feelings of envy and jealousy leading him to betray his brother more than once. Now Rollo is married to the Frankish princess Gisla, and his betrayals still enrage some, notably Floki.

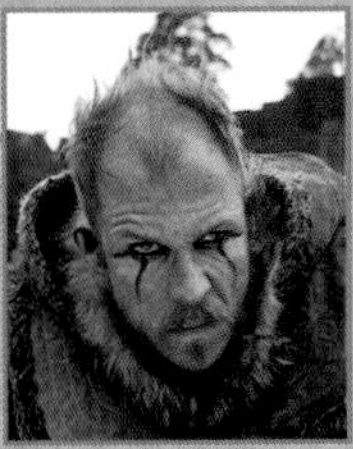

## FLOKI

A skilled shipwright and engineer, Floki's genius borders on madness. A close advisor to Ragnar, he is tormented by his friend's closeness to the English king and his increasing acceptance of Christianity. Floki has been estranged from his friend since he killed Ragnar's confidant, the former slave Athelstan.

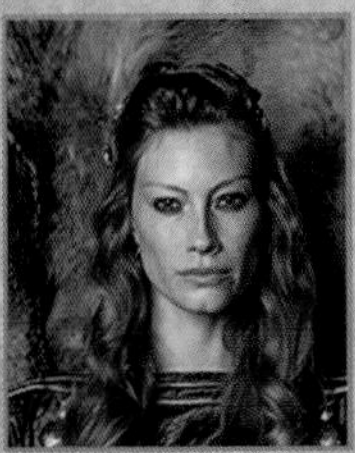

## QUEEN ASLAUG

Ragnar's second wife, she has an illustrious family history, as well as the gift of a völva – to see the future. She is the mother of Ragnar's crippled son, Ivar, who is prophesied to become a great leader. The couple's relationship has been strained by their infidelities and Ragnar's current state of mind.

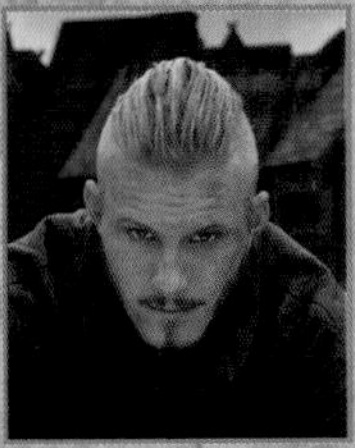

## BJORN IRONSIDE

Ragnar's eldest son by his first wife Lagertha, Bjorn idolizes his father and wants to be a renowned warrior and leader like him. The events of the Paris raid have affected Bjorn's bond with his father, as he struggles to understand why Ragnar is so broken.

# CHAPTER 1

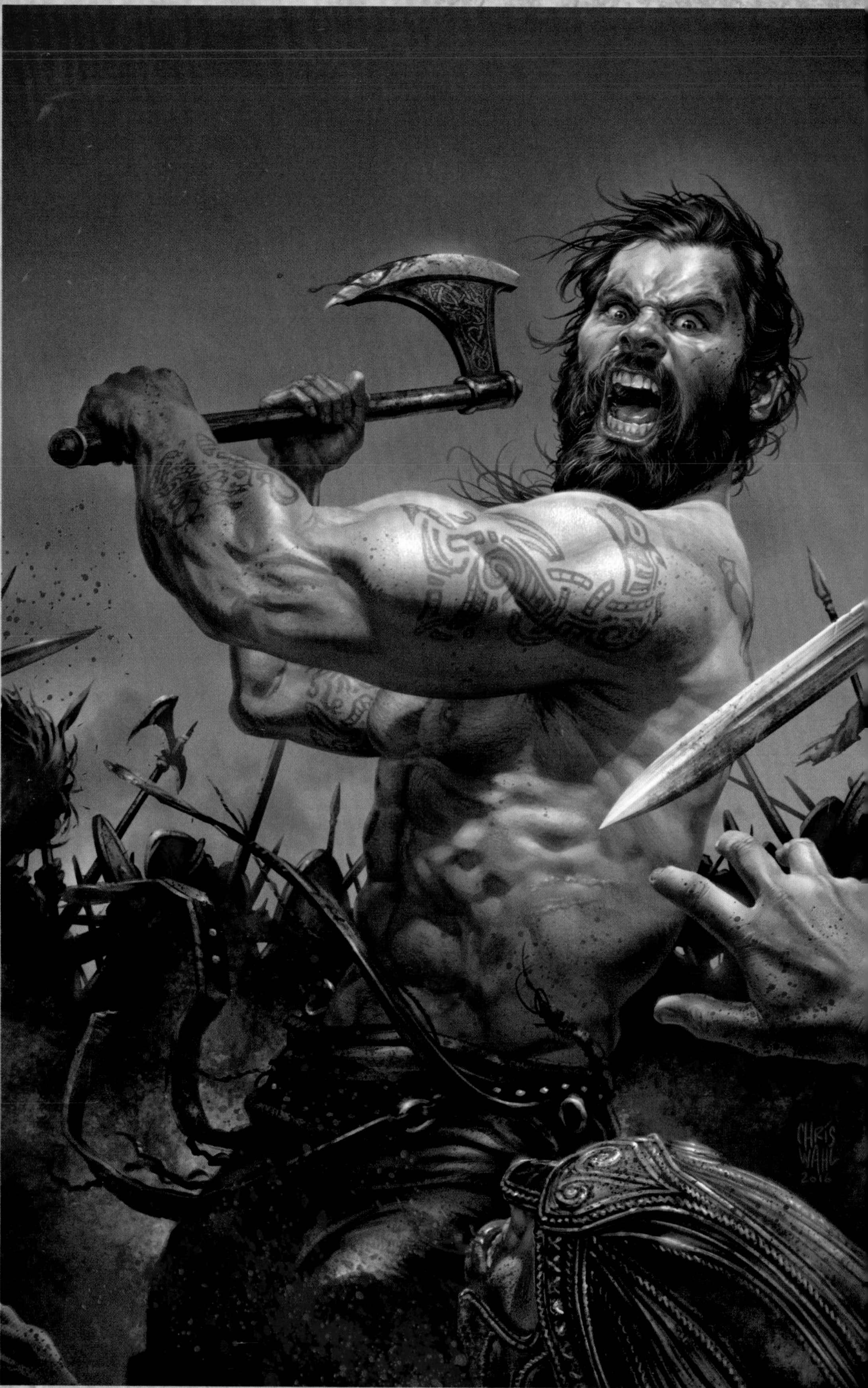
CHRIS WAHL 2016

ILLUSTRATION BY CHRIS WAHL

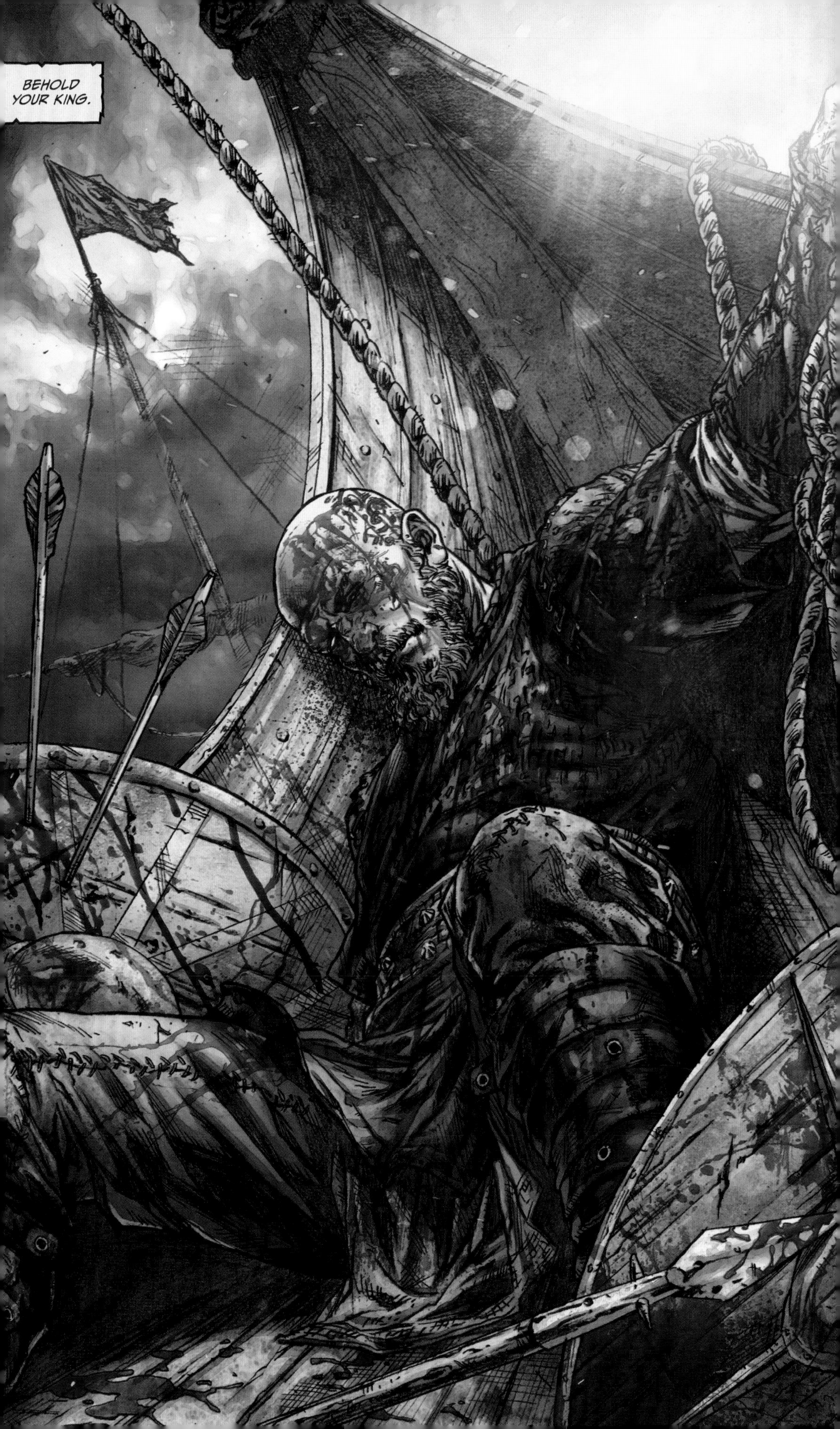
BEHOLD YOUR KING.

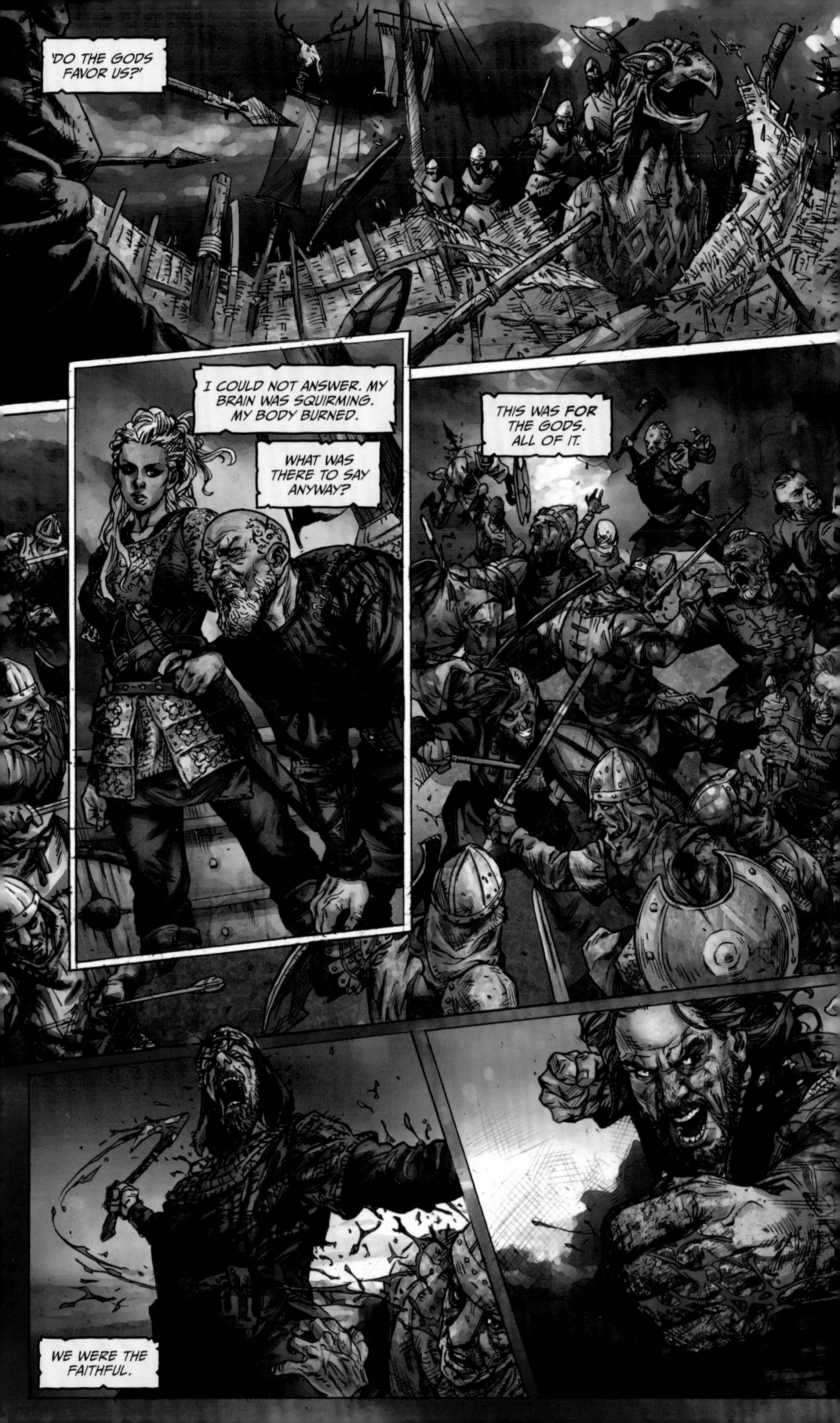
'DO THE GODS FAVOR US?'
I COULD NOT ANSWER. MY BRAIN WAS SQUIRMING. MY BODY BURNED.
WHAT WAS THERE TO SAY ANYWAY?
THIS WAS FOR THE GODS. ALL OF IT.
WE WERE THE FAITHFUL.

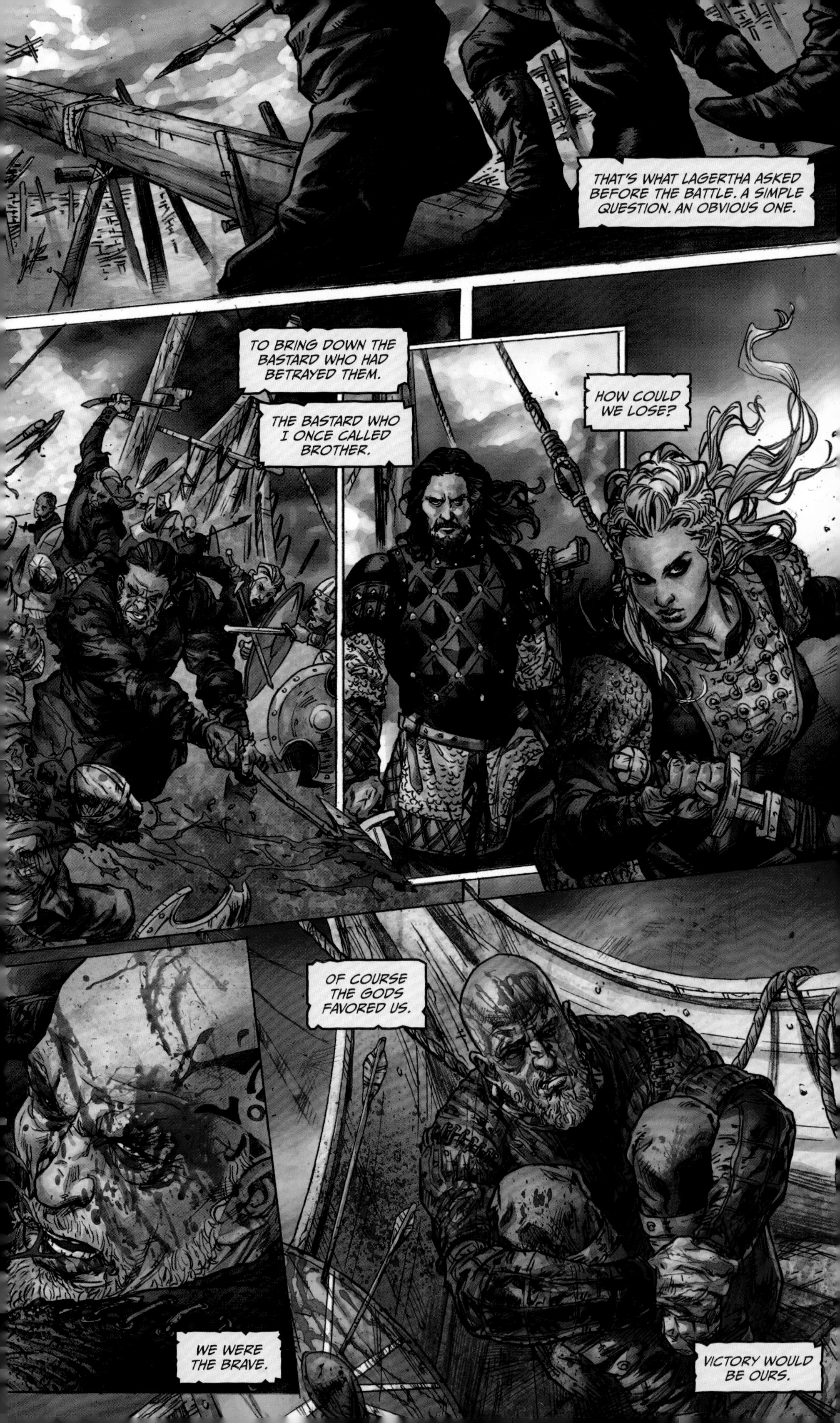
THAT'S WHAT LAGERTHA ASKED BEFORE THE BATTLE. A SIMPLE QUESTION. AN OBVIOUS ONE.
TO BRING DOWN THE BASTARD WHO HAD BETRAYED THEM.
THE BASTARD WHO I ONCE CALLED BROTHER.
HOW COULD WE LOSE?
OF COURSE THE GODS FAVORED US.
WE WERE THE BRAVE.
VICTORY WOULD BE OURS.

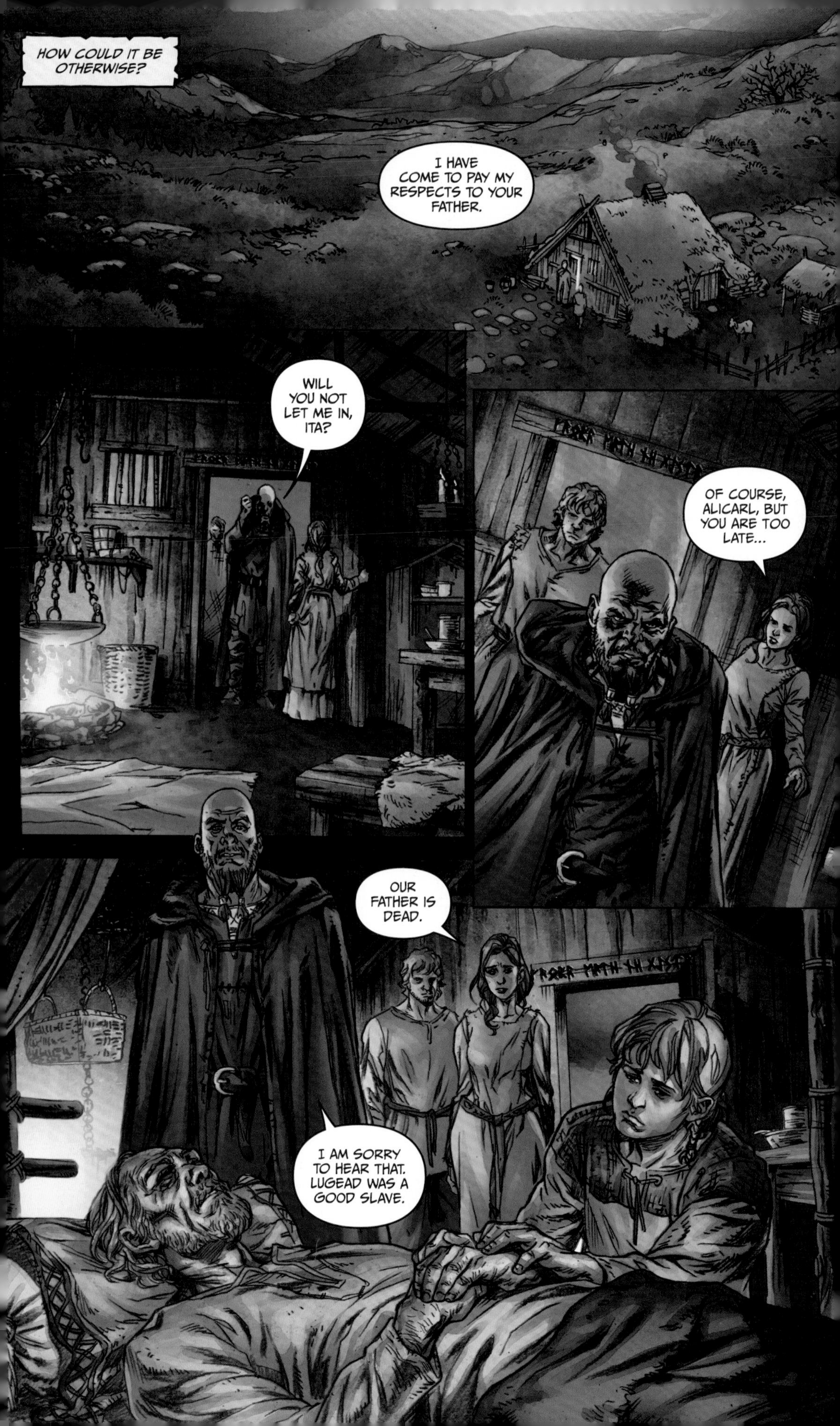
HOW COULD IT BE OTHERWISE?
I HAVE COME TO PAY MY RESPECTS TO YOUR FATHER.
WILL YOU NOT LET ME IN, ITA?
OF COURSE, ALICARL, BUT YOU ARE TOO LATE...
OUR FATHER IS DEAD.
I AM SORRY TO HEAR THAT. LUGEAD WAS A GOOD SLAVE.

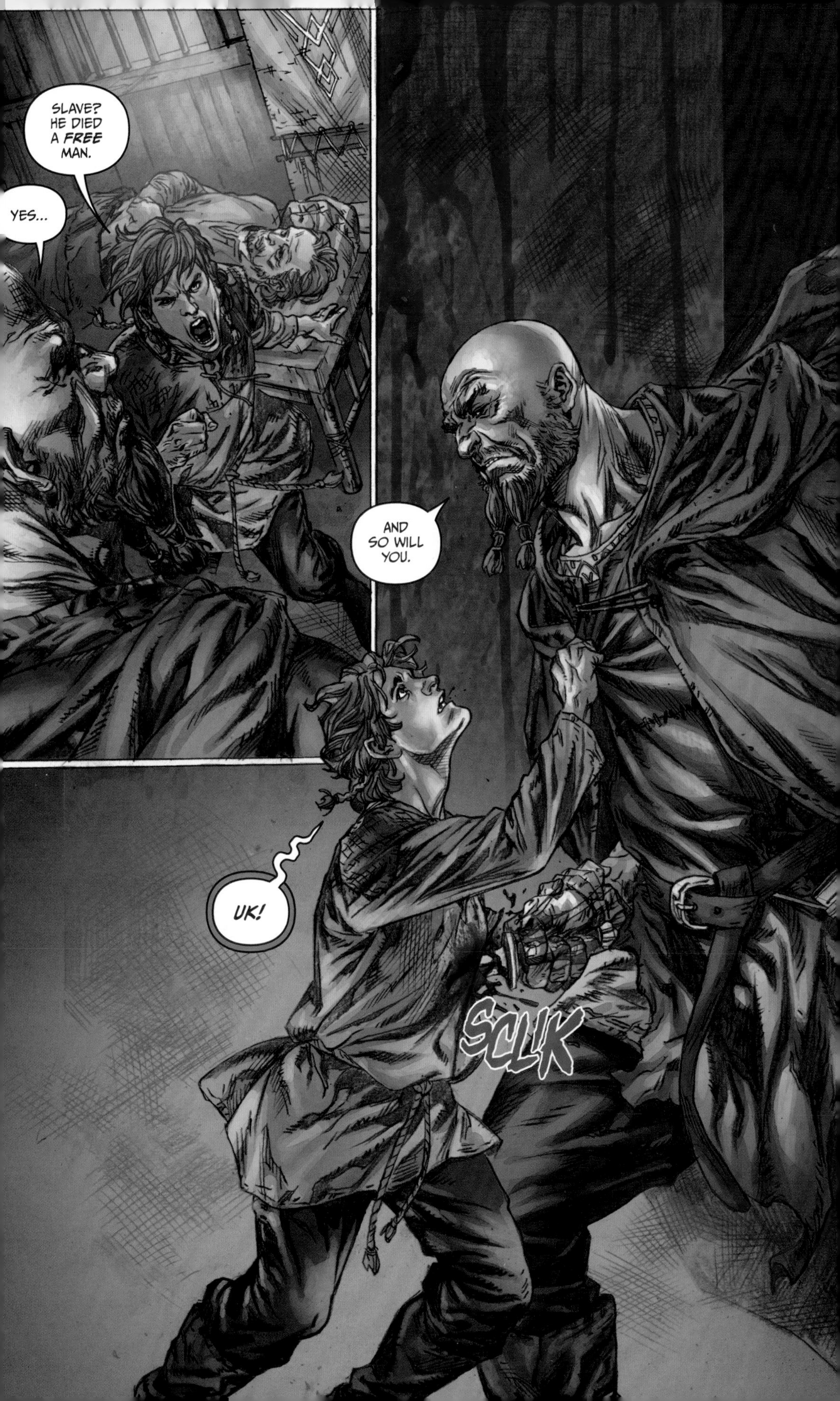
SLAVE? HE DIED A FREE MAN.
YES...
AND SO WILL YOU.
UK!
SCLIK

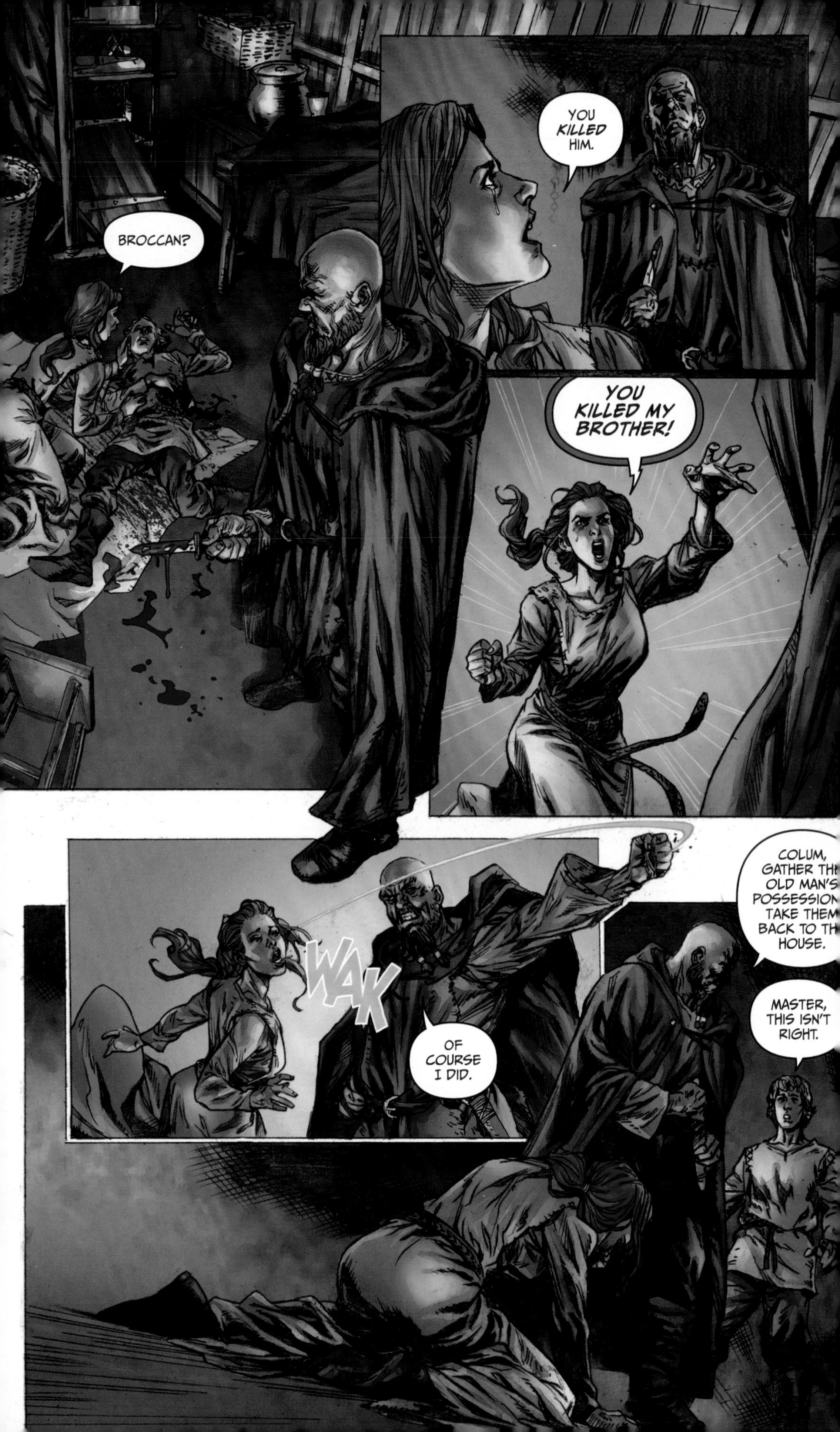
BROCCAN?
YOU KILLED HIM.
YOU KILLED MY BROTHER!
WAK
OF COURSE I DID.
COLUM, GATHER TH OLD MAN'S POSSESSION TAKE THEM BACK TO TH HOUSE.
MASTER, THIS ISN'T RIGHT.

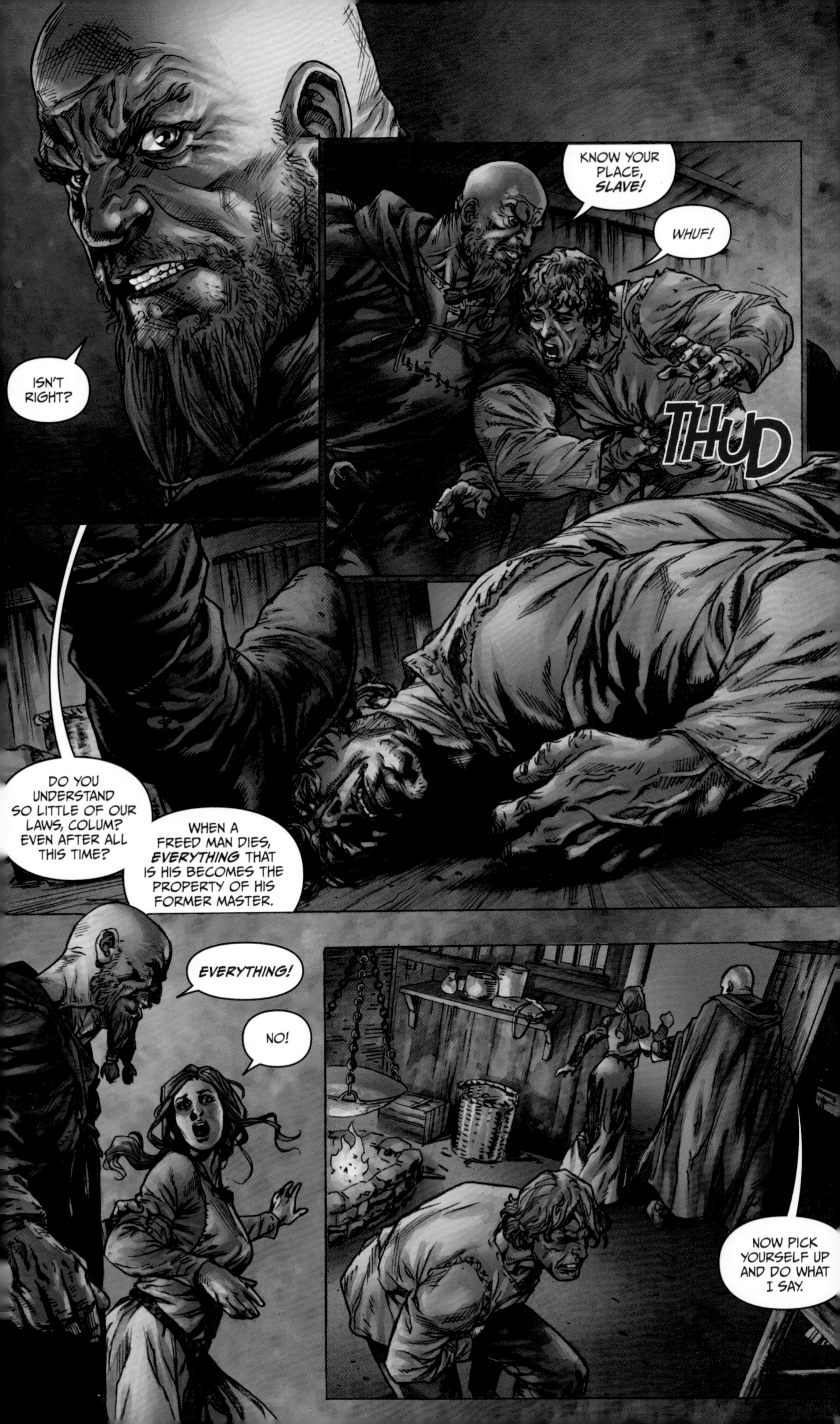
ISN'T RIGHT?
KNOW YOUR PLACE, SLAVE!
WHUF!
THUD
DO YOU UNDERSTAND SO LITTLE OF OUR LAWS, COLUM? EVEN AFTER ALL THIS TIME?
WHEN A FREED MAN DIES, EVERYTHING THAT IS HIS BECOMES THE PROPERTY OF HIS FORMER MASTER.
EVERYTHING!
NO!
NOW PICK YOURSELF UP AND DO WHAT I SAY.

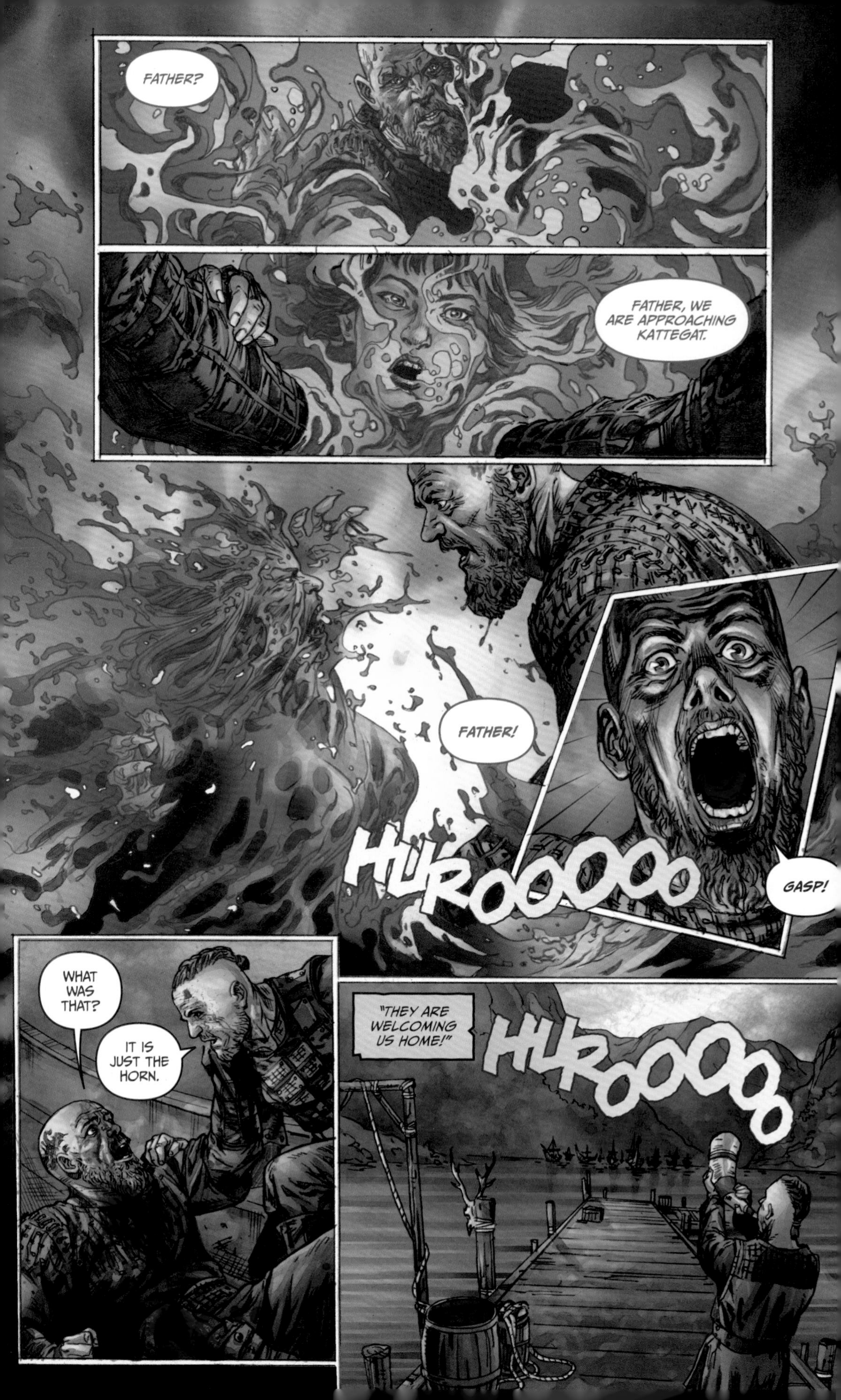
FATHER?
FATHER, WE ARE APPROACHING KATTEGAT.
FATHER!
HUROOOOO
GASP!
WHAT WAS THAT?
IT IS JUST THE HORN.
"THEY ARE WELCOMING US HOME!"
HUROOOOO

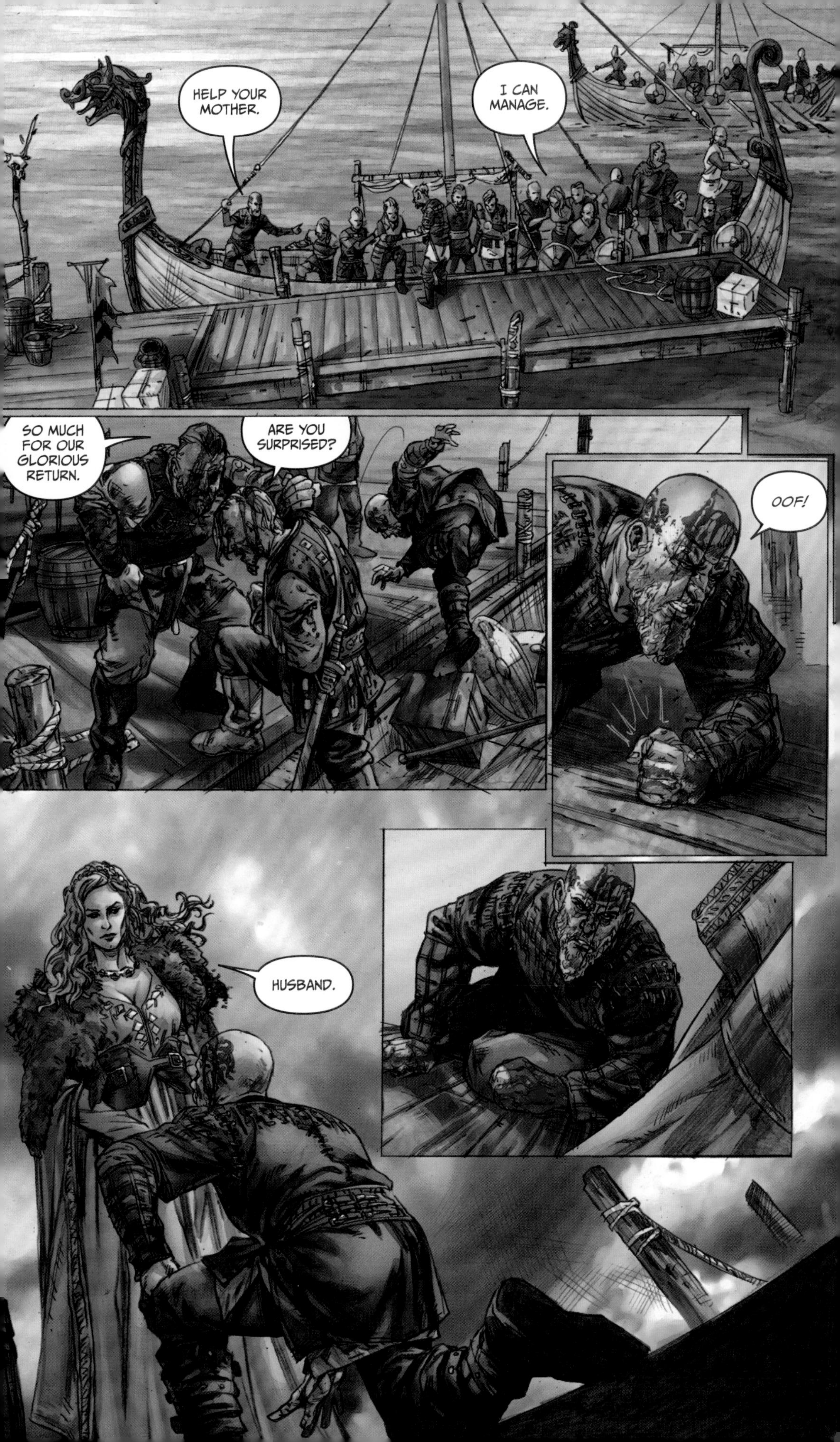
HELP YOUR MOTHER.
I CAN MANAGE.
SO MUCH FOR OUR GLORIOUS RETURN.
ARE YOU SURPRISED?
OOF!
HUSBAND.

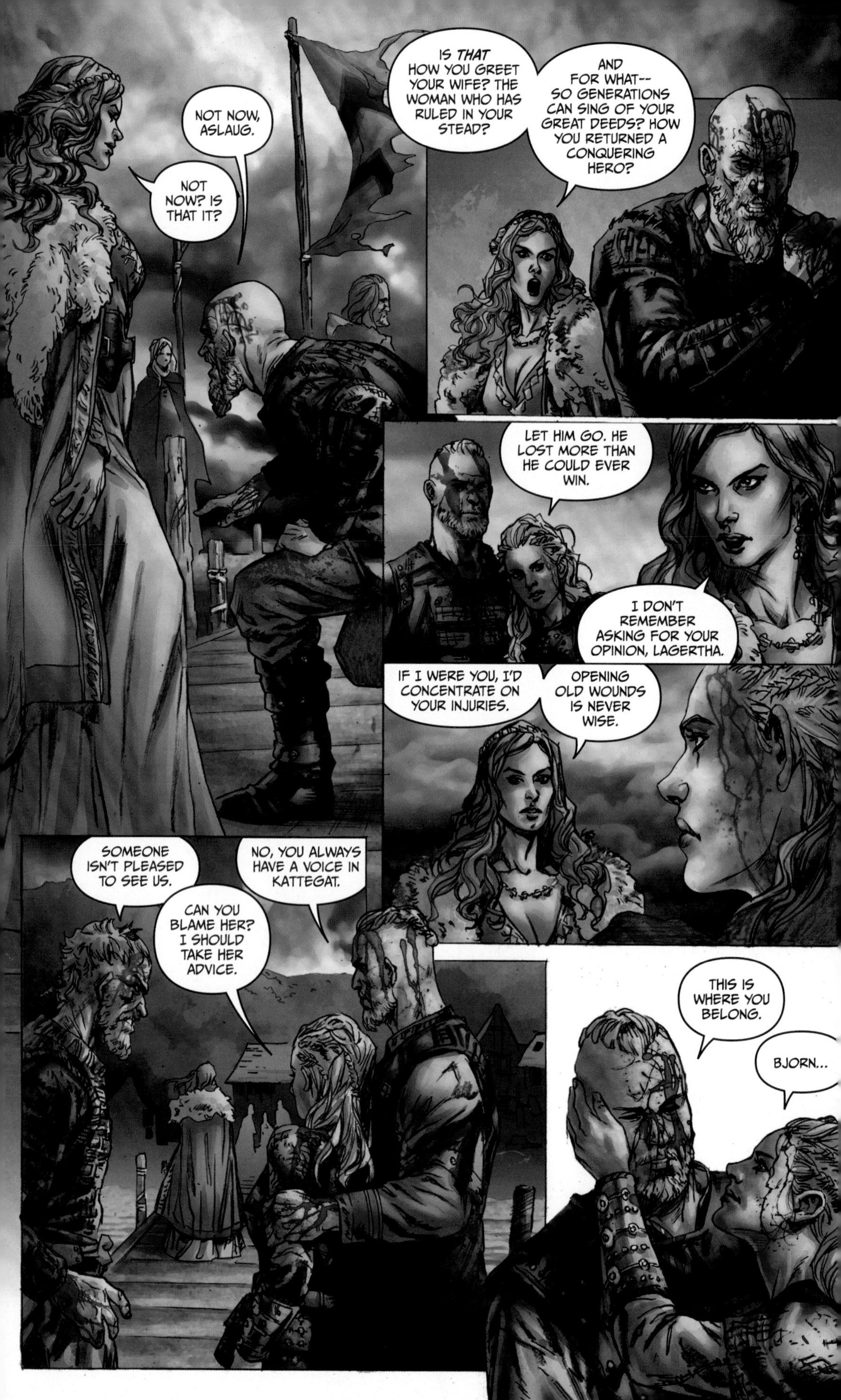
NOT NOW, ASLAUG.
NOT NOW? IS THAT IT?
IS THAT HOW YOU GREET YOUR WIFE? THE WOMAN WHO HAS RULED IN YOUR STEAD?
AND FOR WHAT-- SO GENERATIONS CAN SING OF YOUR GREAT DEEDS? HOW YOU RETURNED A CONQUERING HERO?
LET HIM GO. HE LOST MORE THAN HE COULD EVER WIN.
I DON'T REMEMBER ASKING FOR YOUR OPINION, LAGERTHA.
IF I WERE YOU, I'D CONCENTRATE ON YOUR INJURIES.
OPENING OLD WOUNDS IS NEVER WISE.
SOMEONE ISN'T PLEASED TO SEE US.
CAN YOU BLAME HER? I SHOULD TAKE HER ADVICE.
NO, YOU ALWAYS HAVE A VOICE IN KATTEGAT.
THIS IS WHERE YOU BELONG.
BJORN...

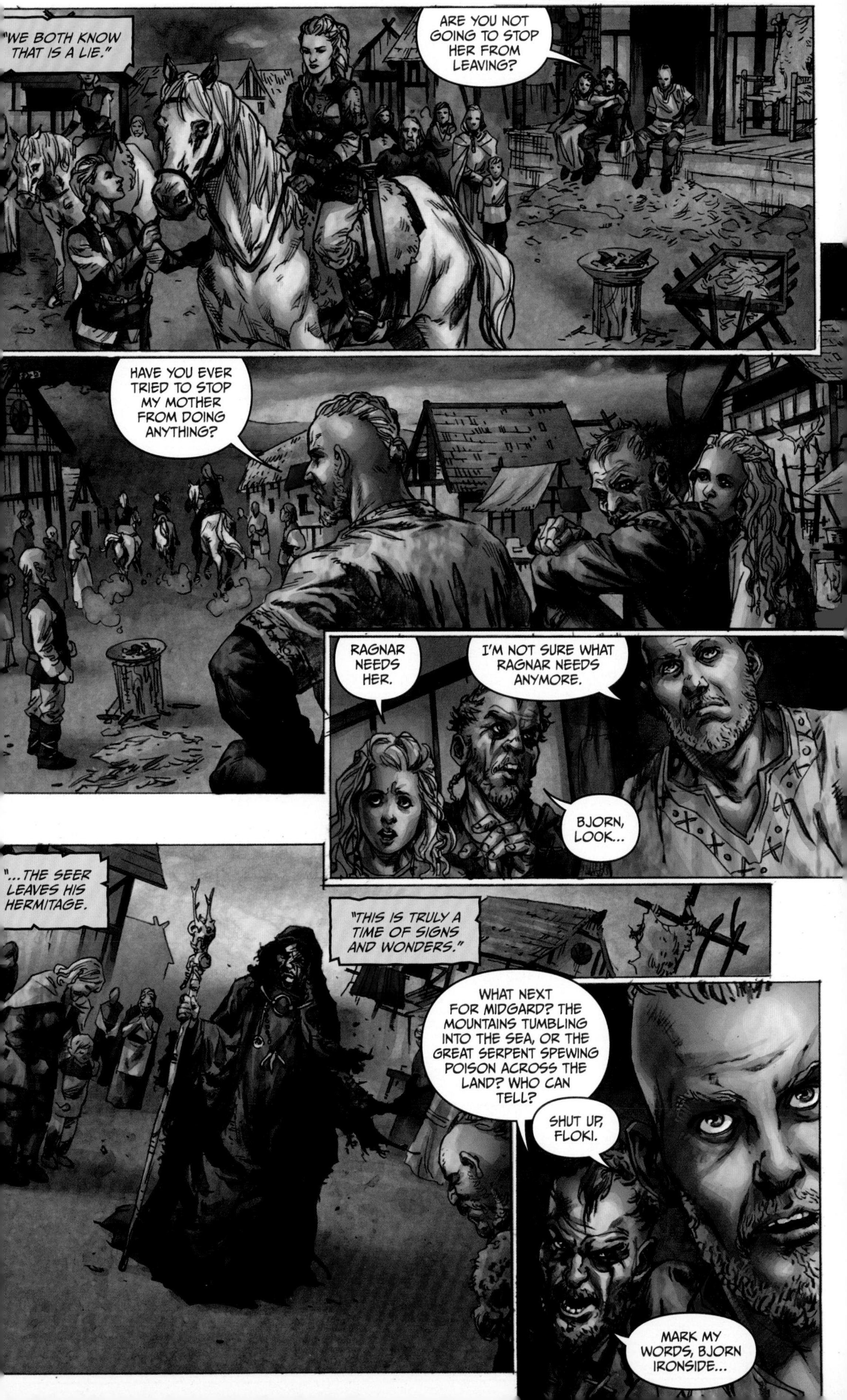
"WE BOTH KNOW THAT IS A LIE."
ARE YOU NOT GOING TO STOP HER FROM LEAVING?
HAVE YOU EVER TRIED TO STOP MY MOTHER FROM DOING ANYTHING?
RAGNAR NEEDS HER.
I'M NOT SURE WHAT RAGNAR NEEDS ANYMORE.
BJORN, LOOK...
"...THE SEER LEAVES HIS HERMITAGE.
"THIS IS TRULY A TIME OF SIGNS AND WONDERS."
WHAT NEXT FOR MIDGARD? THE MOUNTAINS TUMBLING INTO THE SEA, OR THE GREAT SERPENT SPEWING POISON ACROSS THE LAND? WHO CAN TELL?
SHUT UP, FLOKI.
MARK MY WORDS, BJORN IRONSIDE...

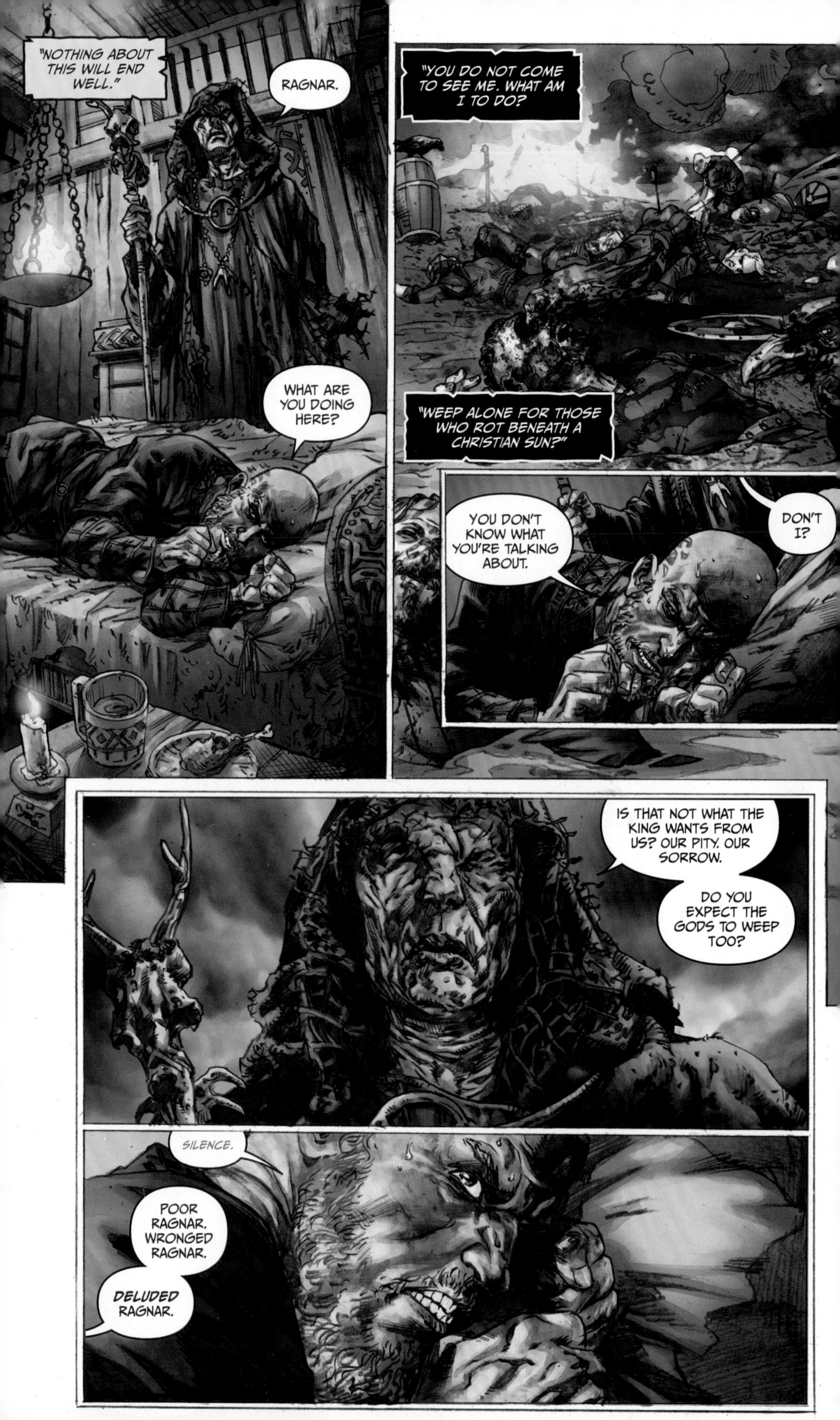
"NOTHING ABOUT THIS WILL END WELL."
RAGNAR.
WHAT ARE YOU DOING HERE?
"YOU DO NOT COME TO SEE ME. WHAT AM I TO DO?
"WEEP ALONE FOR THOSE WHO ROT BENEATH A CHRISTIAN SUN?"
YOU DON'T KNOW WHAT YOU'RE TALKING ABOUT.
DON'T I?
IS THAT NOT WHAT THE KING WANTS FROM US? OUR PITY. OUR SORROW.
DO YOU EXPECT THE GODS TO WEEP TOO?
SILENCE.
POOR RAGNAR. WRONGED RAGNAR.
DELUDED RAGNAR.

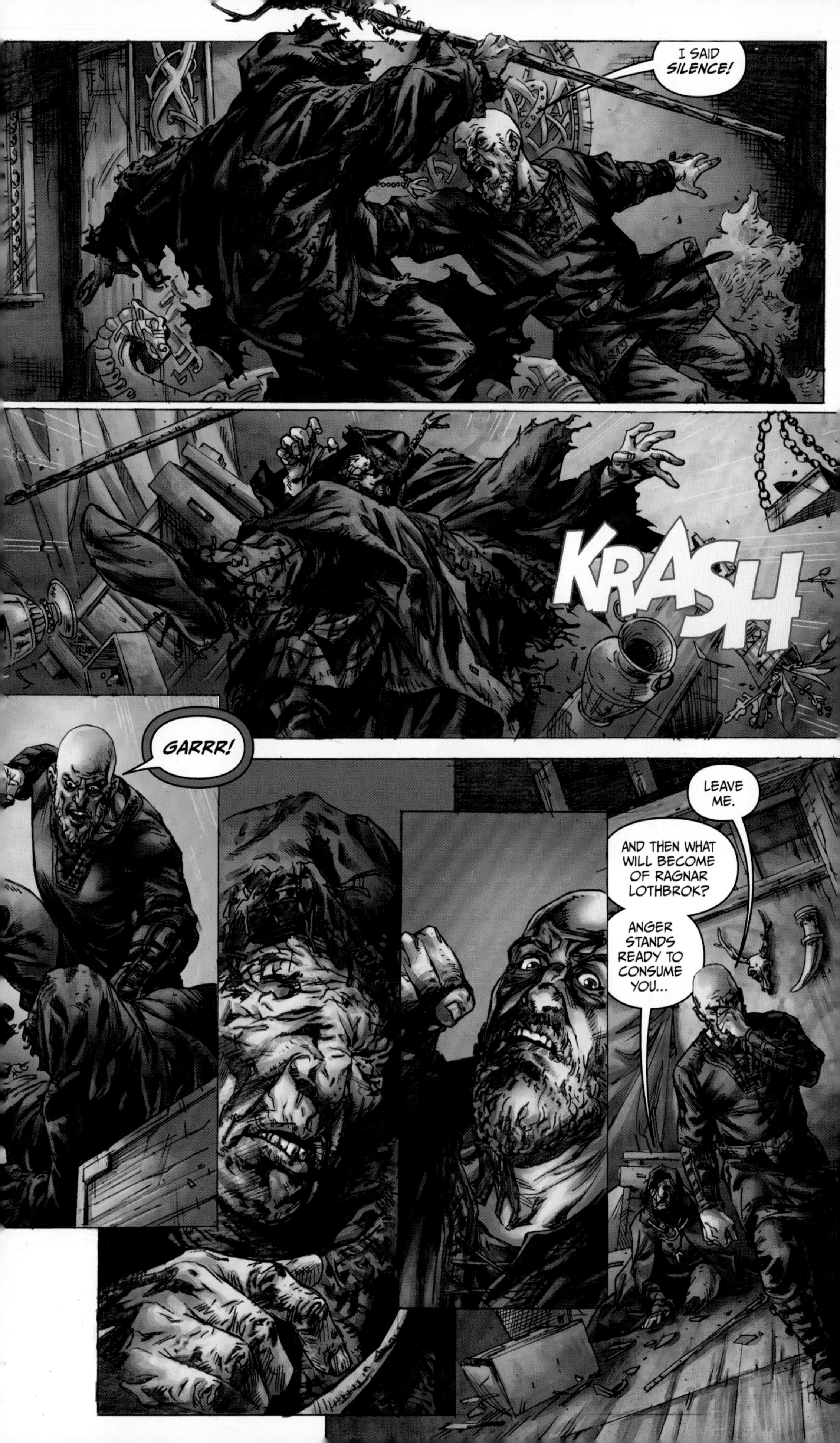
I SAID SILENCE!
KRASH
GARRR!
LEAVE ME.
AND THEN WHAT WILL BECOME OF RAGNAR LOTHBROK?
ANGER STANDS READY TO CONSUME YOU...

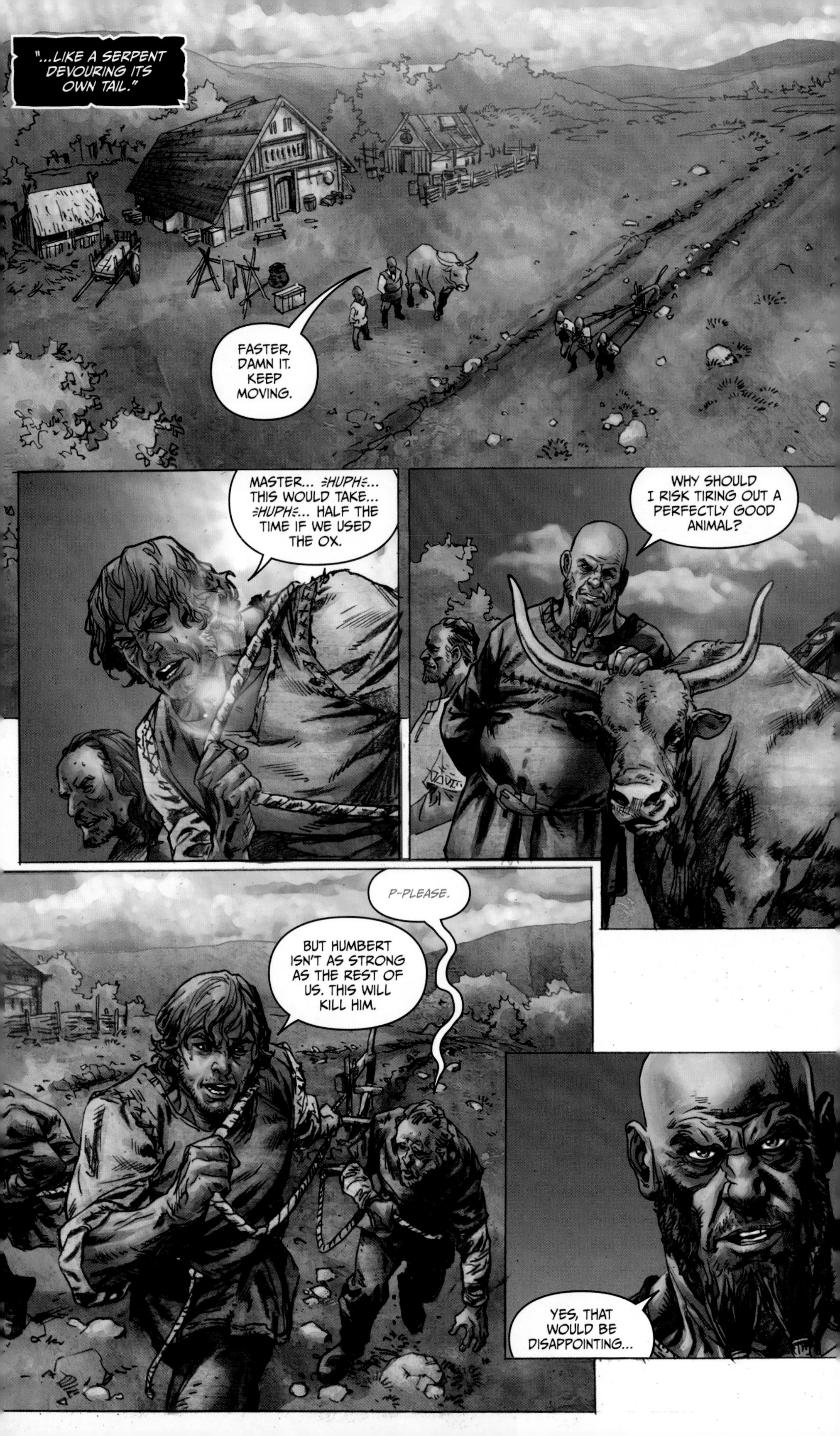
"...LIKE A SERPENT DEVOURING ITS OWN TAIL."
FASTER, DAMN IT. KEEP MOVING.
MASTER... =HUPH=... THIS WOULD TAKE... =HUPH=... HALF THE TIME IF WE USED THE OX.
WHY SHOULD I RISK TIRING OUT A PERFECTLY GOOD ANIMAL?
BUT HUMBERT ISN'T AS STRONG AS THE REST OF US. THIS WILL KILL HIM.
P-PLEASE.
YES, THAT WOULD BE DISAPPOINTING...

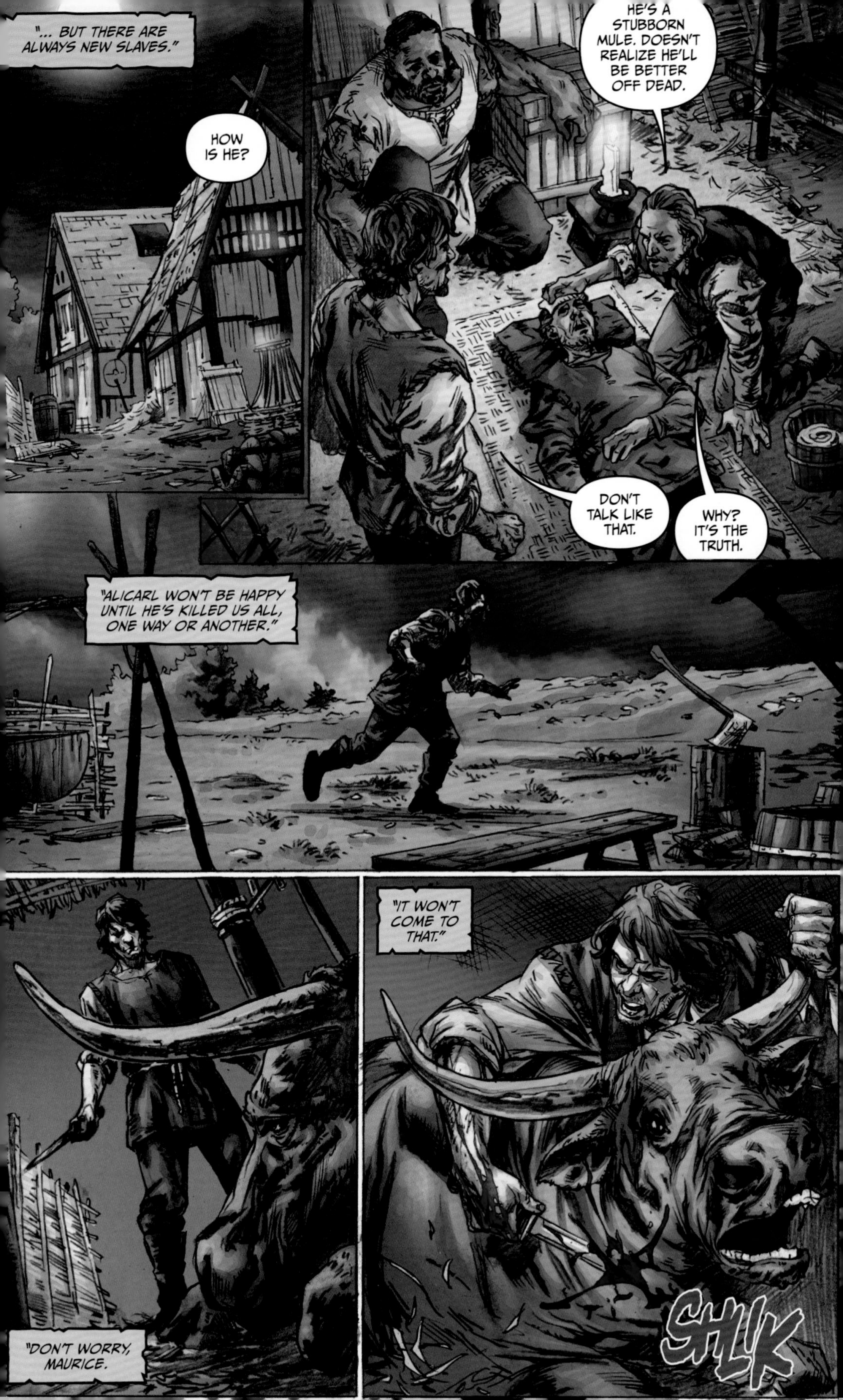
"... BUT THERE ARE ALWAYS NEW SLAVES."
HOW IS HE?
HE'S A STUBBORN MULE. DOESN'T REALIZE HE'LL BE BETTER OFF DEAD.
DON'T TALK LIKE THAT.
WHY? IT'S THE TRUTH.
"ALICARL WON'T BE HAPPY UNTIL HE'S KILLED US ALL, ONE WAY OR ANOTHER."
"DON'T WORRY, MAURICE.
"IT WON'T COME TO THAT."
SHLIK

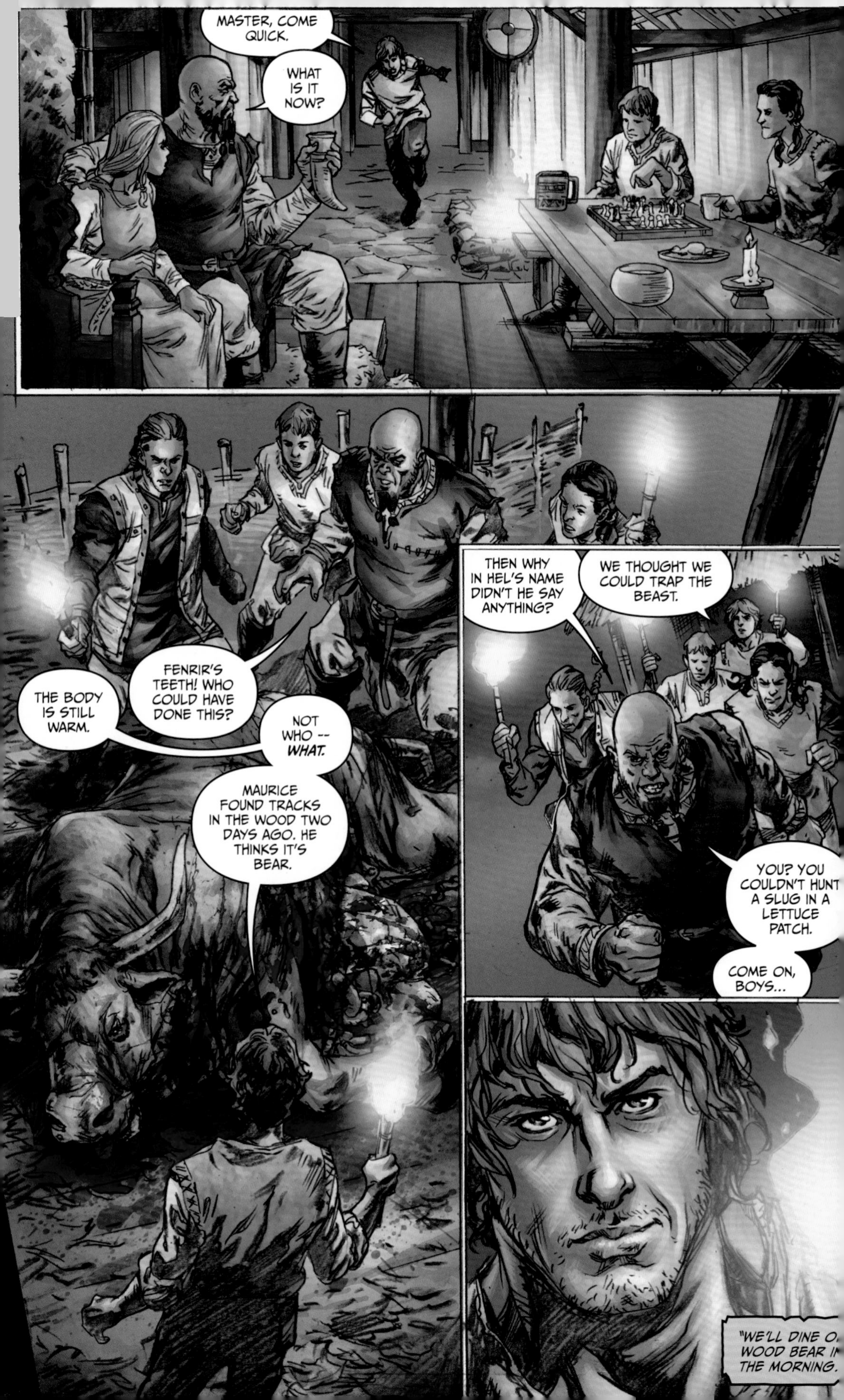
MASTER, COME QUICK.
WHAT IS IT NOW?
FENRIR'S TEETH! WHO COULD HAVE DONE THIS?
THE BODY IS STILL WARM.
NOT WHO -- *WHAT.*
MAURICE FOUND TRACKS IN THE WOOD TWO DAYS AGO. HE THINKS IT'S BEAR.
THEN WHY IN HEL'S NAME DIDN'T HE SAY ANYTHING?
WE THOUGHT WE COULD TRAP THE BEAST.
YOU? YOU COULDN'T HUNT A SLUG IN A LETTUCE PATCH.
COME ON, BOYS...
*"WE'LL DINE O WOOD BEAR I THE MORNING.*

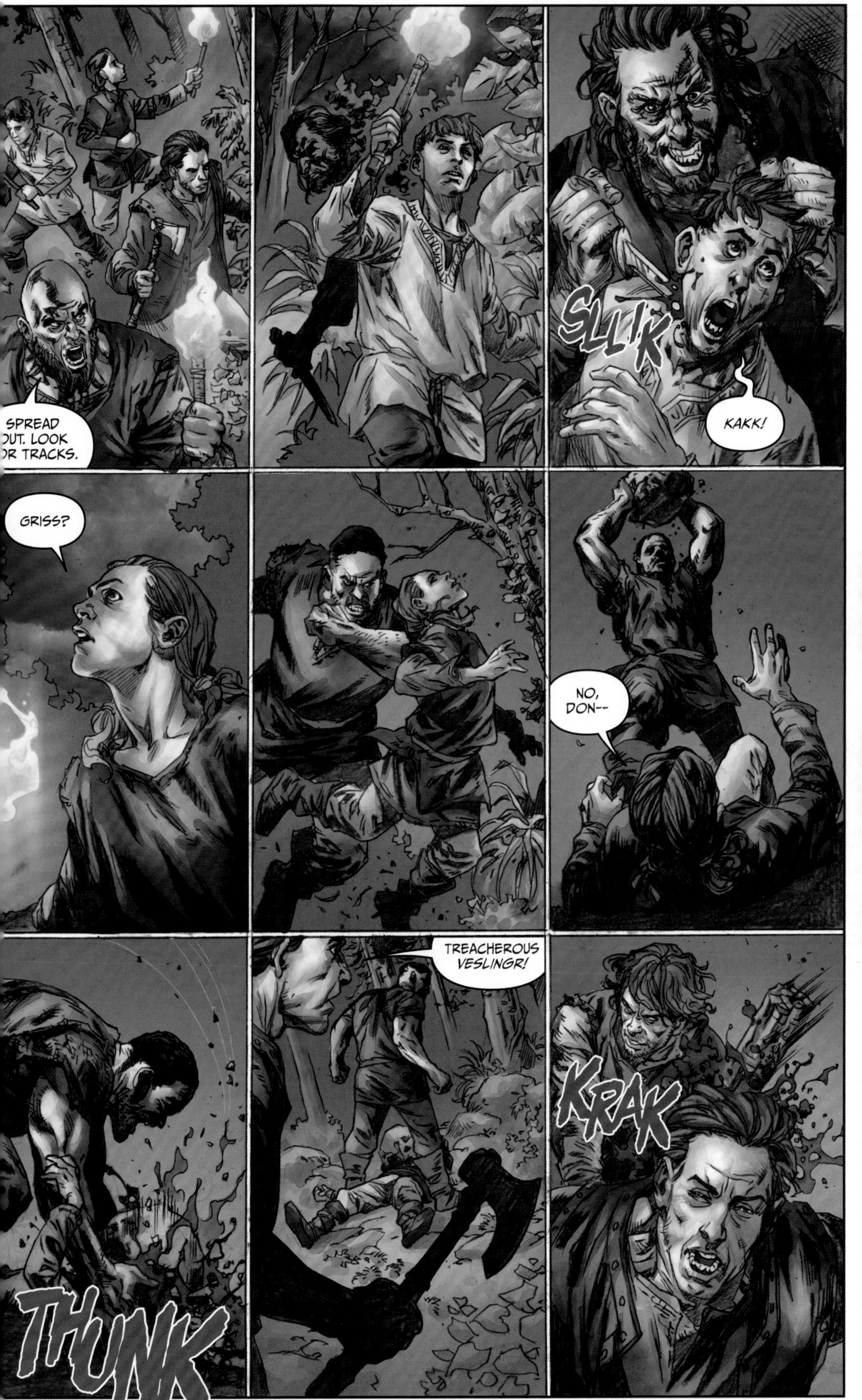

SPREAD OUT. LOOK OR TRACKS.
SLLIK
KAKK!
GRISS?
NO, DON--
THUNK
TREACHEROUS VESLINGR!
KRAK

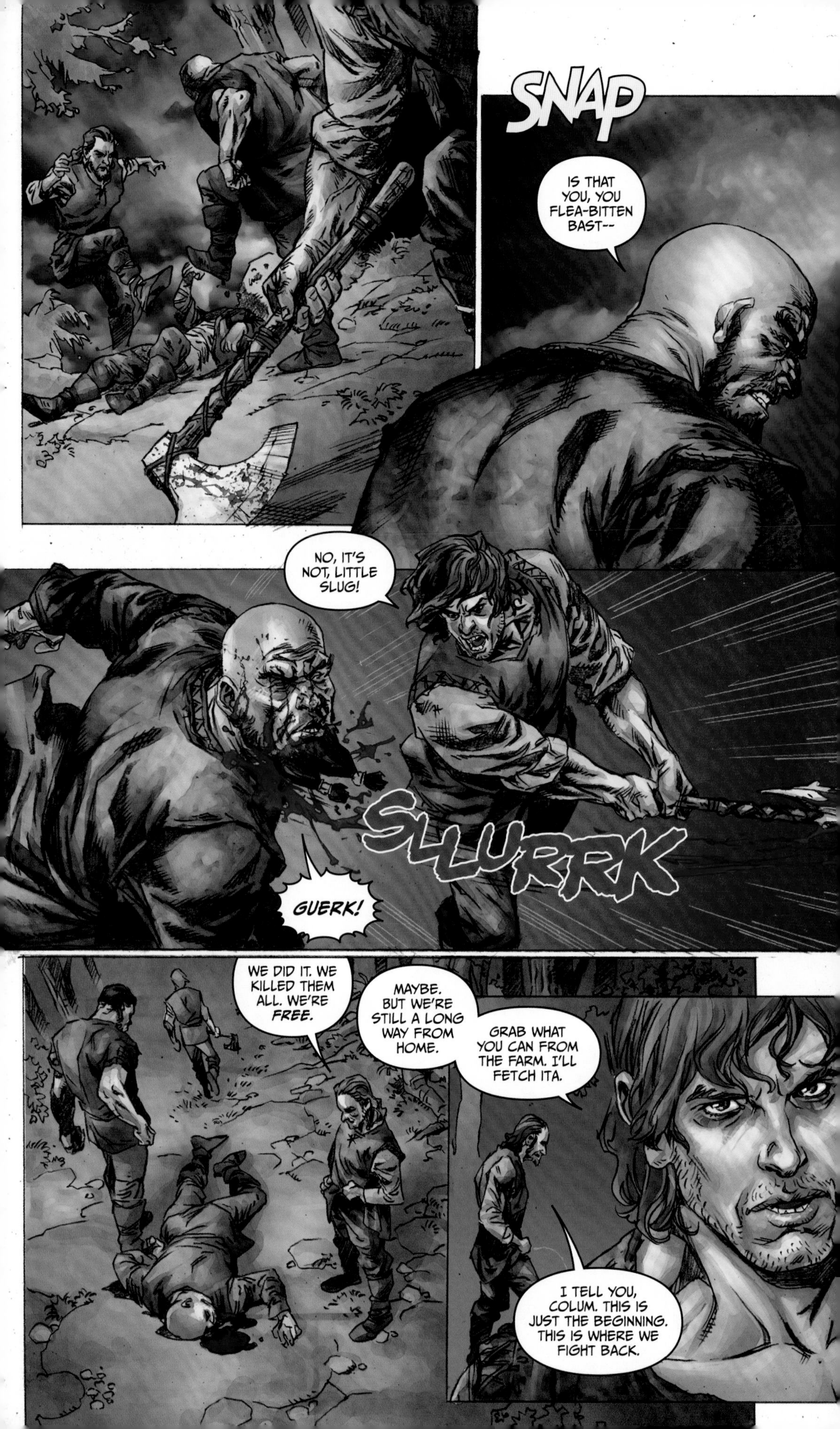
SNAP
IS THAT YOU, YOU FLEA-BITTEN BAST--
NO, IT'S NOT, LITTLE SLUG!
SLLURRK
GUERK!
WE DID IT. WE KILLED THEM ALL. WE'RE FREE.
MAYBE. BUT WE'RE STILL A LONG WAY FROM HOME.
GRAB WHAT YOU CAN FROM THE FARM. I'LL FETCH ITA.
I TELL YOU, COLUM. THIS IS JUST THE BEGINNING. THIS IS WHERE WE FIGHT BACK.

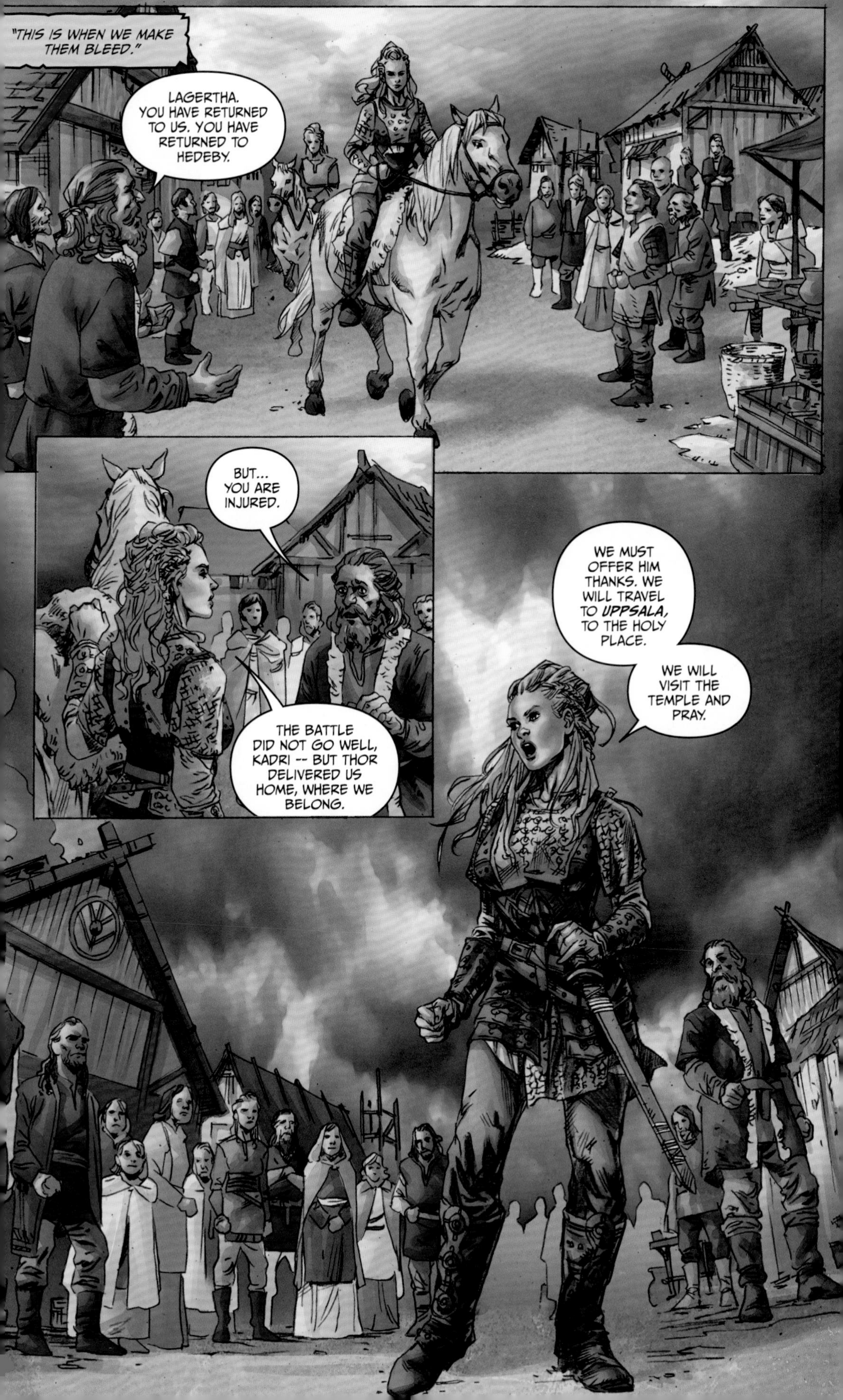
"THIS IS WHEN WE MAKE THEM BLEED."
LAGERTHA. YOU HAVE RETURNED TO US. YOU HAVE RETURNED TO HEDEBY.
BUT... YOU ARE INJURED.
THE BATTLE DID NOT GO WELL, KADRI -- BUT THOR DELIVERED US HOME, WHERE WE BELONG.
WE MUST OFFER HIM THANKS. WE WILL TRAVEL TO UPPSALA, TO THE HOLY PLACE.
WE WILL VISIT THE TEMPLE AND PRAY.

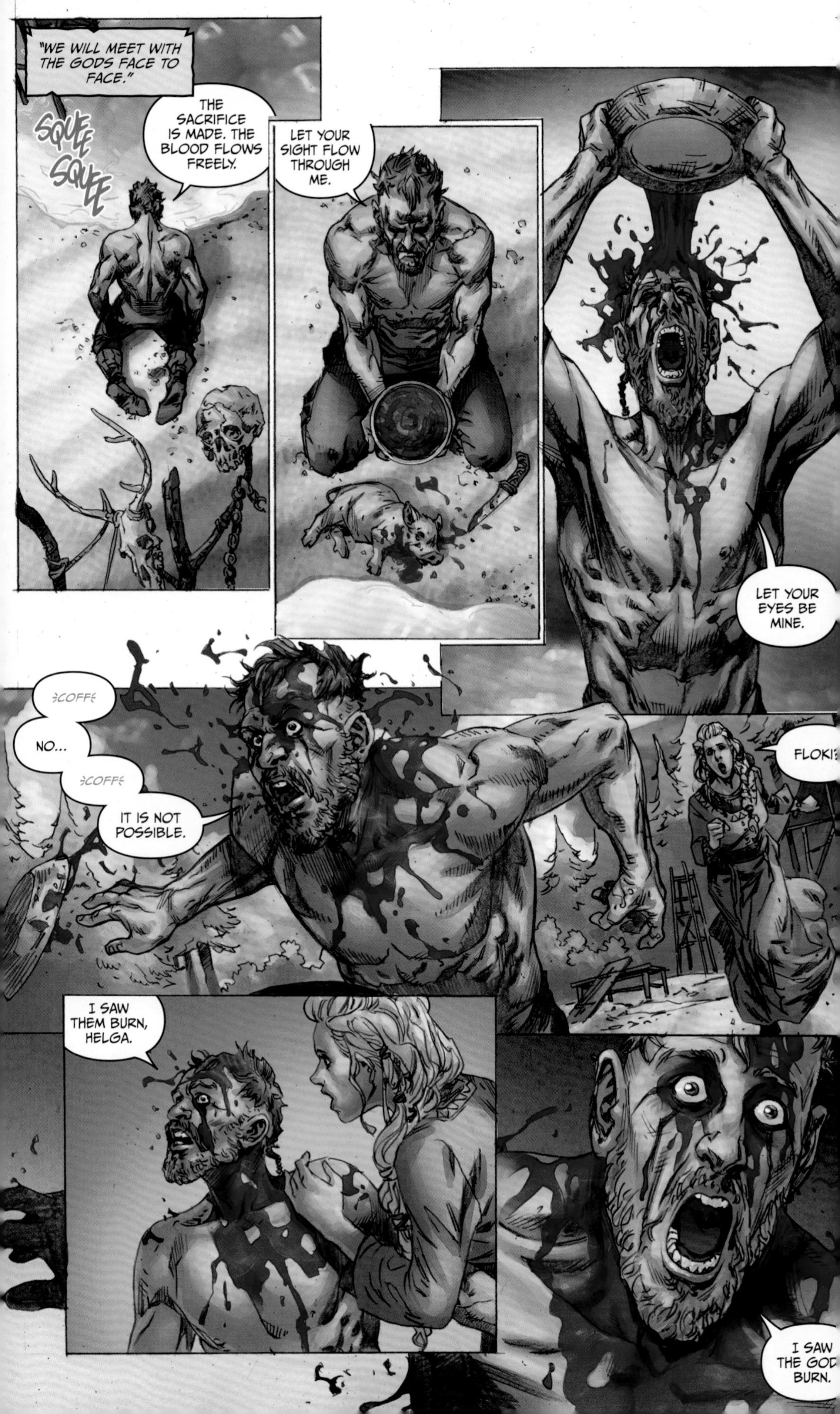
"WE WILL MEET WITH THE GODS FACE TO FACE."
SQUEE
SQUEE
THE SACRIFICE IS MADE. THE BLOOD FLOWS FREELY.
LET YOUR SIGHT FLOW THROUGH ME.
LET YOUR EYES BE MINE.
*COFF*
NO...
*COFF*
IT IS NOT POSSIBLE.
FLOKI?
I SAW THEM BURN, HELGA.
I SAW THE GOD BURN.

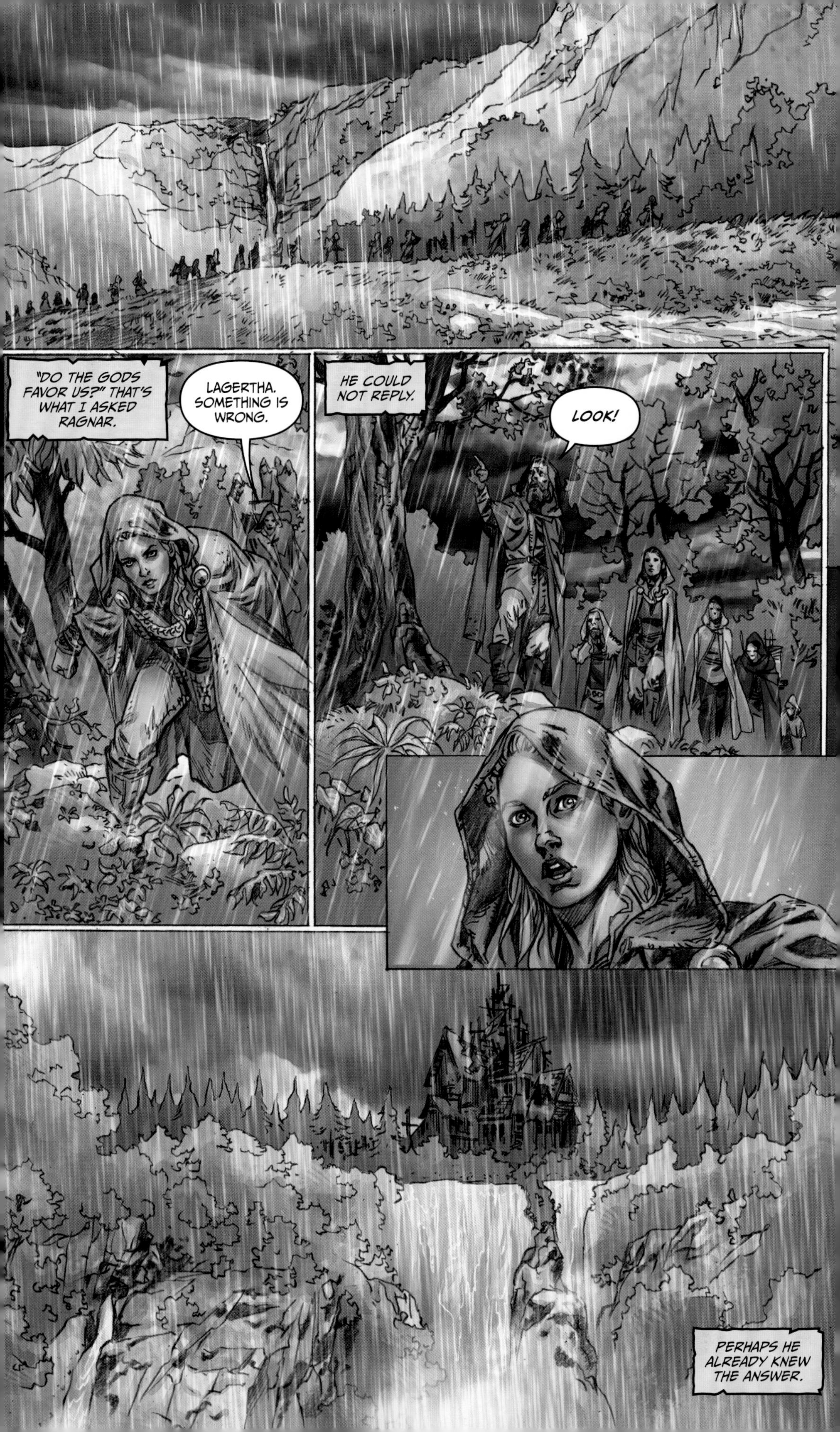
"DO THE GODS FAVOR US?" THAT'S WHAT I ASKED RAGNAR.
LAGERTHA. SOMETHING IS WRONG.
HE COULD NOT REPLY.
LOOK!
PERHAPS HE ALREADY KNEW THE ANSWER.

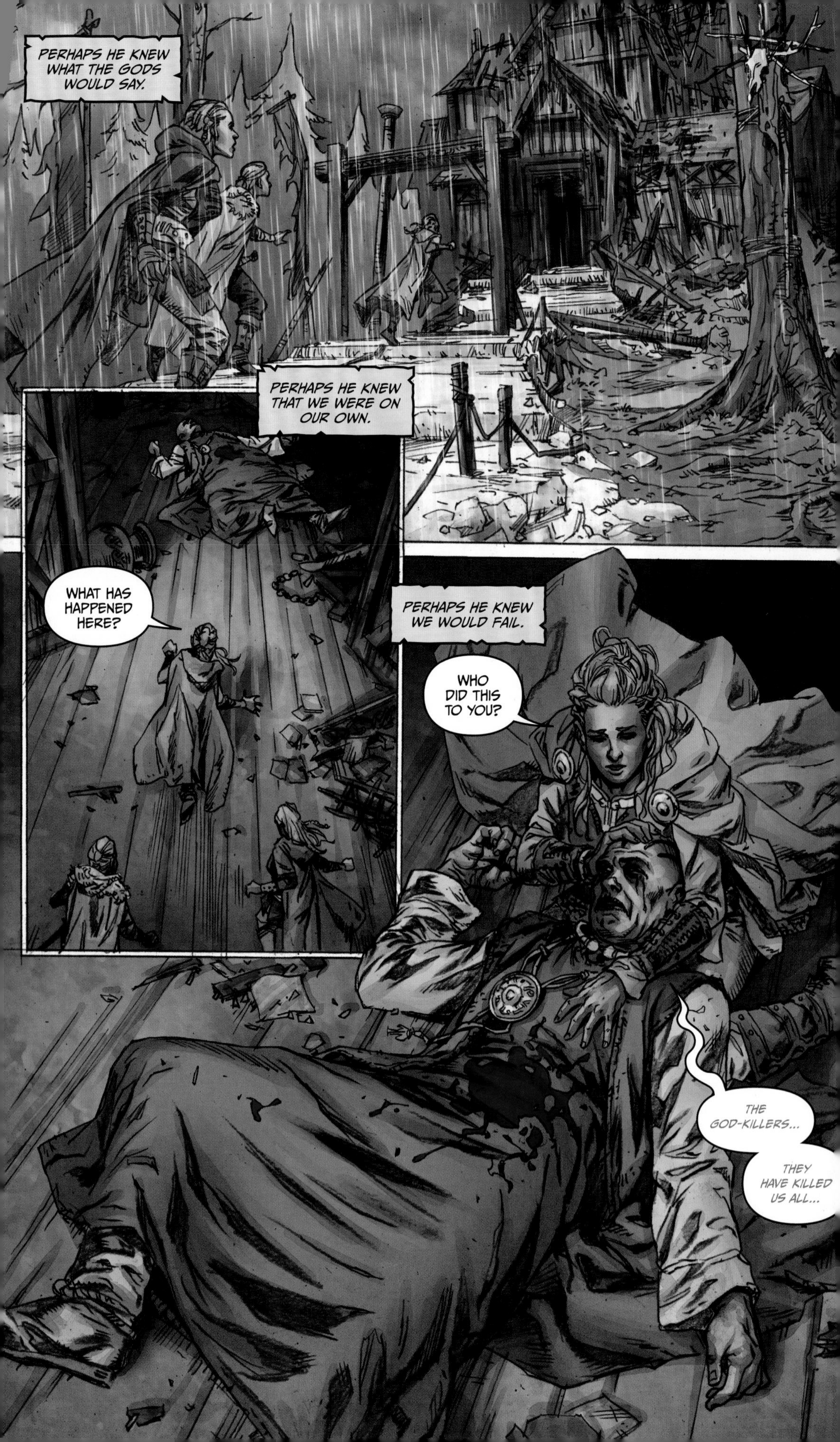
PERHAPS HE KNEW WHAT THE GODS WOULD SAY.
PERHAPS HE KNEW THAT WE WERE ON OUR OWN.
WHAT HAS HAPPENED HERE?
PERHAPS HE KNEW WE WOULD FAIL.
WHO DID THIS TO YOU?
THE GOD-KILLERS...
THEY HAVE KILLED US ALL...

# CHAPTER 2

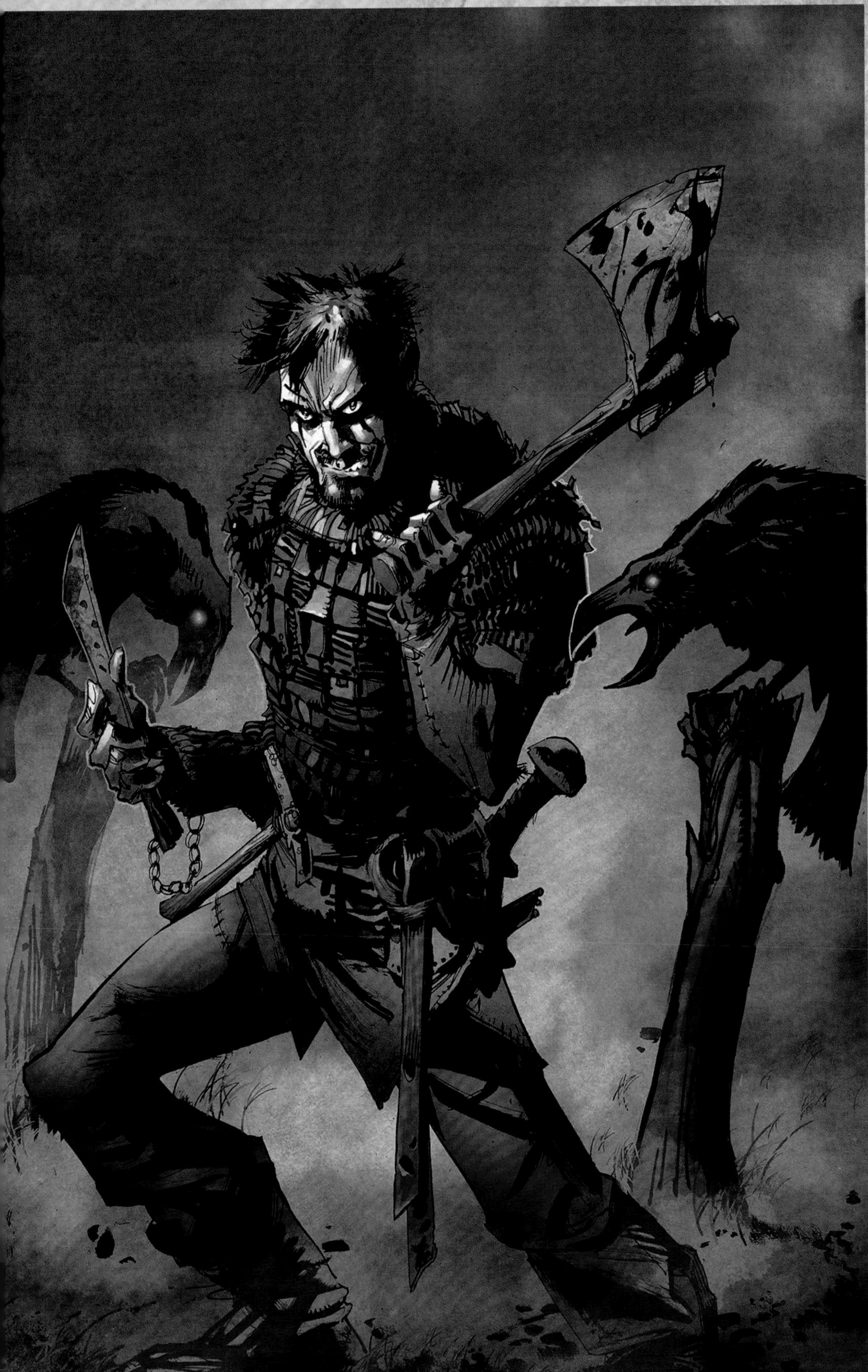

ILLUSTRATION BY JOHN MCCREA

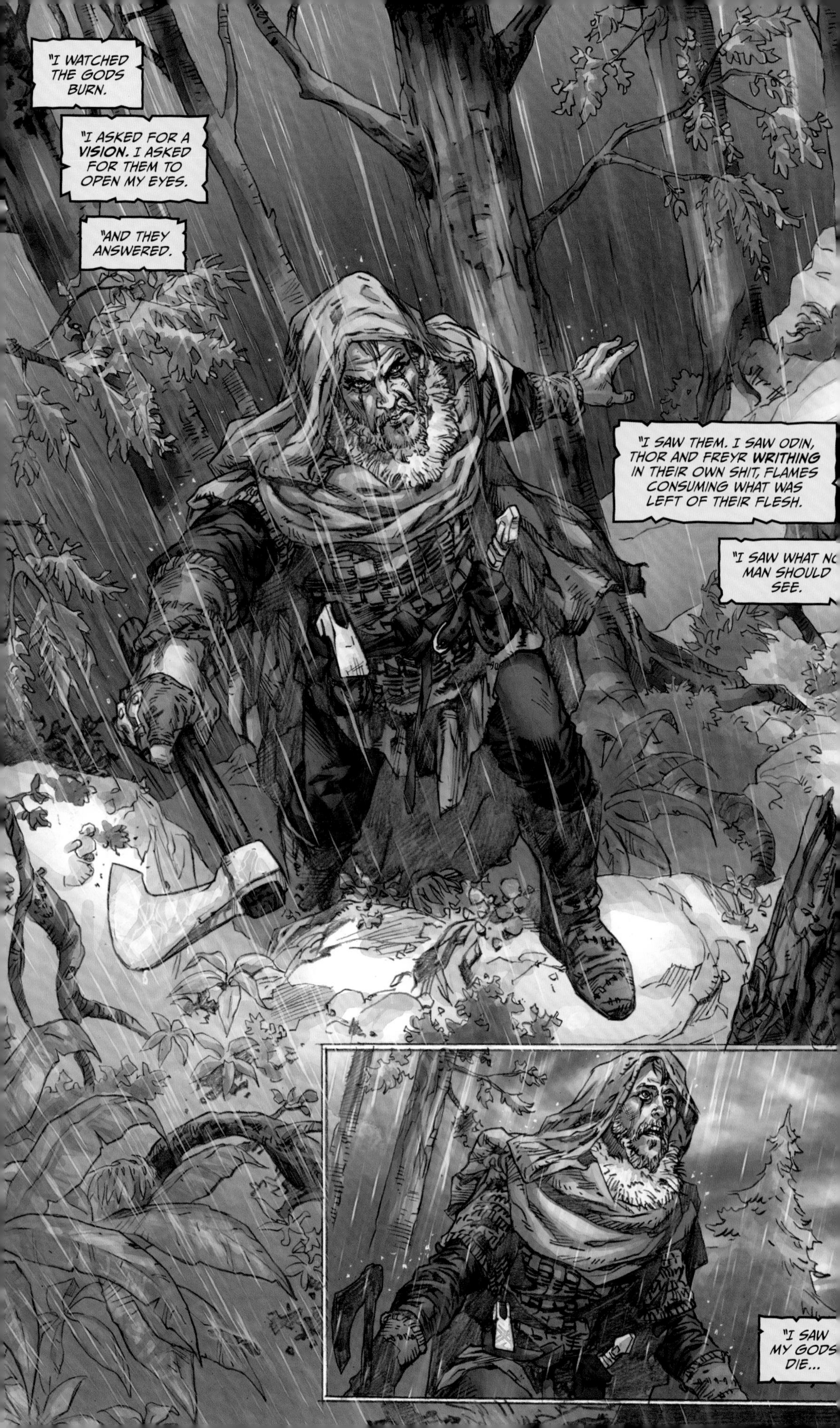
"I WATCHED THE GODS BURN.
"I ASKED FOR A VISION. I ASKED FOR THEM TO OPEN MY EYES.
"AND THEY ANSWERED.
"I SAW THEM. I SAW ODIN, THOR AND FREYR WRITHING IN THEIR OWN SHIT, FLAMES CONSUMING WHAT WAS LEFT OF THEIR FLESH.
"I SAW WHAT NO MAN SHOULD SEE.
"I SAW MY GODS DIE...

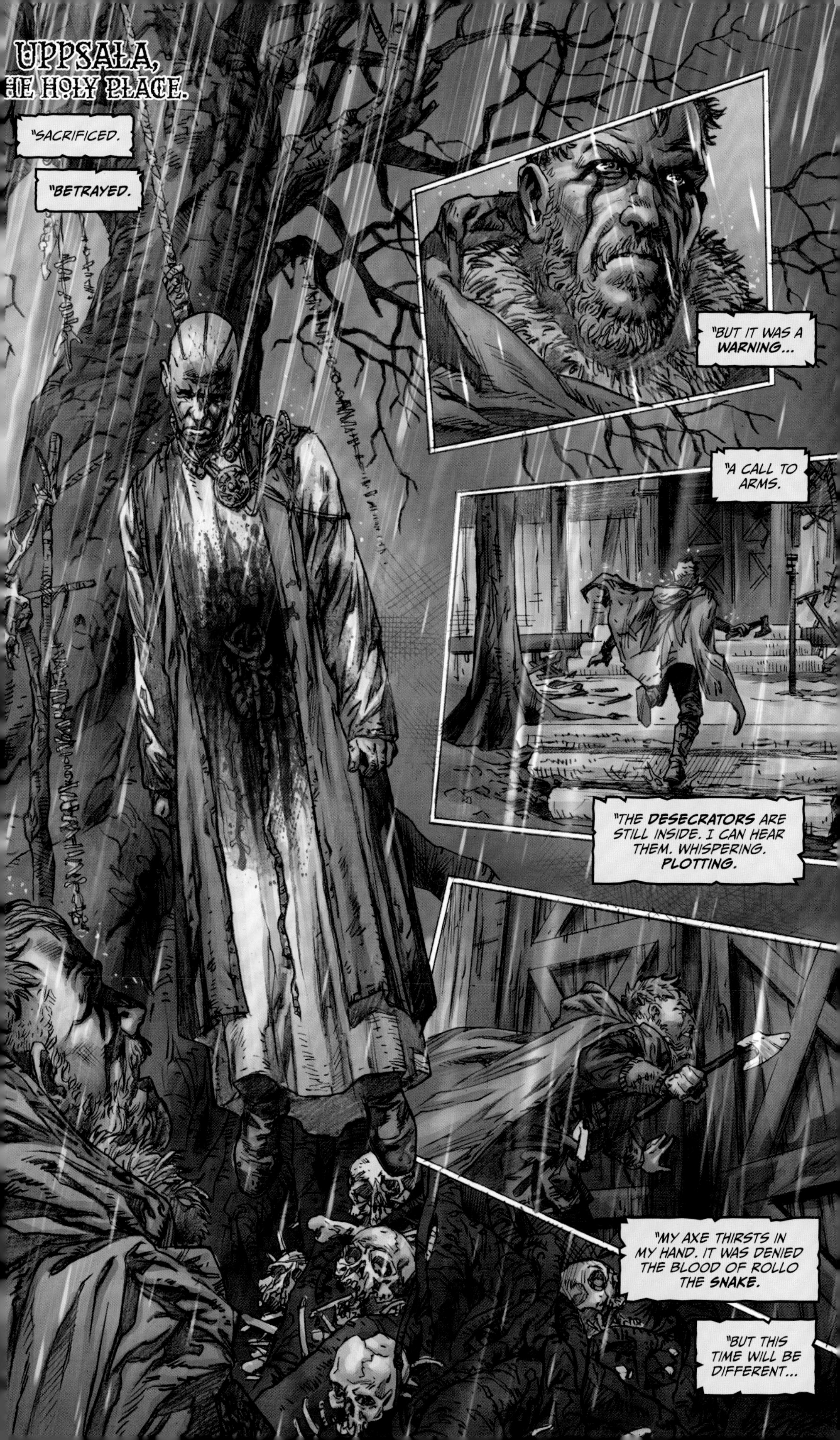
UPPSALA,
HE HOLY PLACE.
"SACRIFICED.
"BETRAYED.
"BUT IT WAS A WARNING...
"A CALL TO ARMS.
"THE DESECRATORS ARE STILL INSIDE. I CAN HEAR THEM. WHISPERING. PLOTTING.
"MY AXE THIRSTS IN MY HAND. IT WAS DENIED THE BLOOD OF ROLLO THE SNAKE.
"BUT THIS TIME WILL BE DIFFERENT...

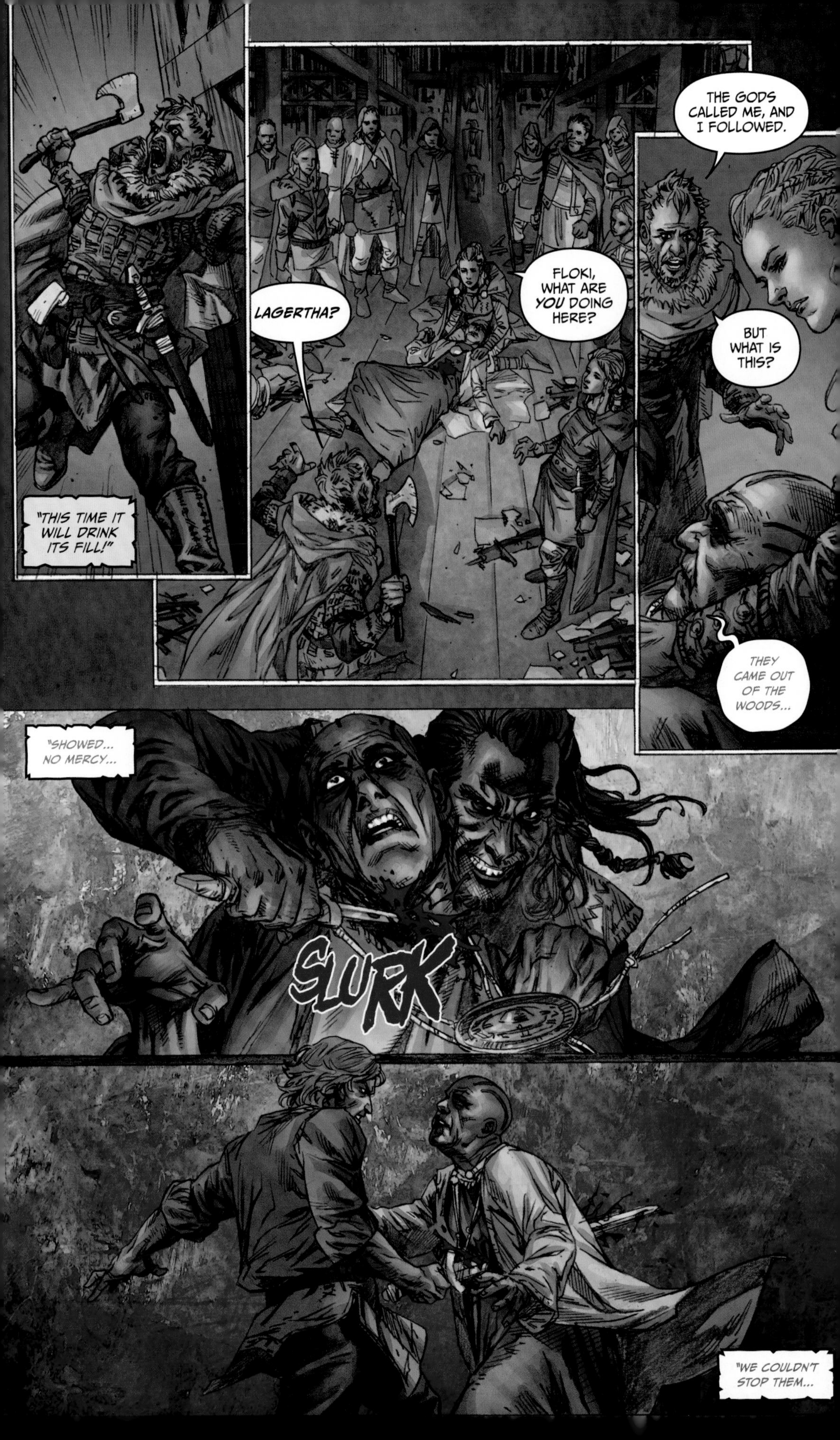

"THIS TIME IT WILL DRINK ITS FILL!"
LAGERTHA?
FLOKI, WHAT ARE YOU DOING HERE?
THE GODS CALLED ME, AND I FOLLOWED.
BUT WHAT IS THIS?
THEY CAME OUT OF THE WOODS...
"SHOWED... NO MERCY...
SLURK
"WE COULDN'T STOP THEM...

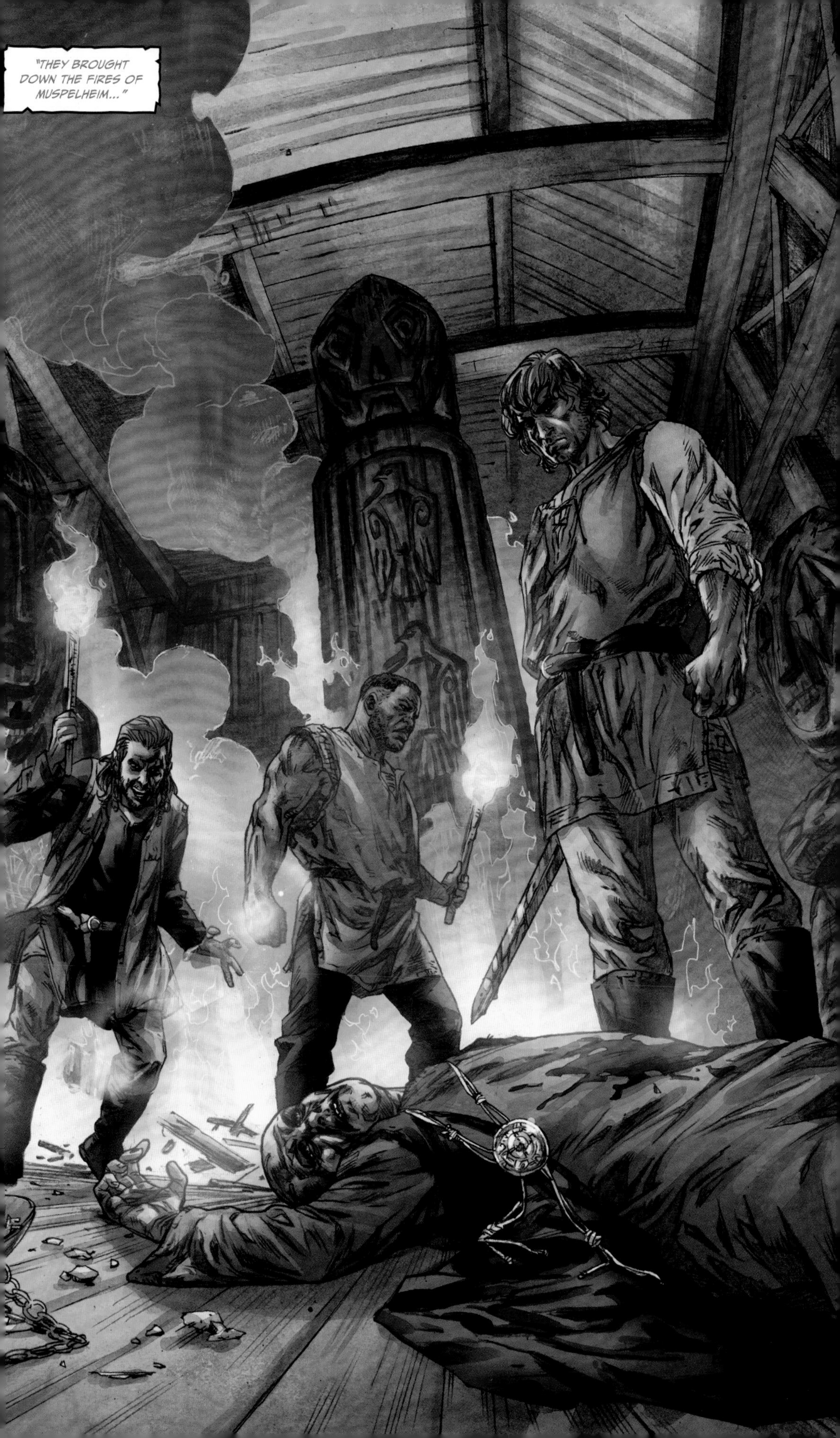
"THEY BROUGHT DOWN THE FIRES OF MUSPELHEIM..."

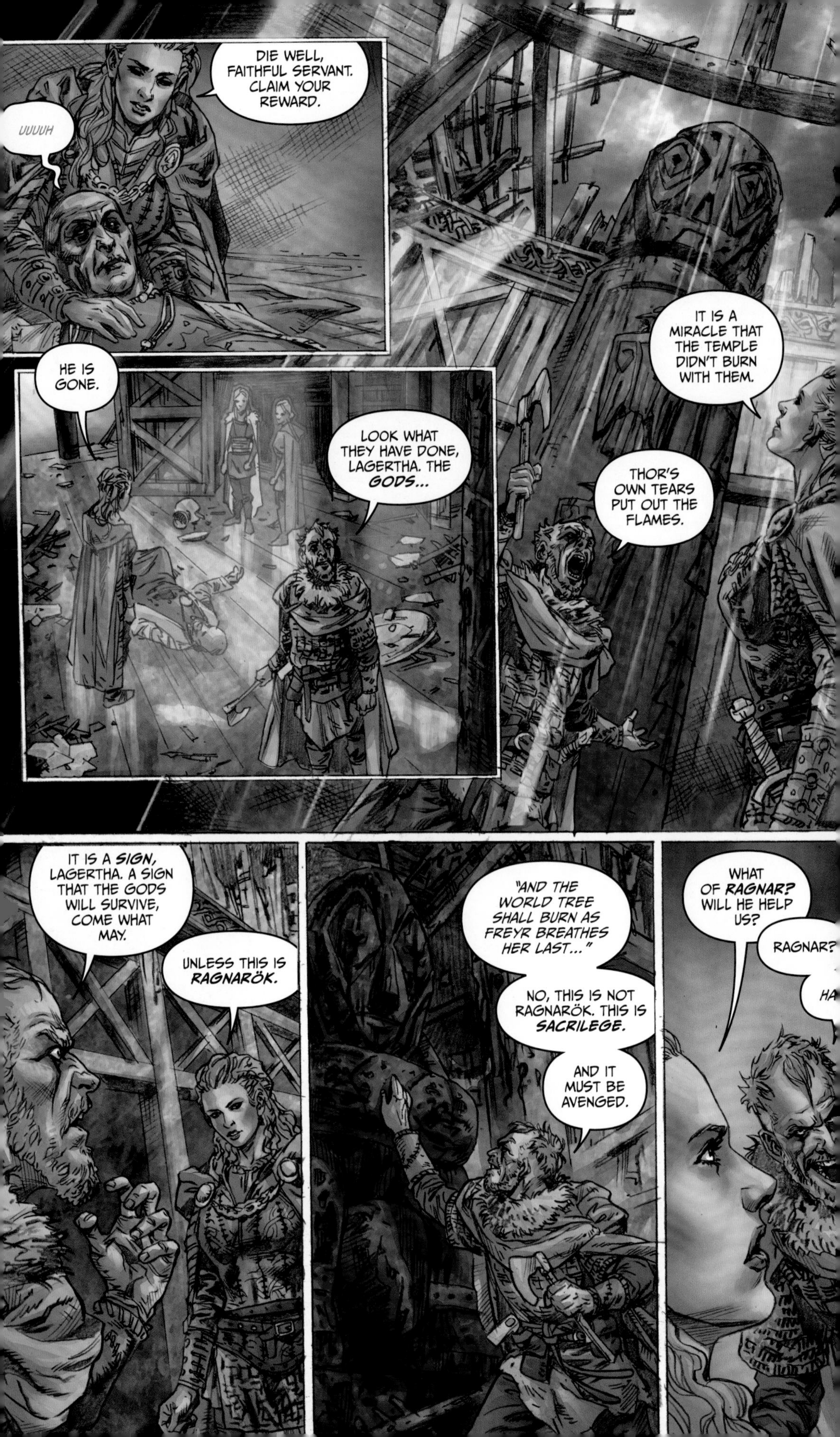
DIE WELL, FAITHFUL SERVANT. CLAIM YOUR REWARD.
UUUUH
HE IS GONE.
LOOK WHAT THEY HAVE DONE, LAGERTHA. THE GODS...
IT IS A MIRACLE THAT THE TEMPLE DIDN'T BURN WITH THEM.
THOR'S OWN TEARS PUT OUT THE FLAMES.
IT IS A SIGN, LAGERTHA. A SIGN THAT THE GODS WILL SURVIVE, COME WHAT MAY.
UNLESS THIS IS RAGNARÖK.
"AND THE WORLD TREE SHALL BURN AS FREYR BREATHES HER LAST..."
NO, THIS IS NOT RAGNARÖK. THIS IS SACRILEGE.
AND IT MUST BE AVENGED.
WHAT OF RAGNAR? WILL HE HELP US?
RAGNAR?

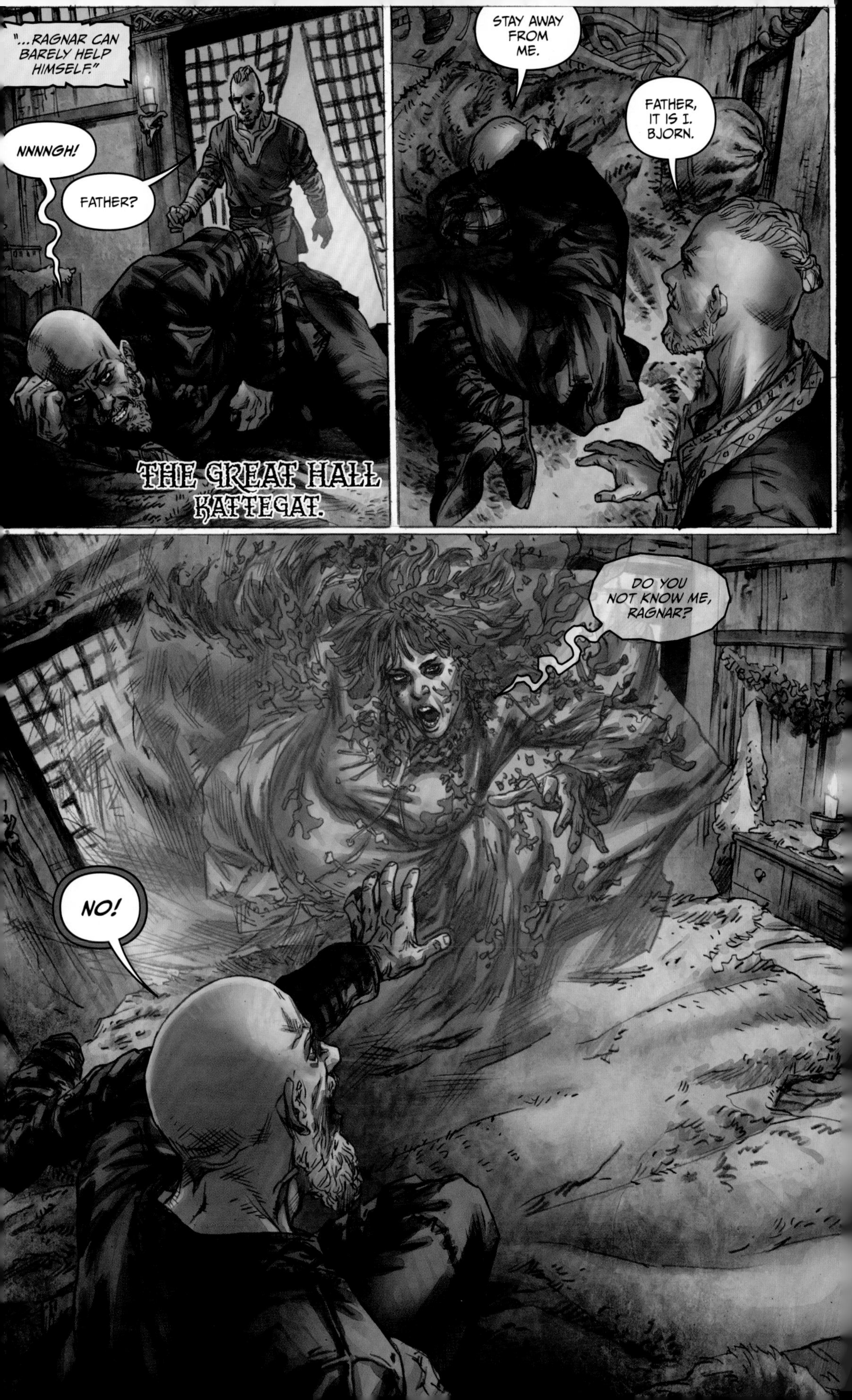
"...RAGNAR CAN BARELY HELP HIMSELF."
NNNNGH!
FATHER?
THE GREAT HALL KATTEGAT.
STAY AWAY FROM ME.
FATHER, IT IS I. BJORN.
DO YOU NOT KNOW ME, RAGNAR?
NO!

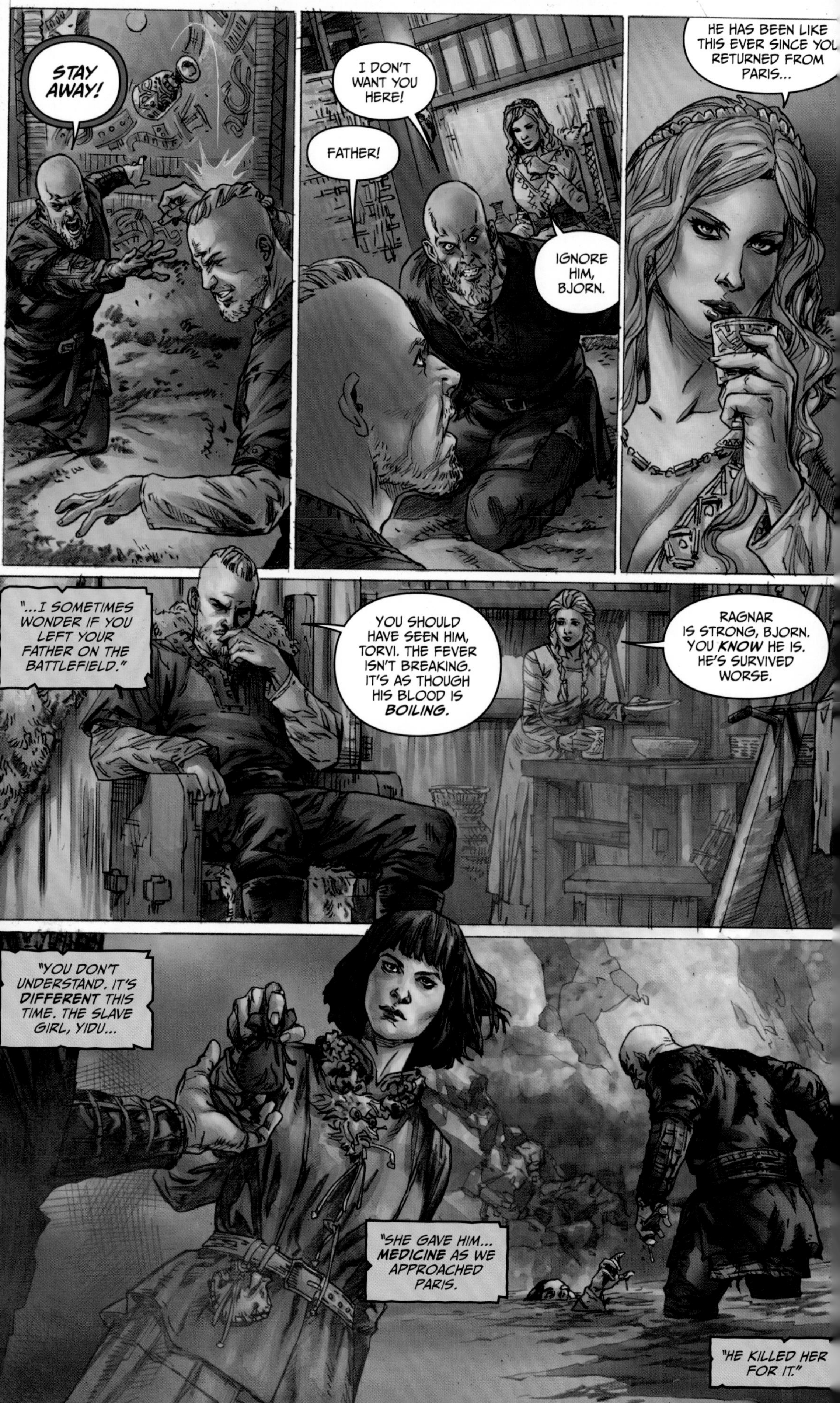
STAY AWAY!
I DON'T WANT YOU HERE!
FATHER!
IGNORE HIM, BJORN.
HE HAS BEEN LIKE THIS EVER SINCE YOU RETURNED FROM PARIS...
"...I SOMETIMES WONDER IF YOU LEFT YOUR FATHER ON THE BATTLEFIELD."
YOU SHOULD HAVE SEEN HIM, TORVI. THE FEVER ISN'T BREAKING. IT'S AS THOUGH HIS BLOOD IS BOILING.
RAGNAR IS STRONG, BJORN. YOU KNOW HE IS. HE'S SURVIVED WORSE.
"YOU DON'T UNDERSTAND. IT'S DIFFERENT THIS TIME. THE SLAVE GIRL, YIDU...
"SHE GAVE HIM... MEDICINE AS WE APPROACHED PARIS.
"HE KILLED HER FOR IT."

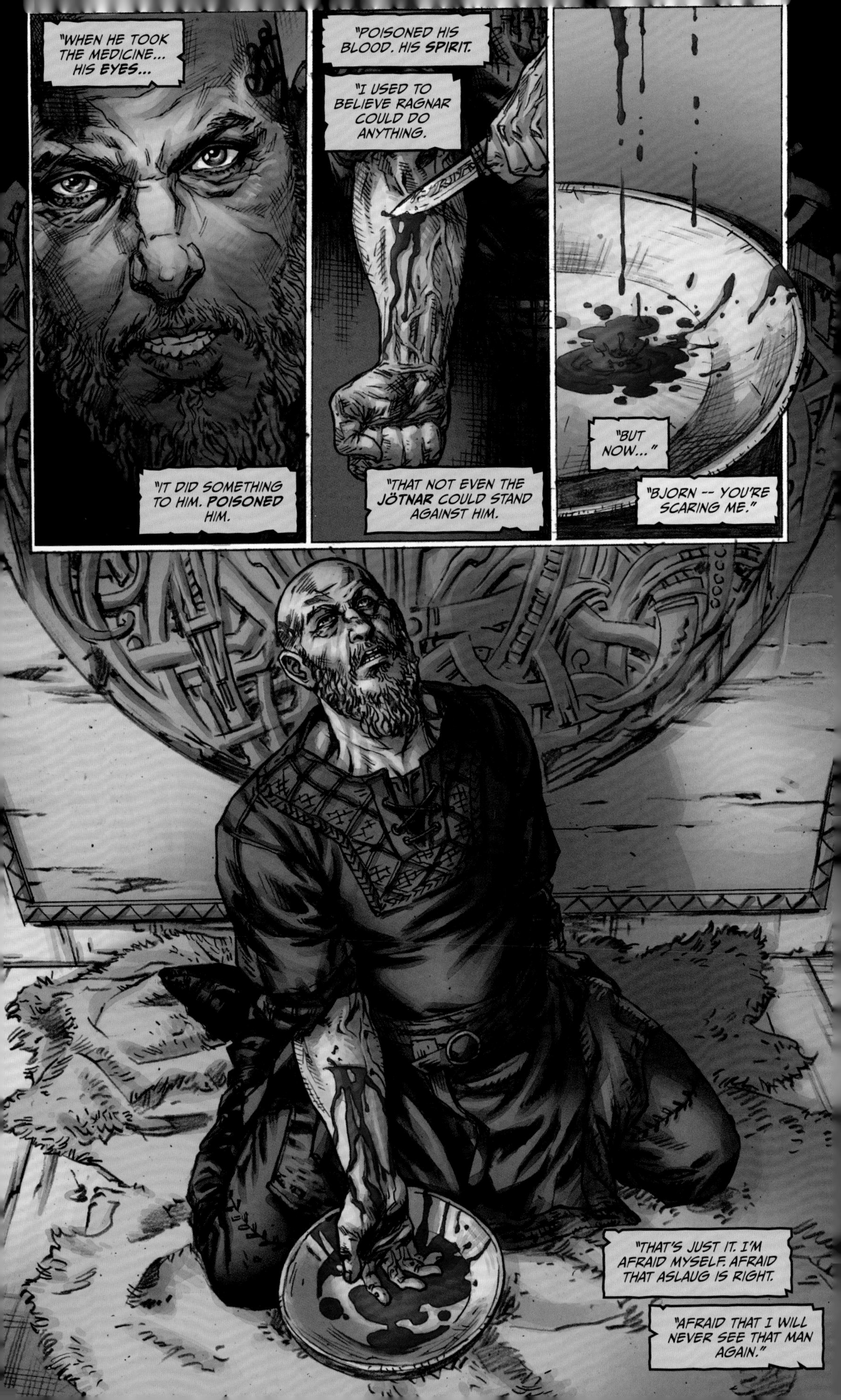

"WHEN HE TOOK THE MEDICINE... HIS EYES...
"IT DID SOMETHING TO HIM. POISONED HIM.
"POISONED HIS BLOOD. HIS SPIRIT.
"I USED TO BELIEVE RAGNAR COULD DO ANYTHING.
"THAT NOT EVEN THE JÖTNAR COULD STAND AGAINST HIM.
"BUT NOW..."
"BJORN -- YOU'RE SCARING ME."
"THAT'S JUST IT. I'M AFRAID MYSELF. AFRAID THAT ASLAUG IS RIGHT.
"AFRAID THAT I WILL NEVER SEE THAT MAN AGAIN."

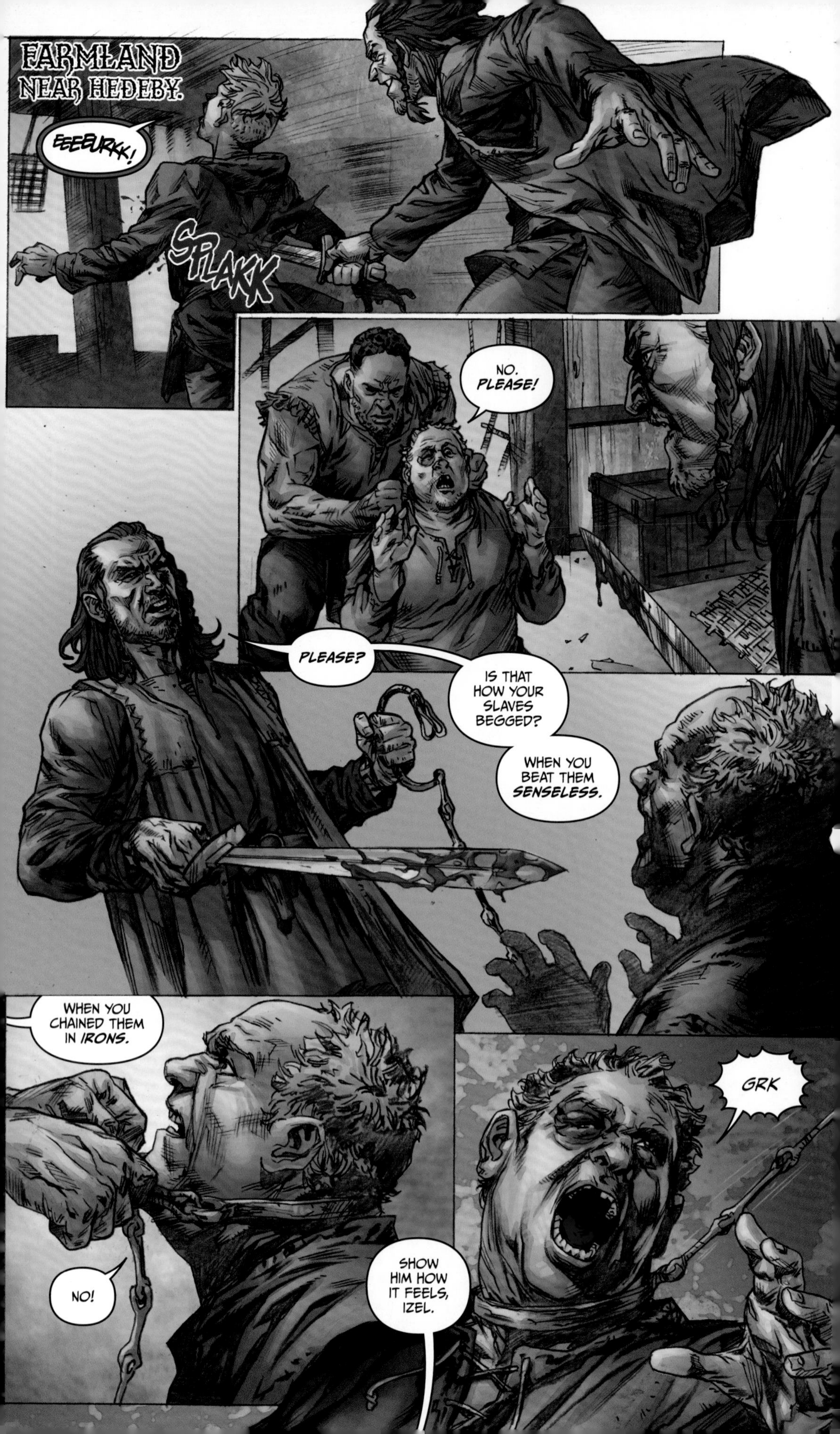
FARMLAND NEAR HEDEBY.
EEEEURKK!
SPLAKK
NO. PLEASE!
PLEASE?
IS THAT HOW YOUR SLAVES BEGGED?
WHEN YOU BEAT THEM SENSELESS.
WHEN YOU CHAINED THEM IN IRONS.
NO!
SHOW HIM HOW IT FEELS, IZEL.
GRK

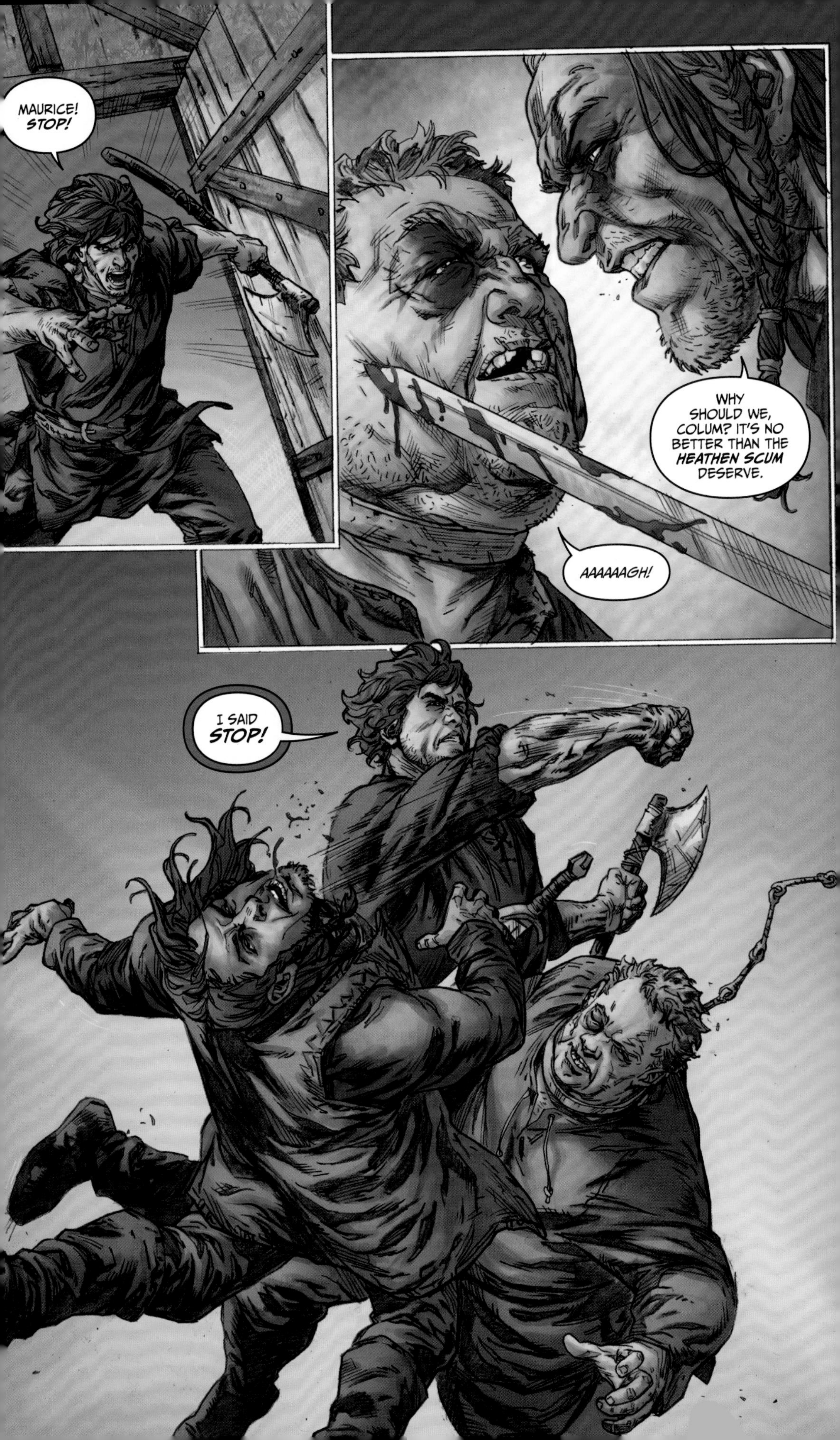
MAURICE! STOP!
WHY SHOULD WE, COLUM? IT'S NO BETTER THAN THE HEATHEN SCUM DESERVE.
AAAAAAGH!
I SAID STOP!

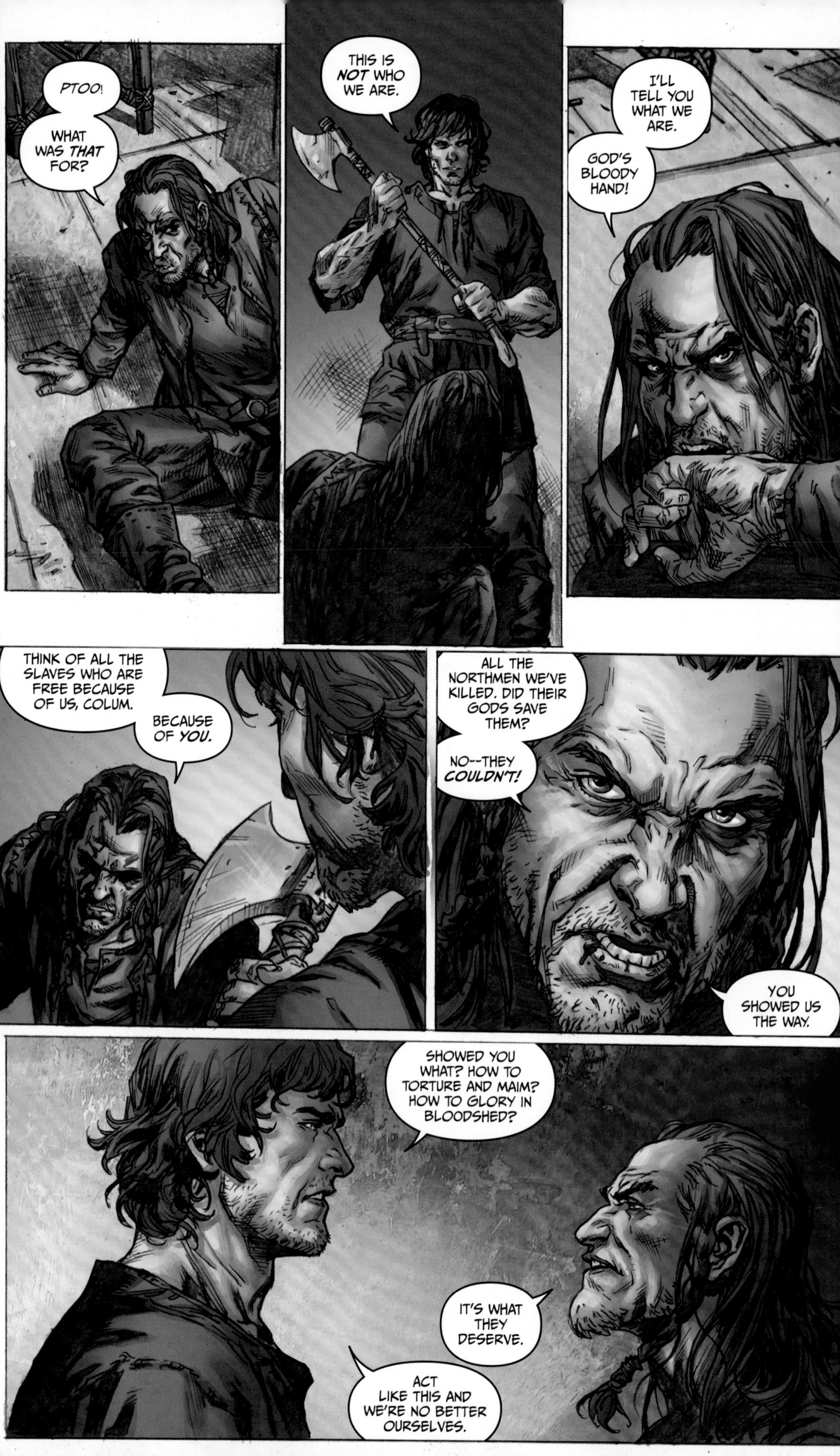
PTOO!
WHAT WAS *THAT* FOR?
THIS IS *NOT* WHO WE ARE.
I'LL TELL YOU WHAT WE ARE.
GOD'S BLOODY HAND!
THINK OF ALL THE SLAVES WHO ARE FREE BECAUSE OF US, COLUM.
BECAUSE OF *YOU.*
ALL THE NORTHMEN WE'VE KILLED. DID THEIR GODS SAVE THEM?
NO--THEY *COULDN'T!*
YOU SHOWED US THE WAY.
SHOWED YOU WHAT? HOW TO TORTURE AND MAIM? HOW TO GLORY IN BLOODSHED?
IT'S WHAT THEY DESERVE.
ACT LIKE THIS AND WE'RE NO BETTER OURSELVES.

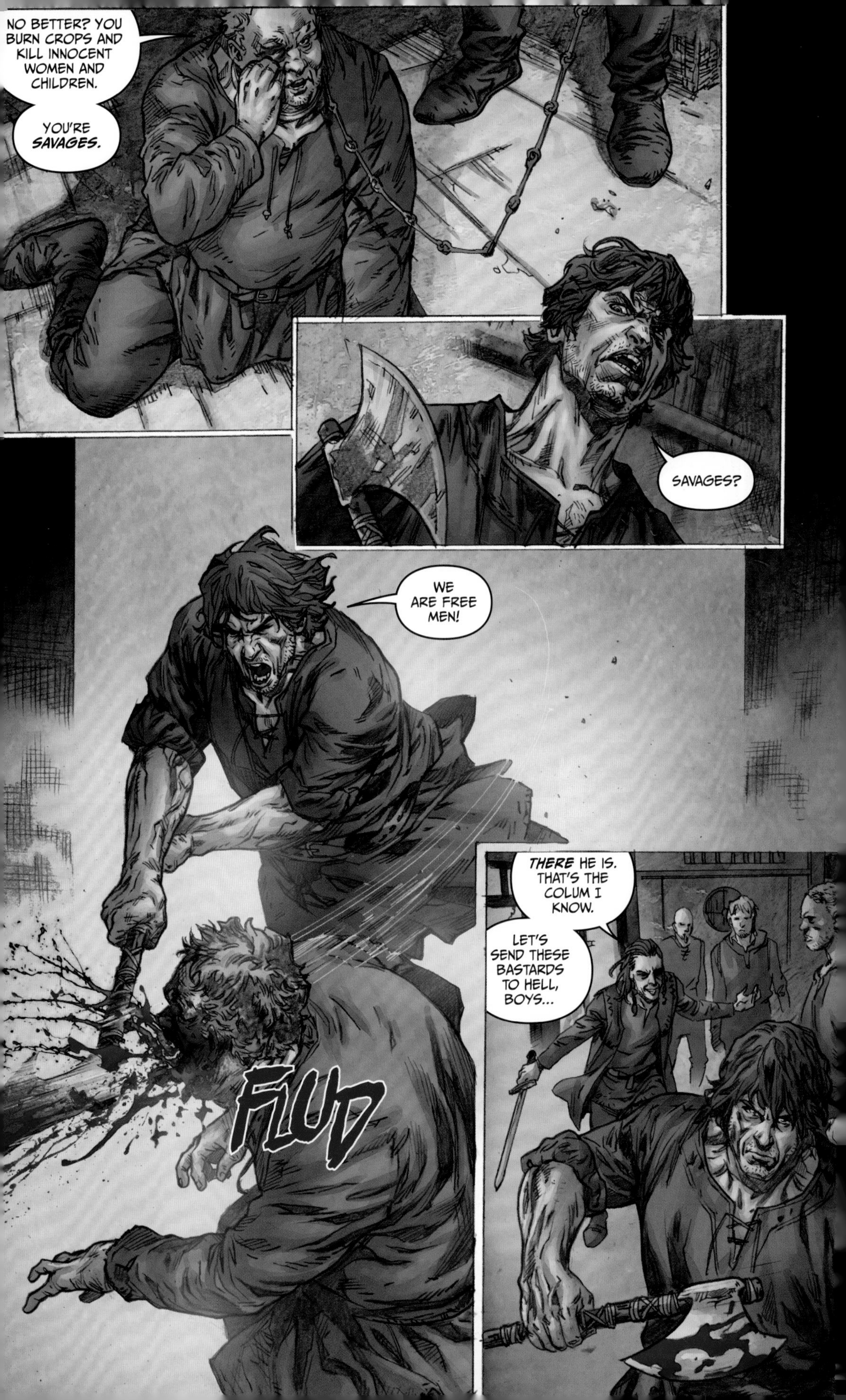
NO BETTER? YOU BURN CROPS AND KILL INNOCENT WOMEN AND CHILDREN.
YOU'RE SAVAGES.
SAVAGES?
WE ARE FREE MEN!
FLUD
THERE HE IS. THAT'S THE COLUM I KNOW.
LET'S SEND THESE BASTARDS TO HELL, BOYS...

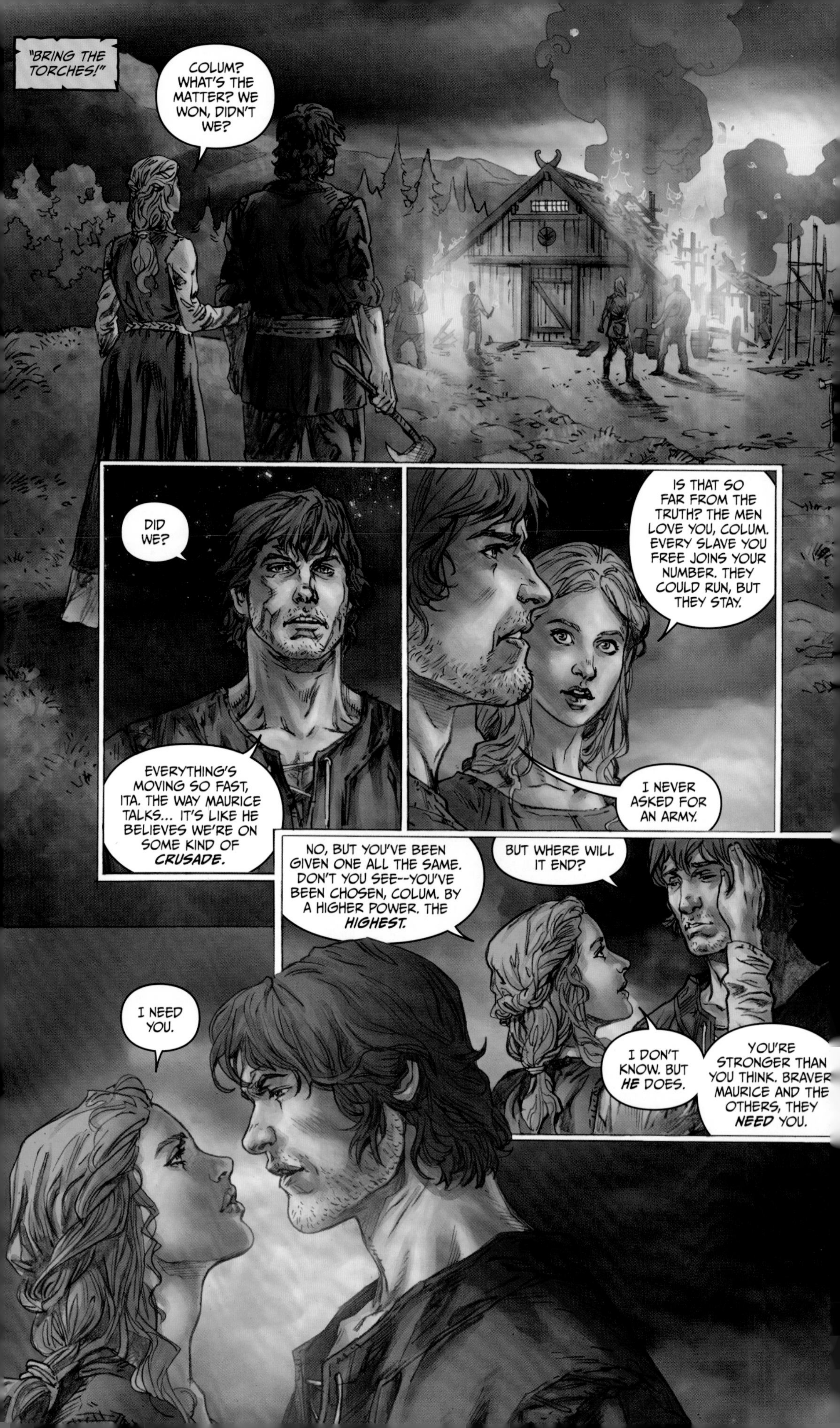
"BRING THE TORCHES!"
COLUM? WHAT'S THE MATTER? WE WON, DIDN'T WE?
DID WE?
EVERYTHING'S MOVING SO FAST, ITA. THE WAY MAURICE TALKS... IT'S LIKE HE BELIEVES WE'RE ON SOME KIND OF CRUSADE.
IS THAT SO FAR FROM THE TRUTH? THE MEN LOVE YOU, COLUM. EVERY SLAVE YOU FREE JOINS YOUR NUMBER. THEY COULD RUN, BUT THEY STAY.
I NEVER ASKED FOR AN ARMY.
NO, BUT YOU'VE BEEN GIVEN ONE ALL THE SAME. DON'T YOU SEE--YOU'VE BEEN CHOSEN, COLUM. BY A HIGHER POWER. THE HIGHEST.
BUT WHERE WILL IT END?
I DON'T KNOW. BUT HE DOES.
YOU'RE STRONGER THAN YOU THINK. BRAVER. MAURICE AND THE OTHERS, THEY NEED YOU.
I NEED YOU.

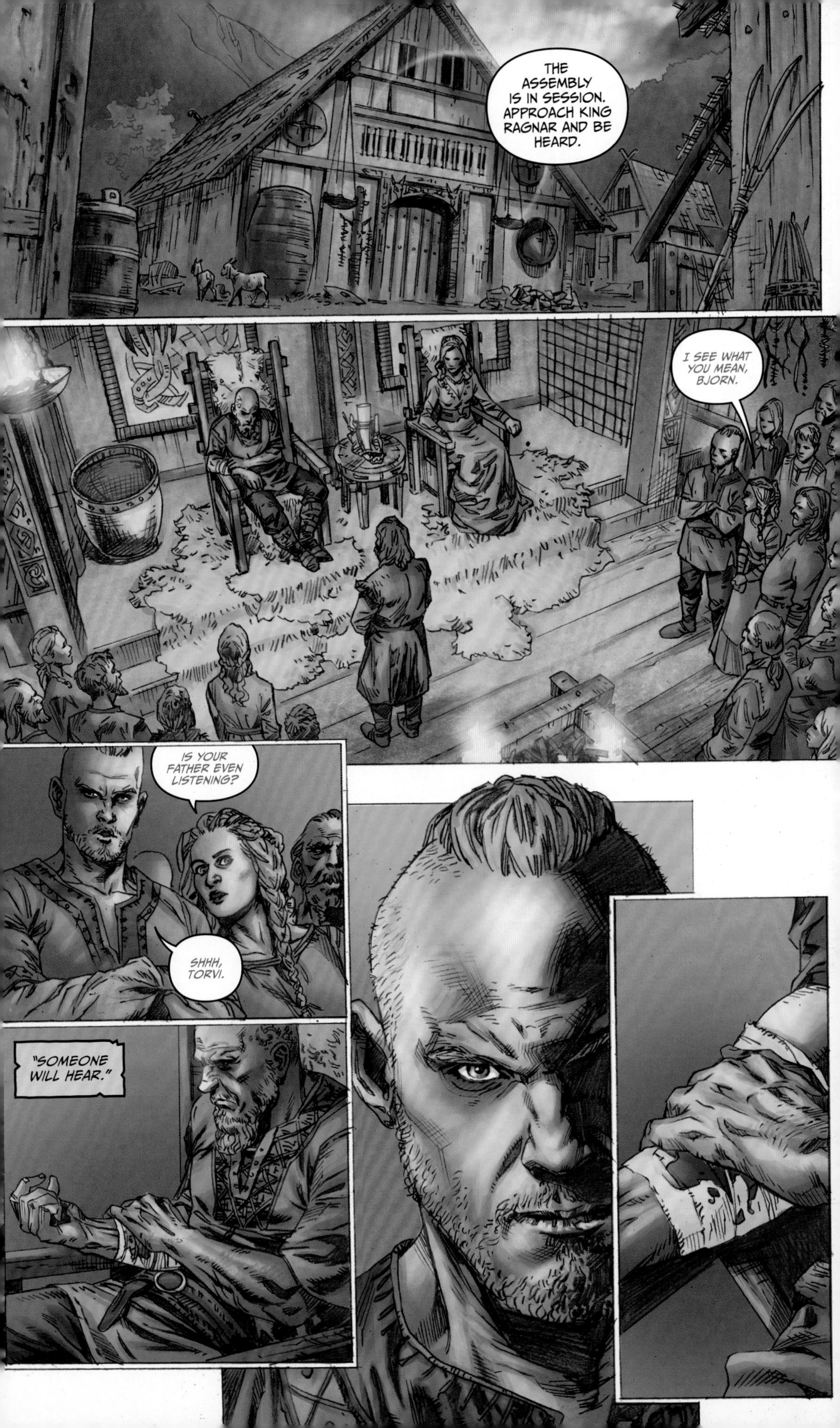
THE ASSEMBLY IS IN SESSION. APPROACH KING RAGNAR AND BE HEARD.
I SEE WHAT YOU MEAN, BJORN.
IS YOUR FATHER EVEN LISTENING?
SHHH, TORVI.
"SOMEONE WILL HEAR."

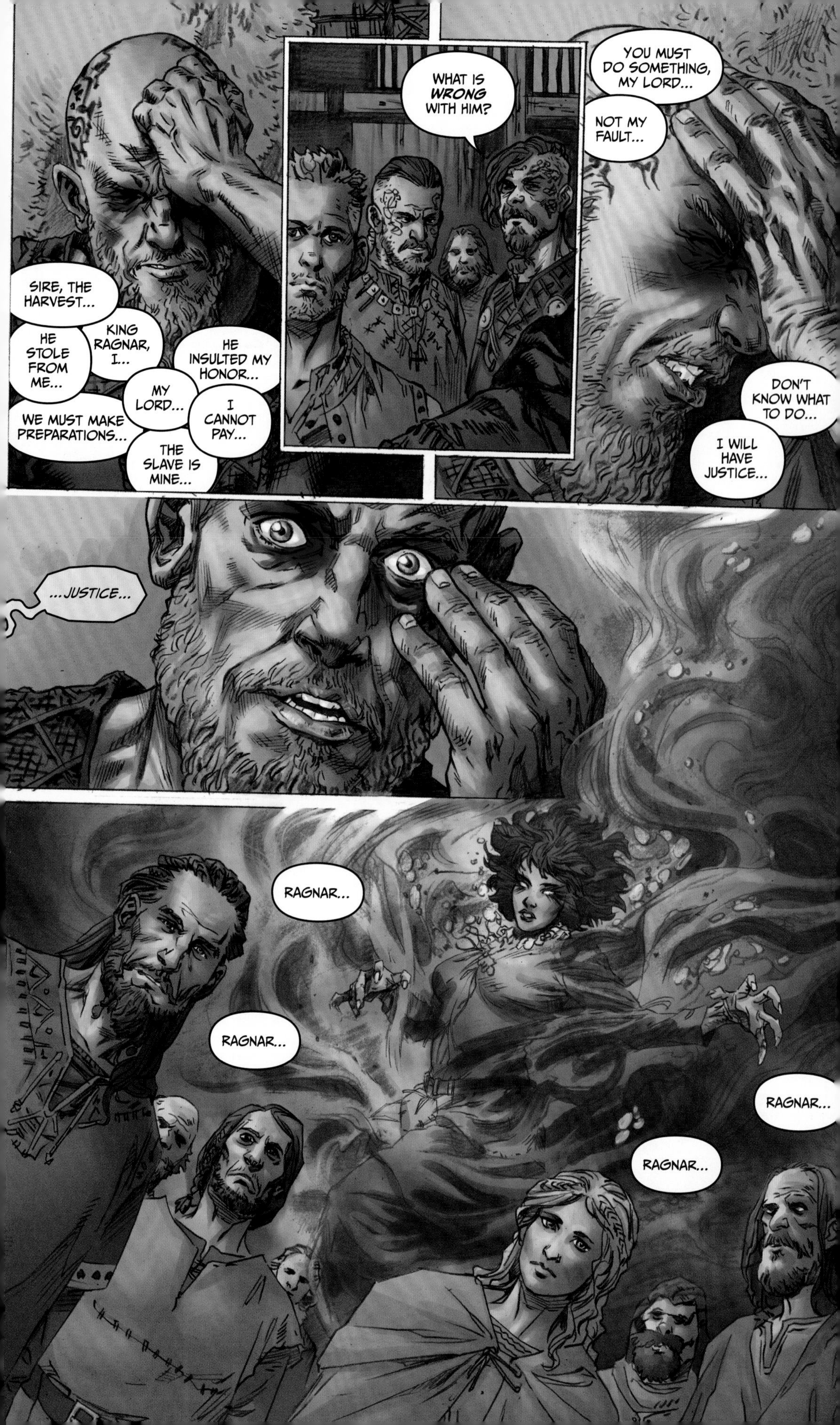
SIRE, THE HARVEST...
HE STOLE FROM ME...
KING RAGNAR, I...
HE INSULTED MY HONOR...
MY LORD...
WE MUST MAKE PREPARATIONS...
I CANNOT PAY...
THE SLAVE IS MINE...
WHAT IS *WRONG* WITH HIM?
YOU MUST DO SOMETHING, MY LORD...
NOT MY FAULT...
DON'T KNOW WHAT TO DO...
I WILL HAVE JUSTICE...
...JUSTICE...
RAGNAR...
RAGNAR...
RAGNAR...
RAGNAR...

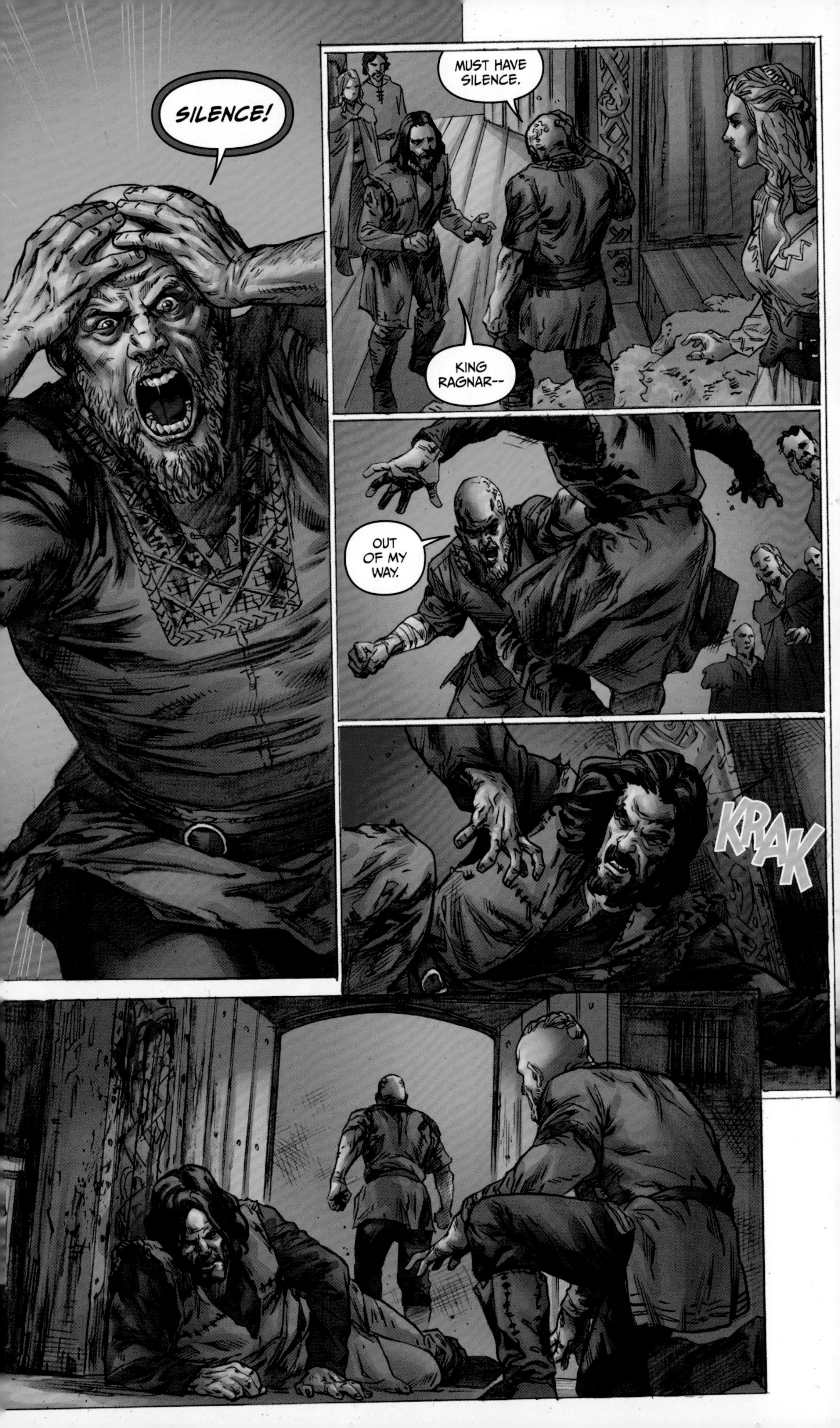
SILENCE!
MUST HAVE SILENCE.
KING RAGNAR--
OUT OF MY WAY.
KRAK

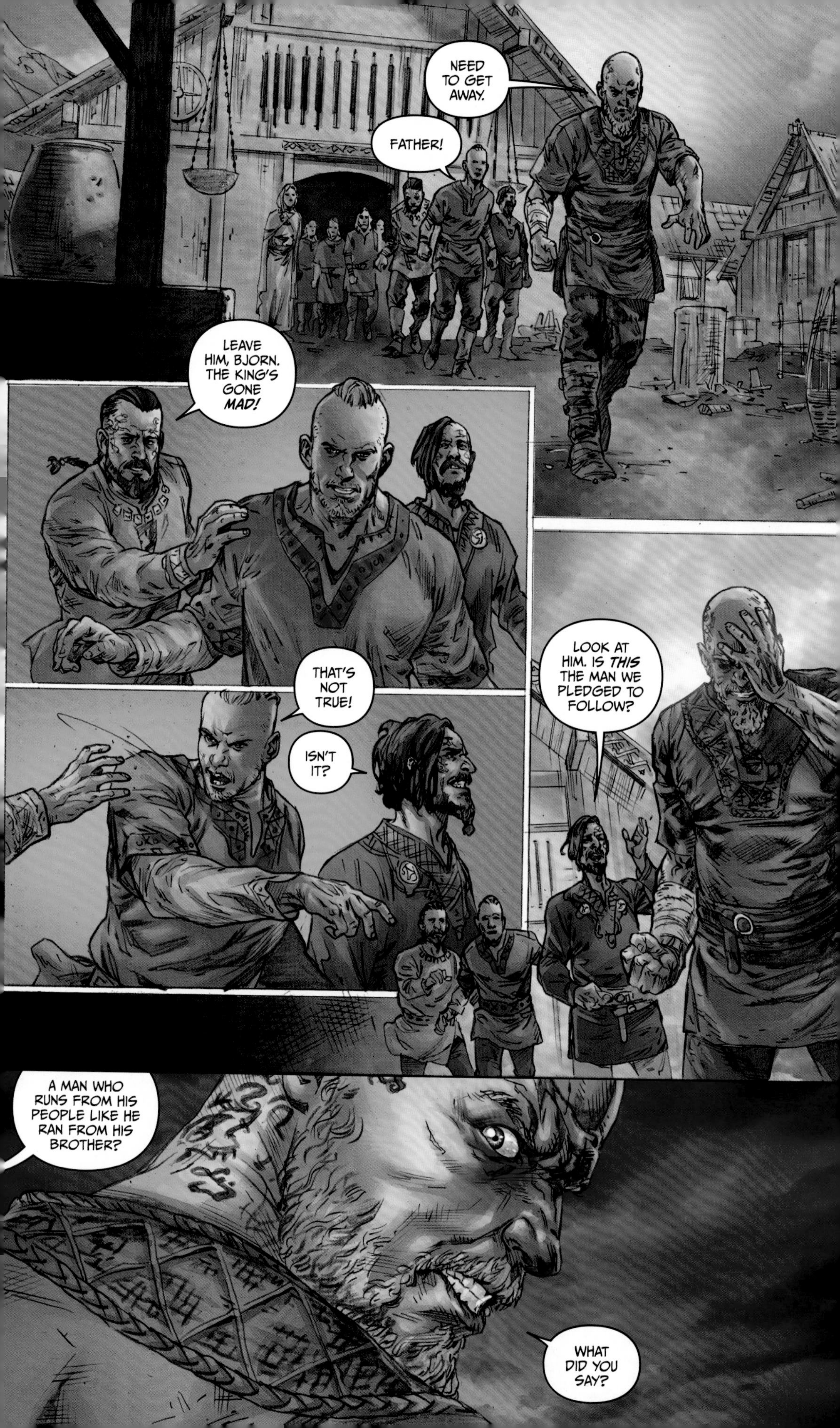
NEED TO GET AWAY.
FATHER!
LEAVE HIM, BJORN. THE KING'S GONE *MAD!*
THAT'S NOT TRUE!
ISN'T IT?
LOOK AT HIM. IS *THIS* THE MAN WE PLEDGED TO FOLLOW?
A MAN WHO RUNS FROM HIS PEOPLE LIKE HE RAN FROM HIS BROTHER?
WHAT DID YOU SAY?

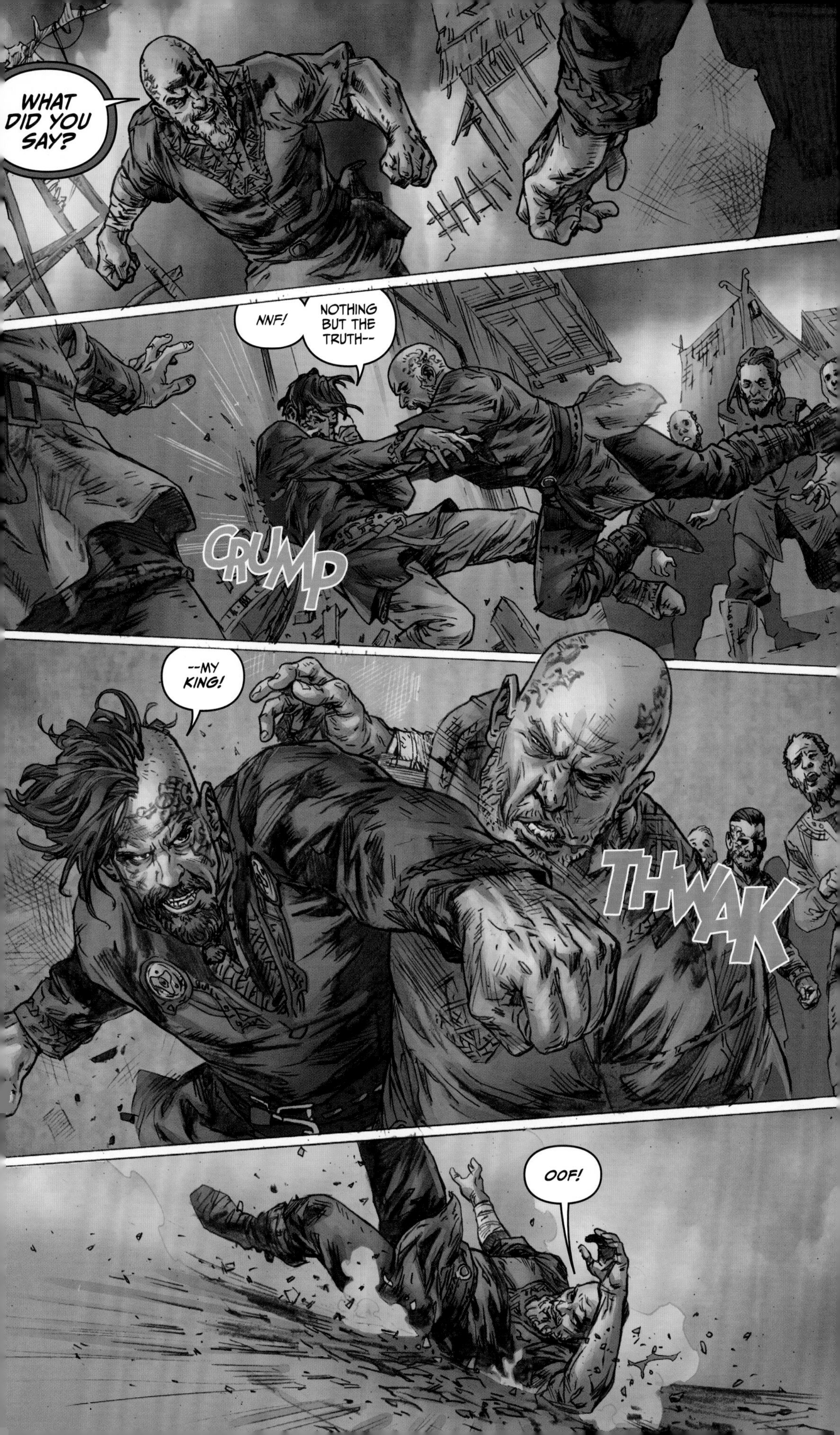
WHAT DID YOU SAY?
NNF!
NOTHING BUT THE TRUTH--
CRUMP
--MY KING!
THWAK
OOF!

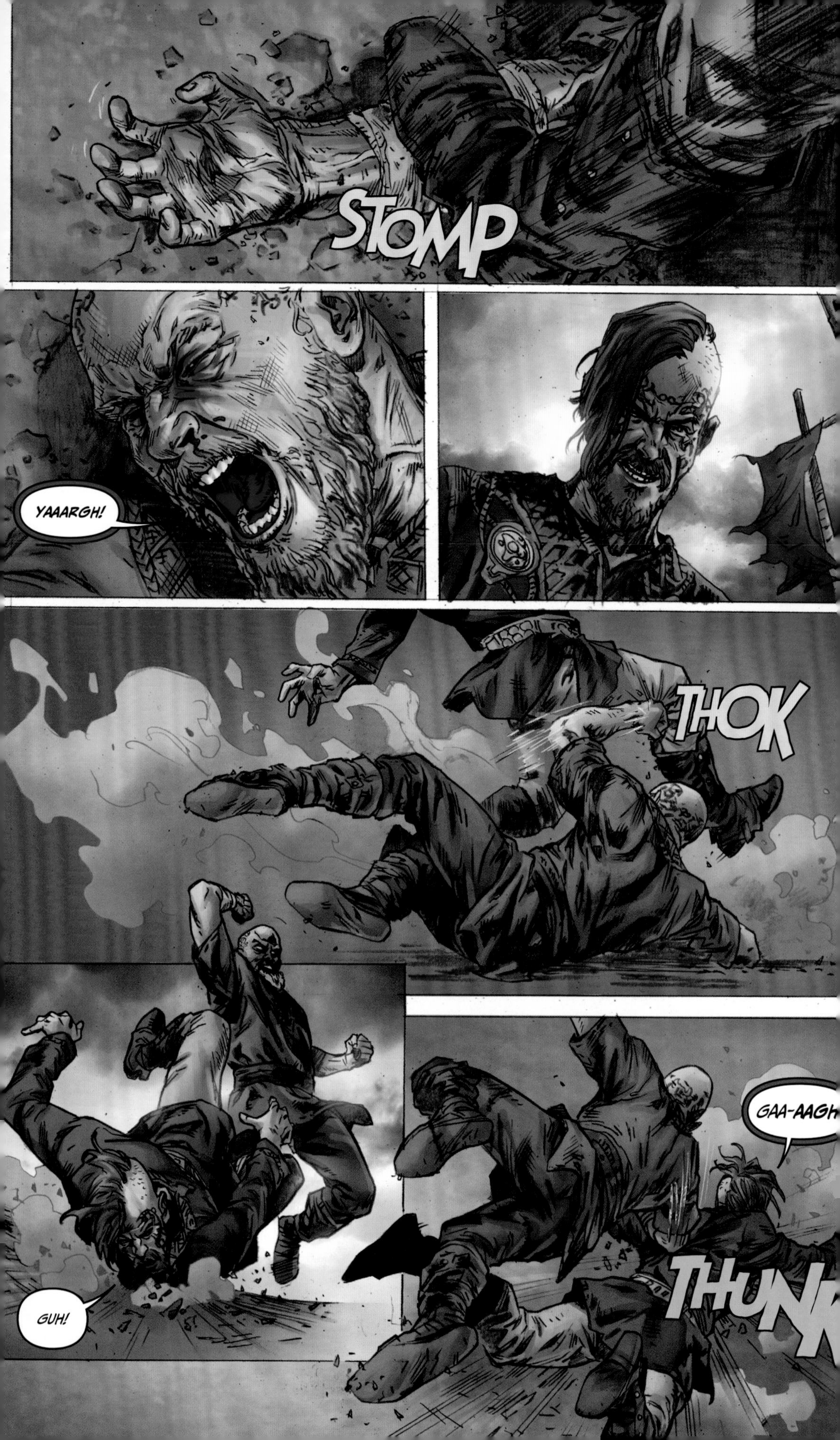
STOMP
YAAARGH!
THOK
GUH!
GAA-AAGH
THUNK

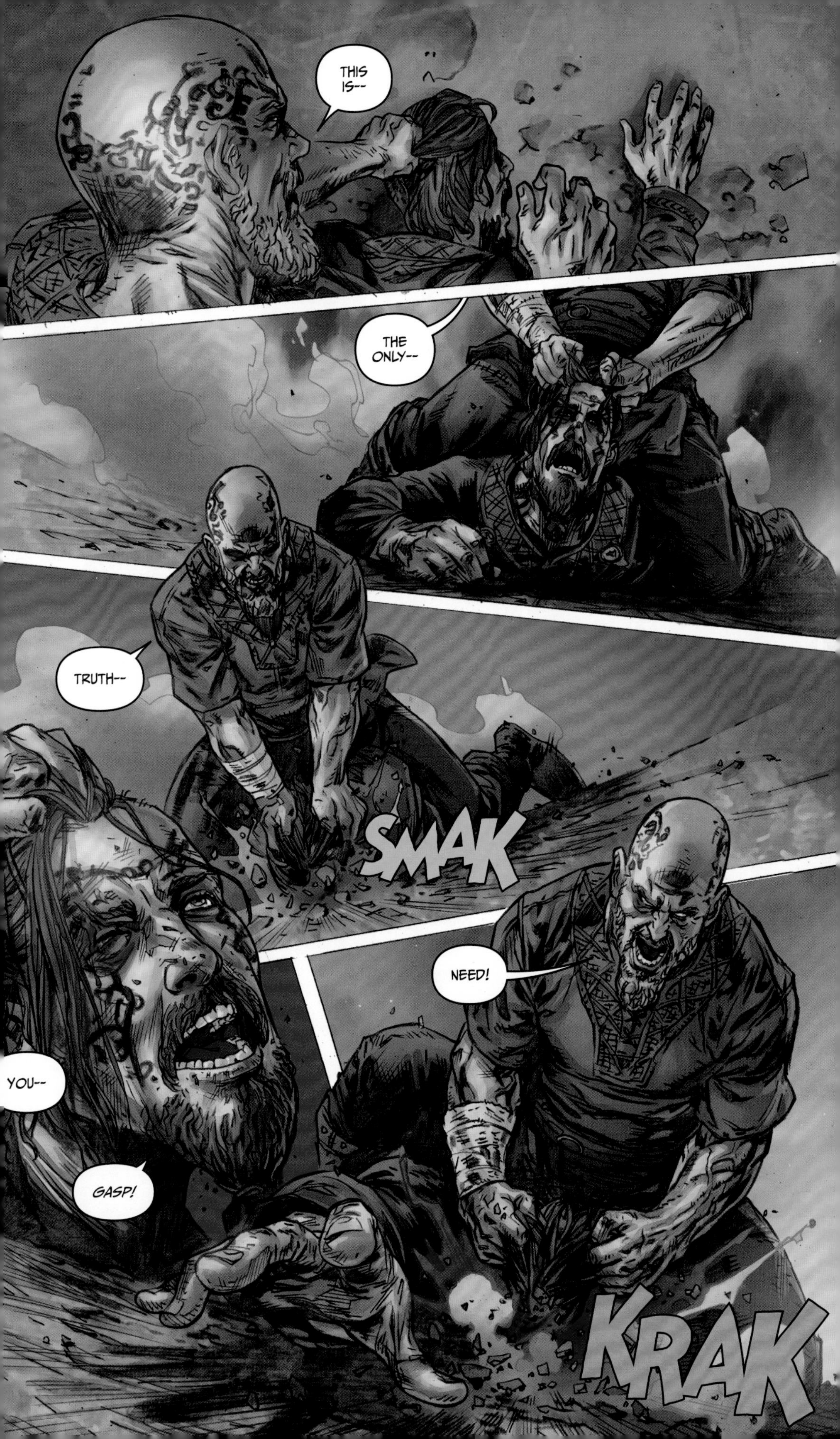
THIS IS--
THE ONLY--
TRUTH--
SMAK
NEED!
YOU--
GASP!
KRAK

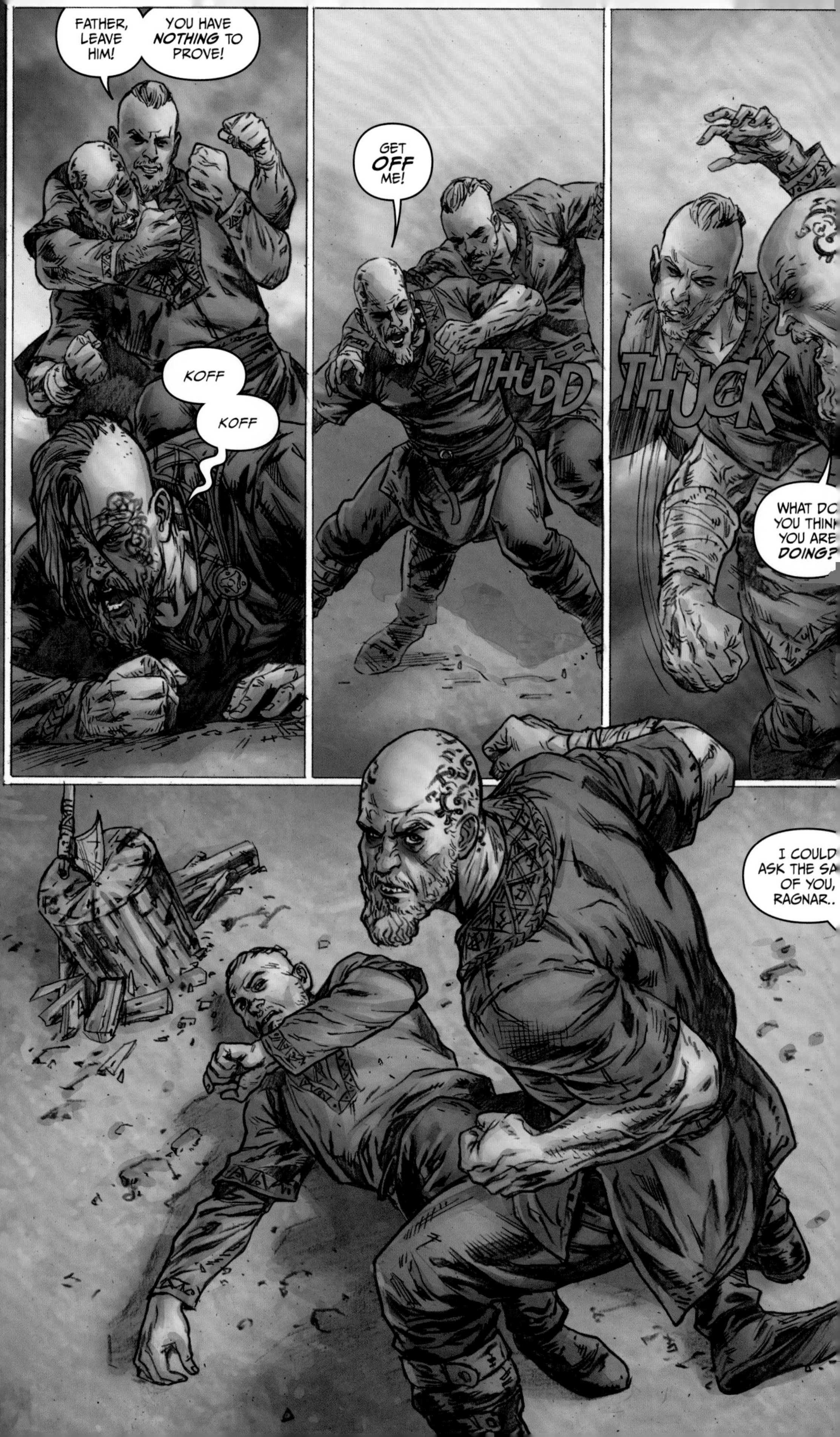

FATHER, LEAVE HIM!
YOU HAVE NOTHING TO PROVE!
KOFF
KOFF
GET OFF ME!
THUDD
THUCK
WHAT DO YOU THINK YOU ARE DOING?
I COULD ASK THE SA OF YOU, RAGNAR..

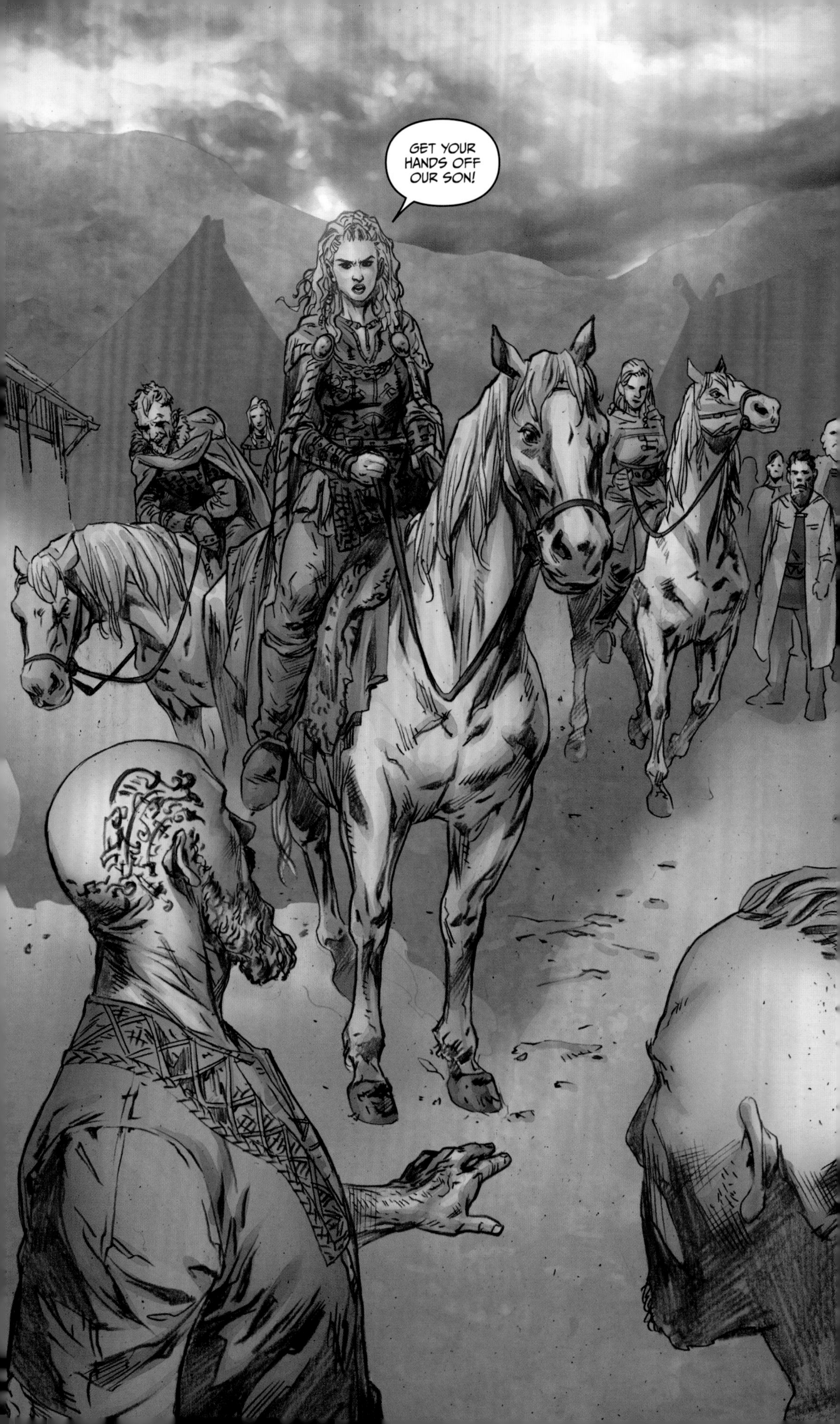
GET YOUR HANDS OFF OUR SON!

# CHAPTER 3

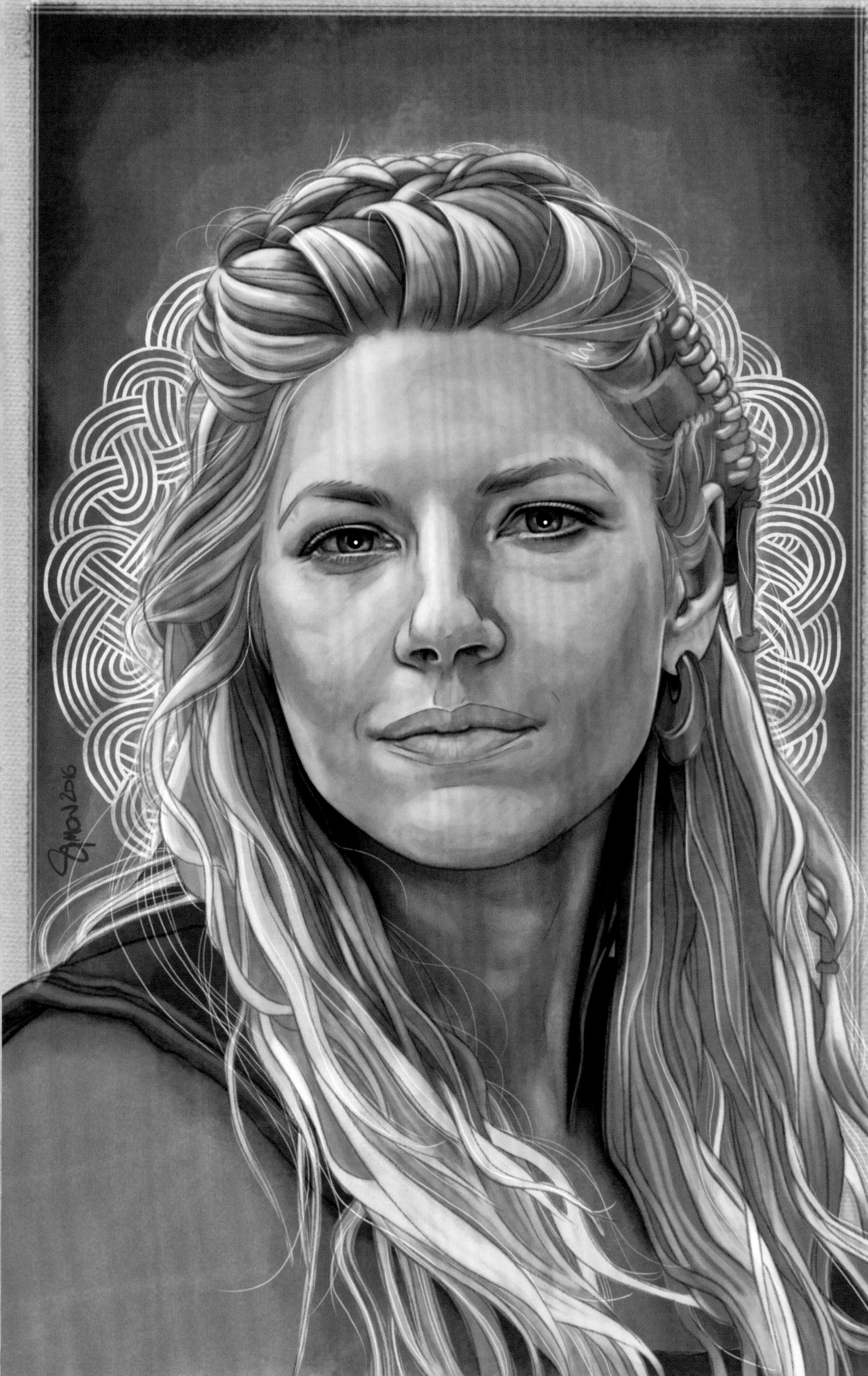
SIMON 2016

ILLUSTRATION BY SIMON MYERS

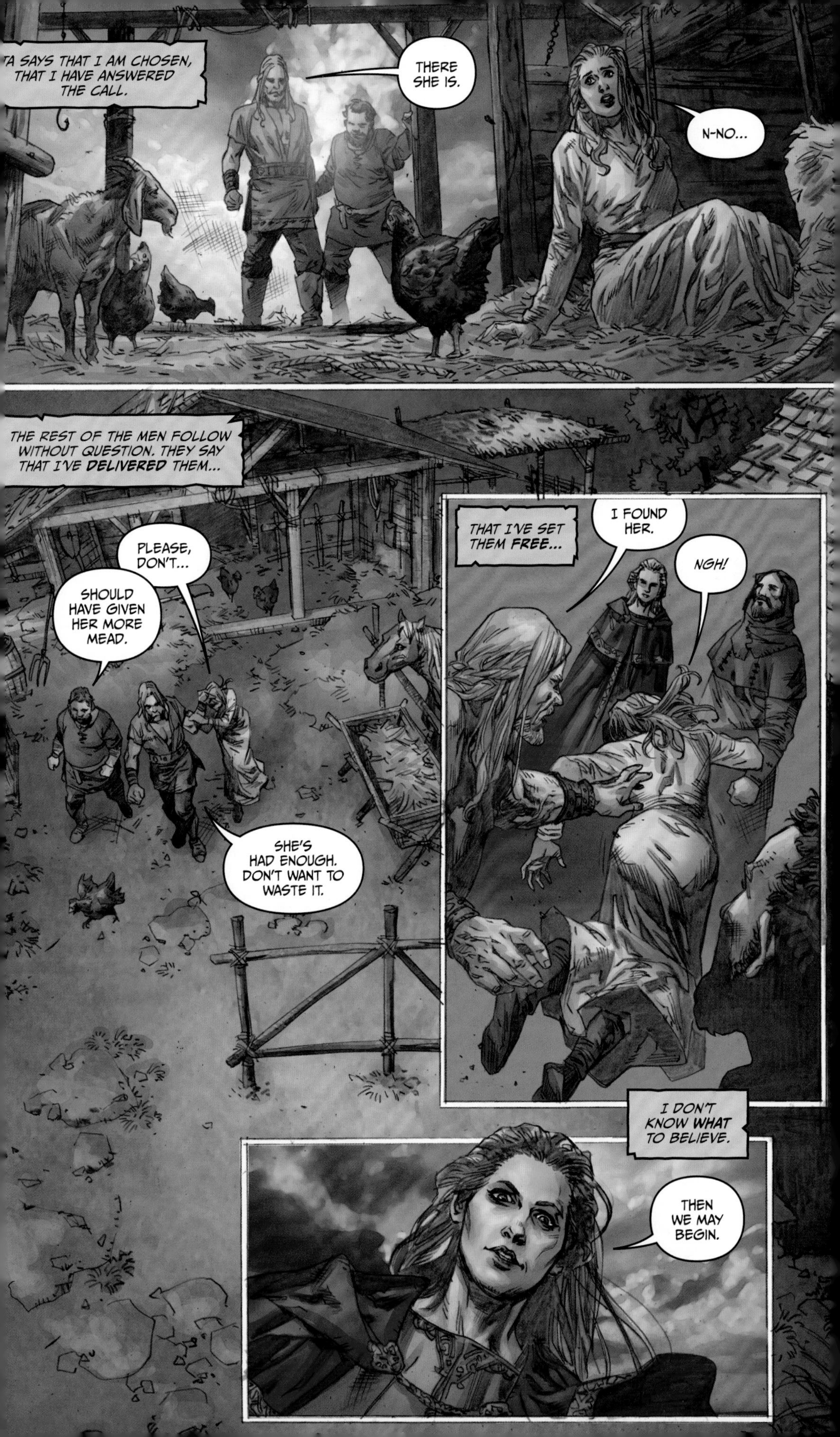
TA SAYS THAT I AM CHOSEN, THAT I HAVE ANSWERED THE CALL.
THERE SHE IS.
N-NO...
THE REST OF THE MEN FOLLOW WITHOUT QUESTION. THEY SAY THAT I'VE **DELIVERED** THEM...
PLEASE, DON'T...
SHOULD HAVE GIVEN HER MORE MEAD.
SHE'S HAD ENOUGH. DON'T WANT TO WASTE IT.
THAT I'VE SET THEM **FREE**...
I FOUND HER.
NGH!
I DON'T KNOW **WHAT** TO BELIEVE.
THEN WE MAY BEGIN.

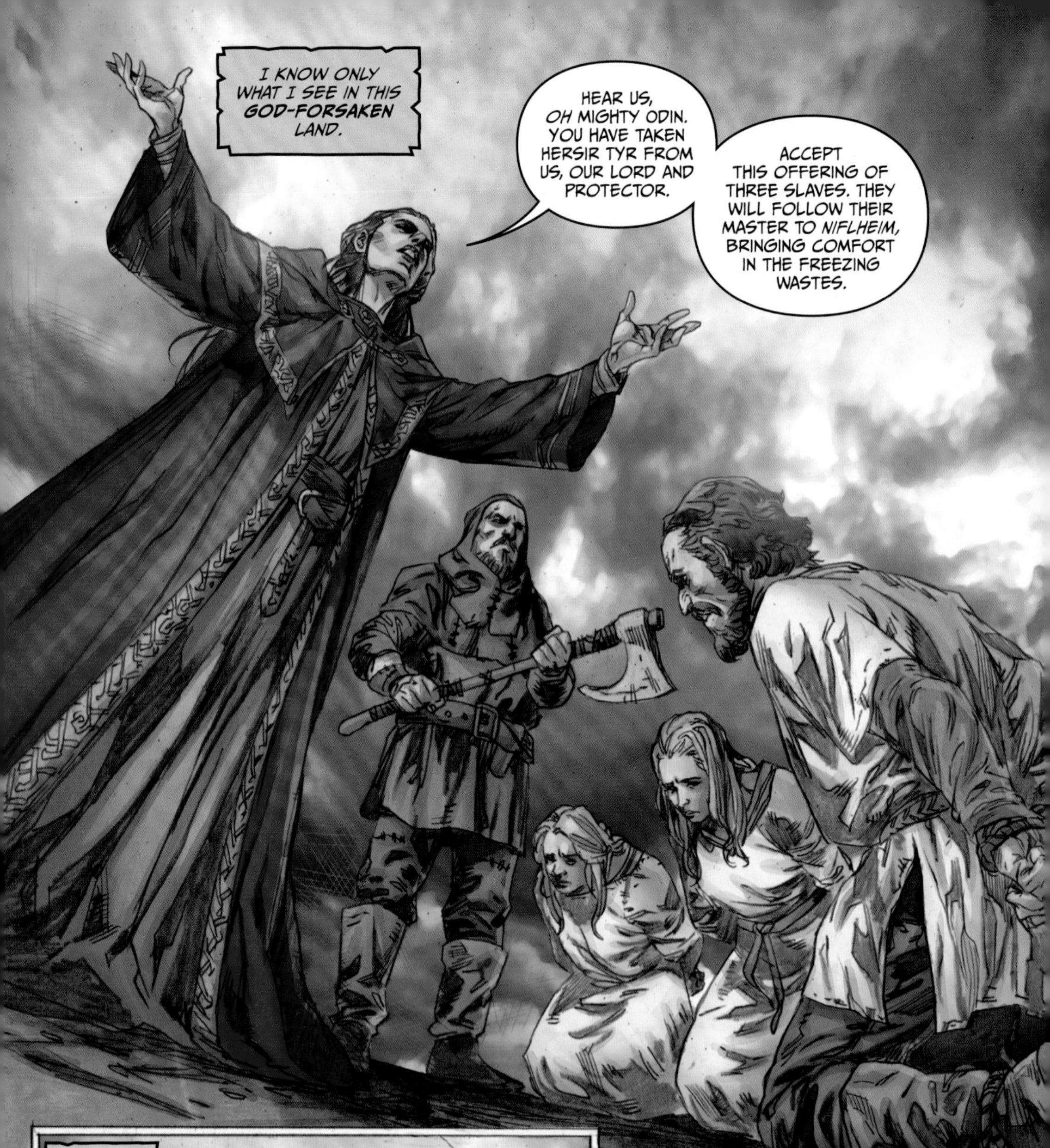
I KNOW ONLY WHAT I SEE IN THIS GOD-FORSAKEN LAND.
HEAR US, OH MIGHTY ODIN. YOU HAVE TAKEN HERSIR TYR FROM US, OUR LORD AND PROTECTOR.
ACCEPT THIS OFFERING OF THREE SLAVES. THEY WILL FOLLOW THEIR MASTER TO NIFLHEIM, BRINGING COMFORT IN THE FREEZING WASTES.

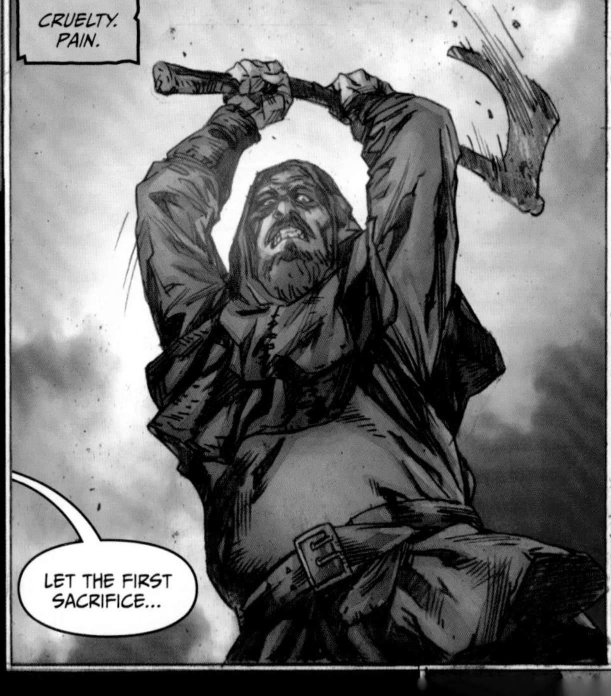
CRUELTY. PAIN.
LET THE FIRST SACRIFICE...

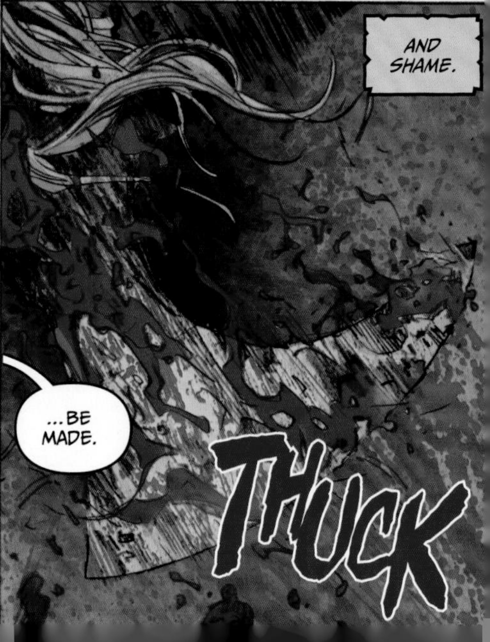
AND SHAME.
...BE MADE.
THUCK

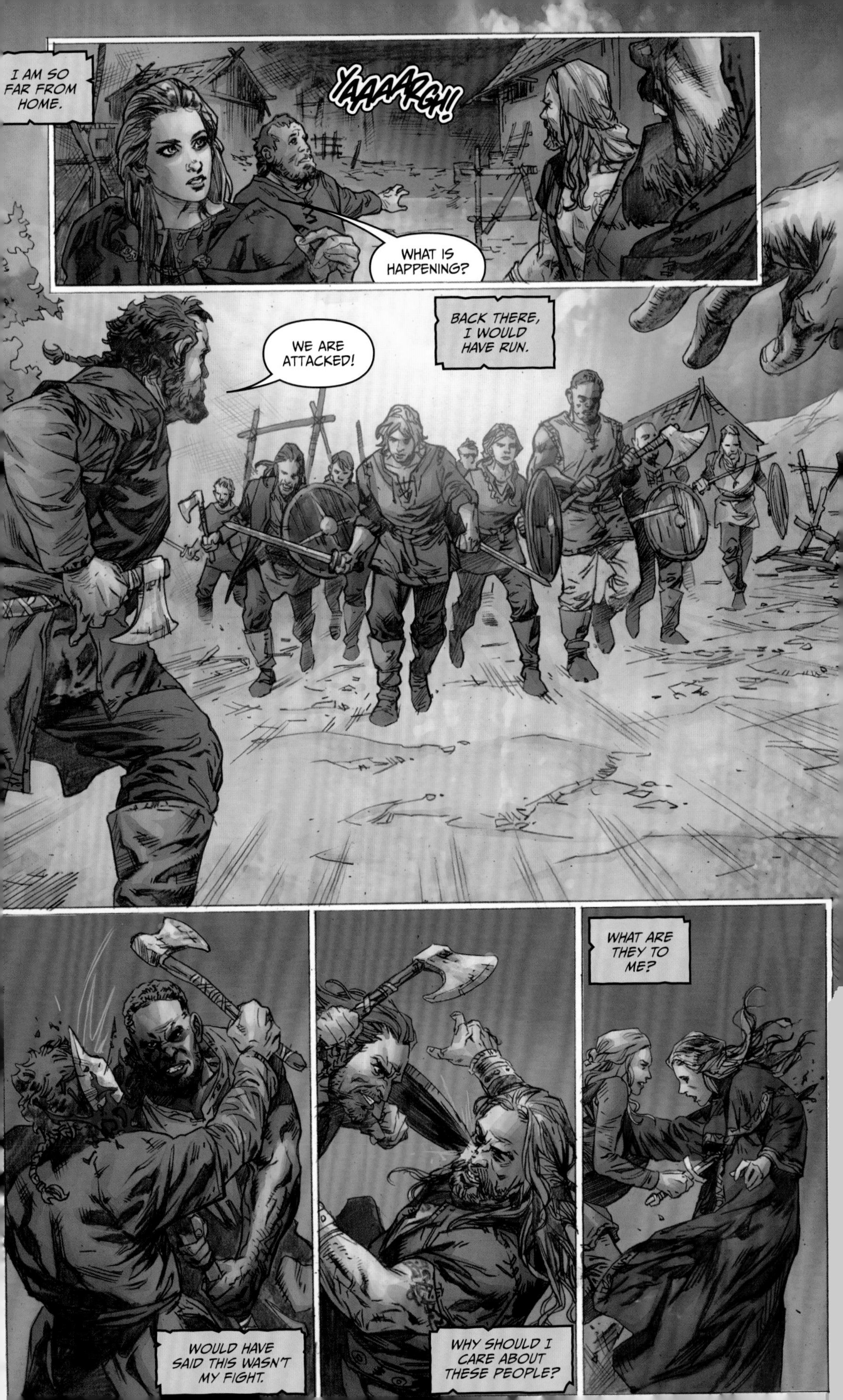
I AM SO FAR FROM HOME.
YAAAARGH!!
WHAT IS HAPPENING?
WE ARE ATTACKED!
BACK THERE, I WOULD HAVE RUN.
WOULD HAVE SAID THIS WASN'T MY FIGHT.
WHY SHOULD I CARE ABOUT THESE PEOPLE?
WHAT ARE THEY TO ME?

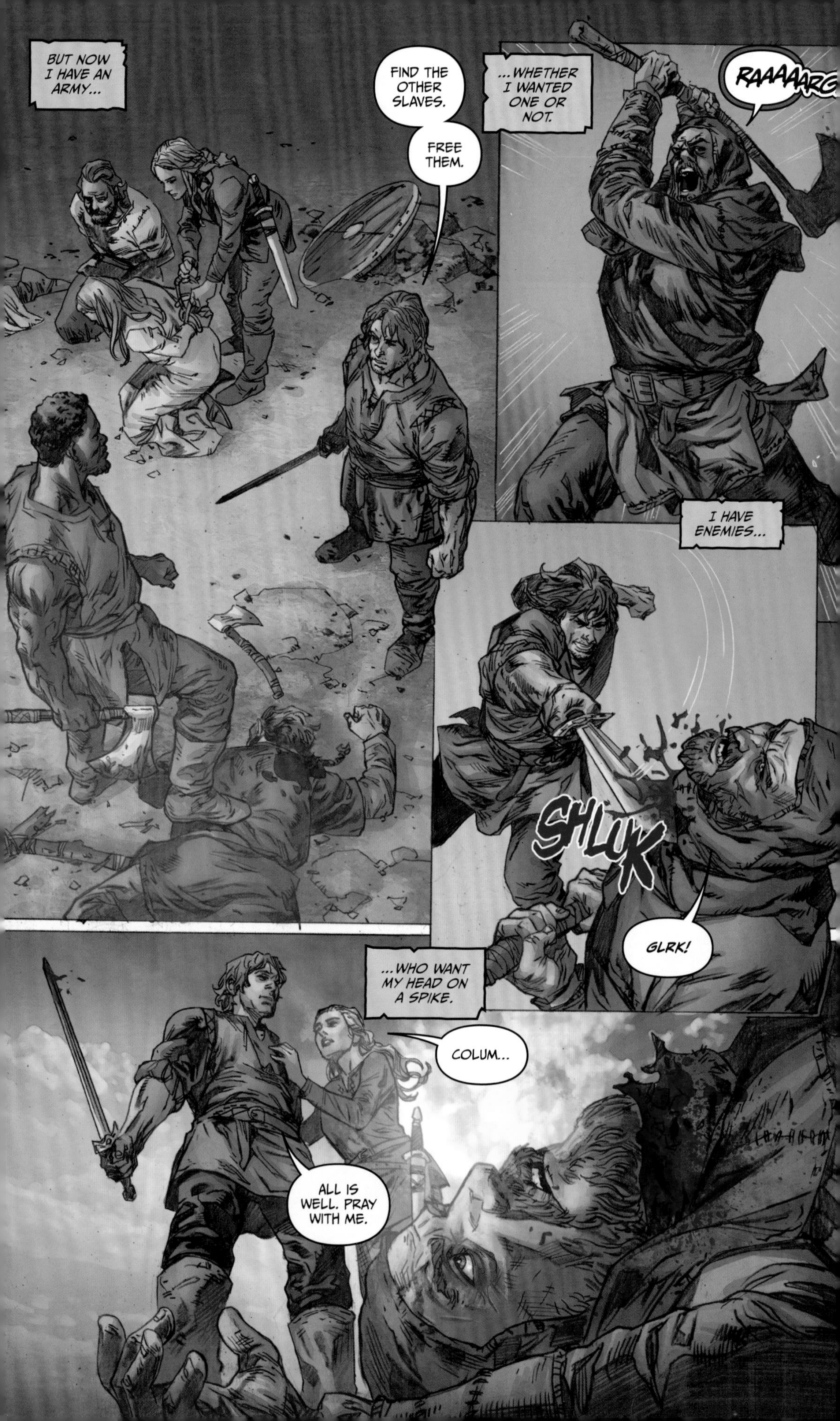

BUT NOW I HAVE AN ARMY...
FIND THE OTHER SLAVES.
FREE THEM.
...WHETHER I WANTED ONE OR NOT.
RAAAAARG
I HAVE ENEMIES...
SHLUK
GLRK!
...WHO WANT MY HEAD ON A SPIKE.
COLUM...
ALL IS WELL. PRAY WITH ME.

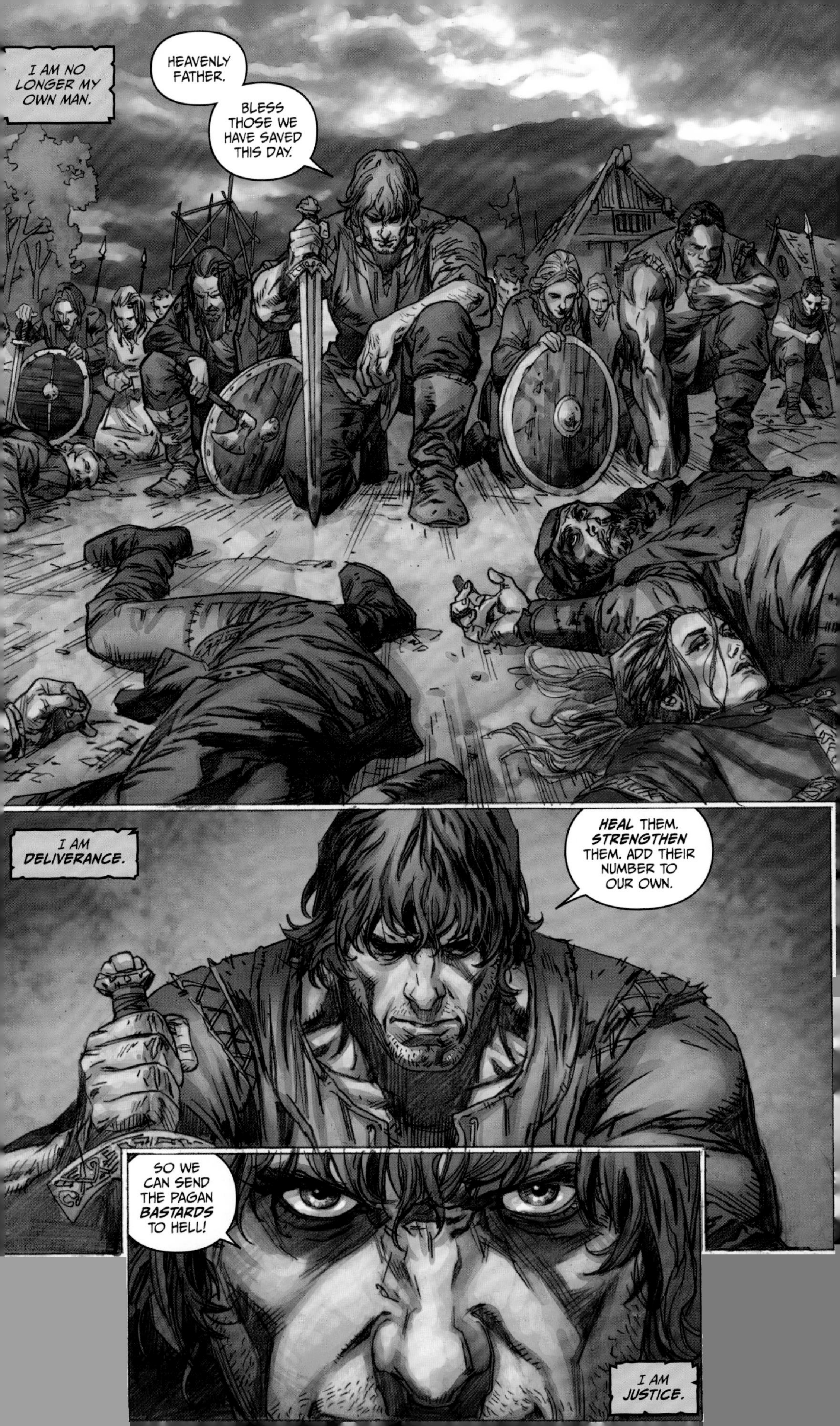
I AM NO LONGER MY OWN MAN.
HEAVENLY FATHER.
BLESS THOSE WE HAVE SAVED THIS DAY.
I AM DELIVERANCE.
HEAL THEM. STRENGTHEN THEM. ADD THEIR NUMBER TO OUR OWN.
SO WE CAN SEND THE PAGAN BASTARDS TO HELL!
I AM JUSTICE.

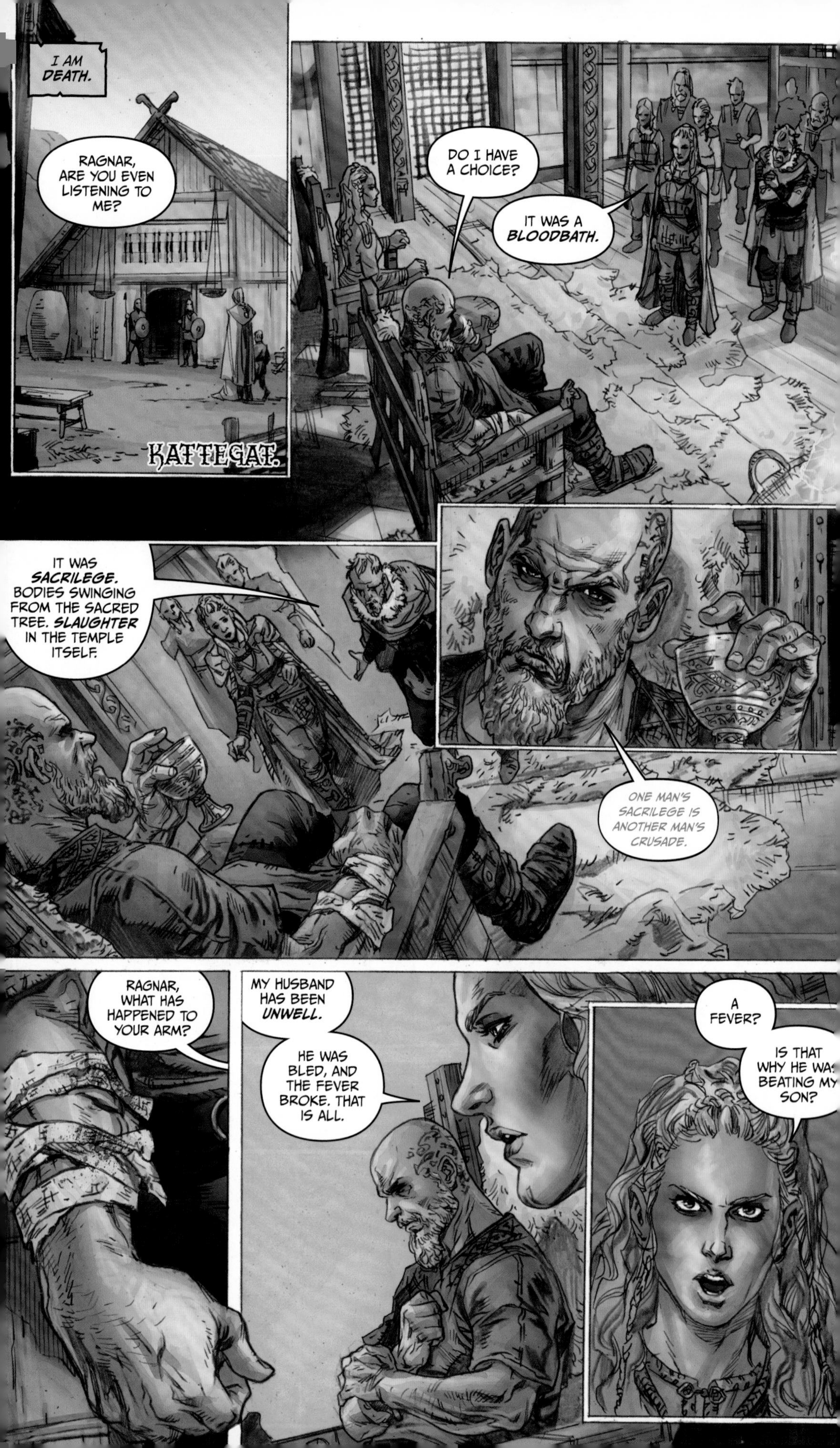
I AM DEATH.
RAGNAR, ARE YOU EVEN LISTENING TO ME?
KATTEGAT.
DO I HAVE A CHOICE?
IT WAS A BLOODBATH.
IT WAS SACRILEGE. BODIES SWINGING FROM THE SACRED TREE. SLAUGHTER IN THE TEMPLE ITSELF.
ONE MAN'S SACRILEGE IS ANOTHER MAN'S CRUSADE.
RAGNAR, WHAT HAS HAPPENED TO YOUR ARM?
MY HUSBAND HAS BEEN UNWELL.
HE WAS BLED, AND THE FEVER BROKE. THAT IS ALL.
A FEVER?
IS THAT WHY HE WAS BEATING MY SON?

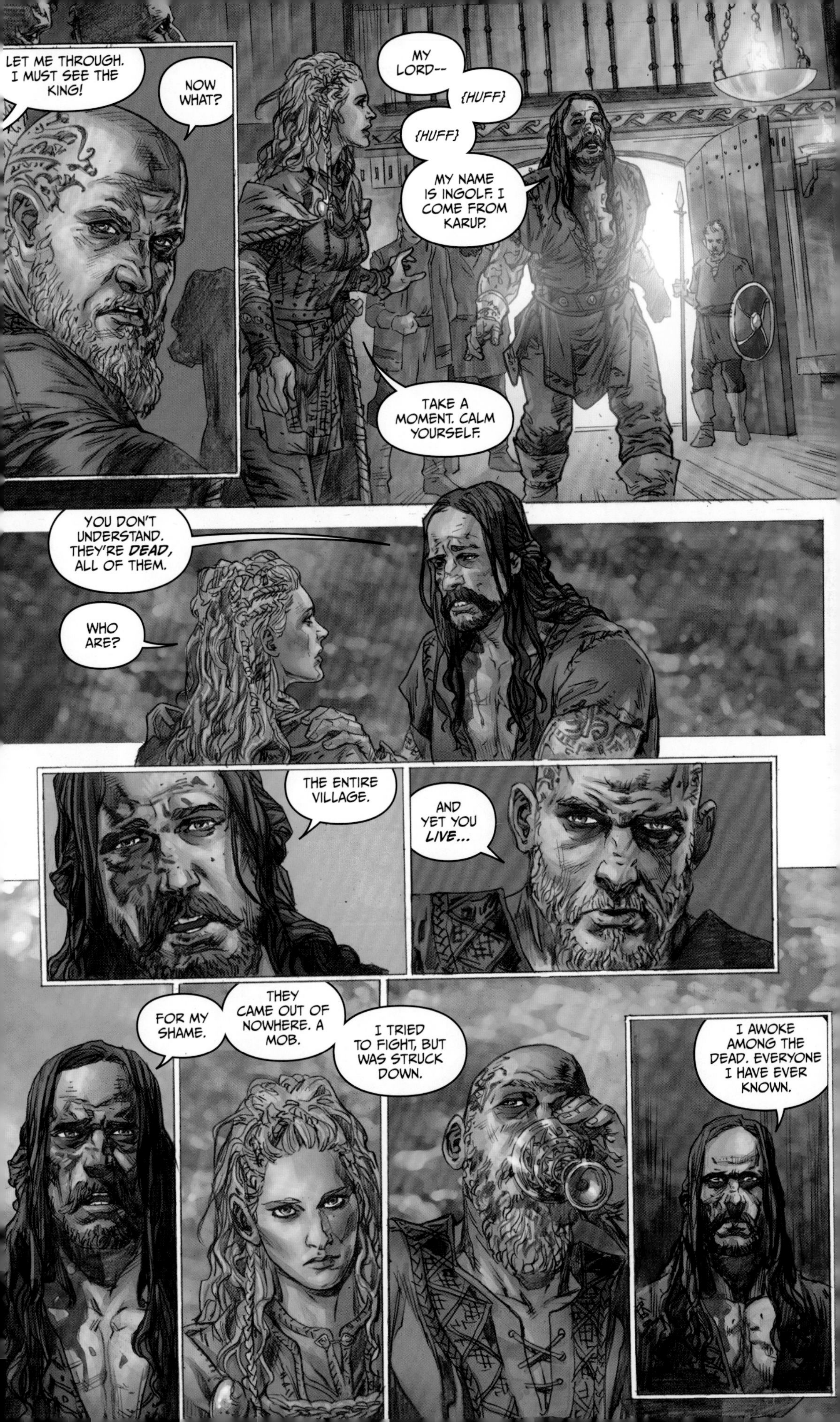
LET ME THROUGH. I MUST SEE THE KING!
NOW WHAT?
MY LORD--
{HUFF}
{HUFF}
MY NAME IS INGOLF. I COME FROM KARUP.
TAKE A MOMENT. CALM YOURSELF.
YOU DON'T UNDERSTAND. THEY'RE *DEAD,* ALL OF THEM.
WHO ARE?
THE ENTIRE VILLAGE.
AND YET YOU *LIVE...*
FOR MY SHAME.
THEY CAME OUT OF NOWHERE. A MOB.
I TRIED TO FIGHT, BUT WAS STRUCK DOWN.
I AWOKE AMONG THE DEAD. EVERYONE I HAVE EVER KNOWN.

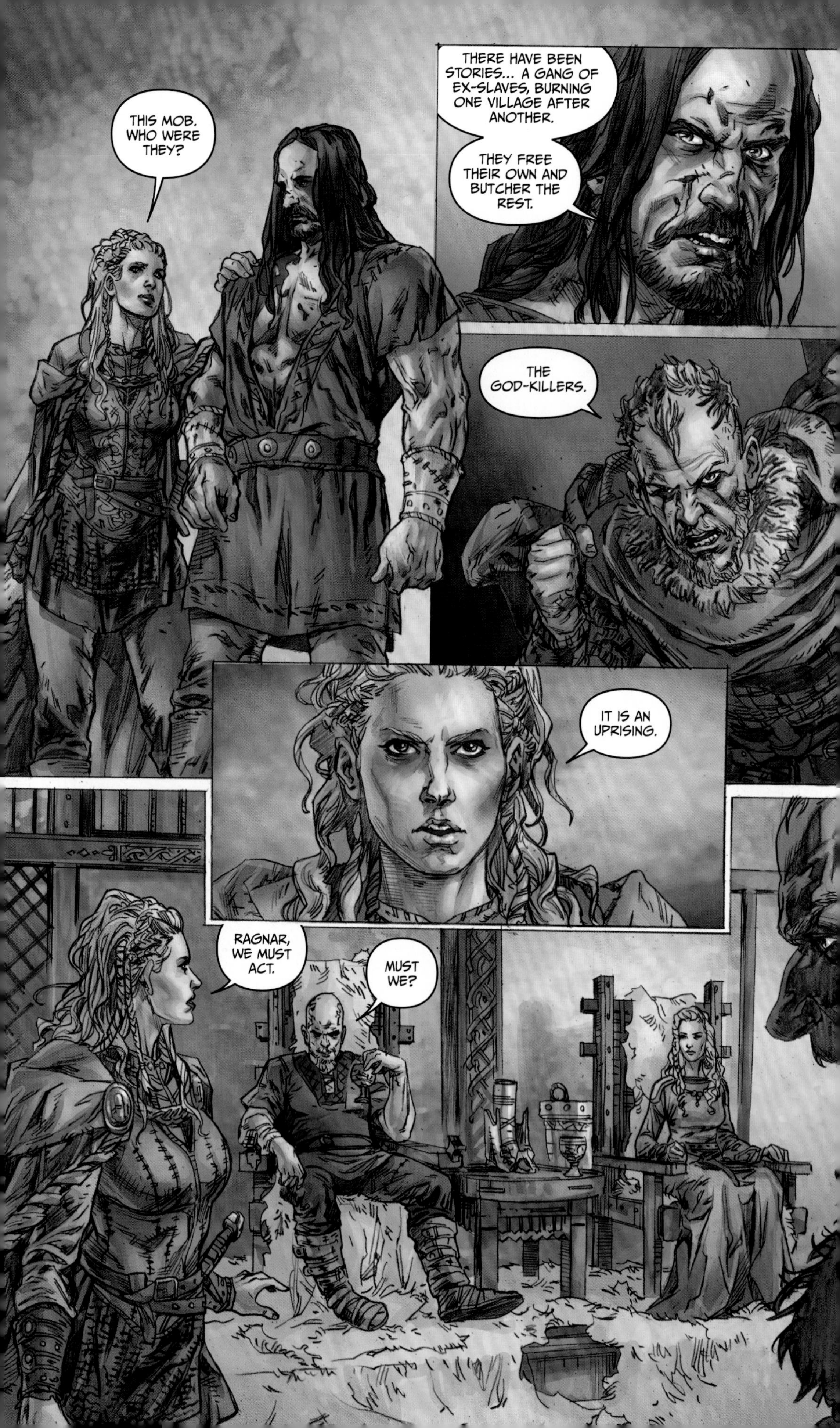
THIS MOB. WHO WERE THEY?
THERE HAVE BEEN STORIES... A GANG OF EX-SLAVES, BURNING ONE VILLAGE AFTER ANOTHER.
THEY FREE THEIR OWN AND BUTCHER THE REST.
THE GOD-KILLERS.
IT IS AN UPRISING.
RAGNAR, WE MUST ACT.
MUST WE?

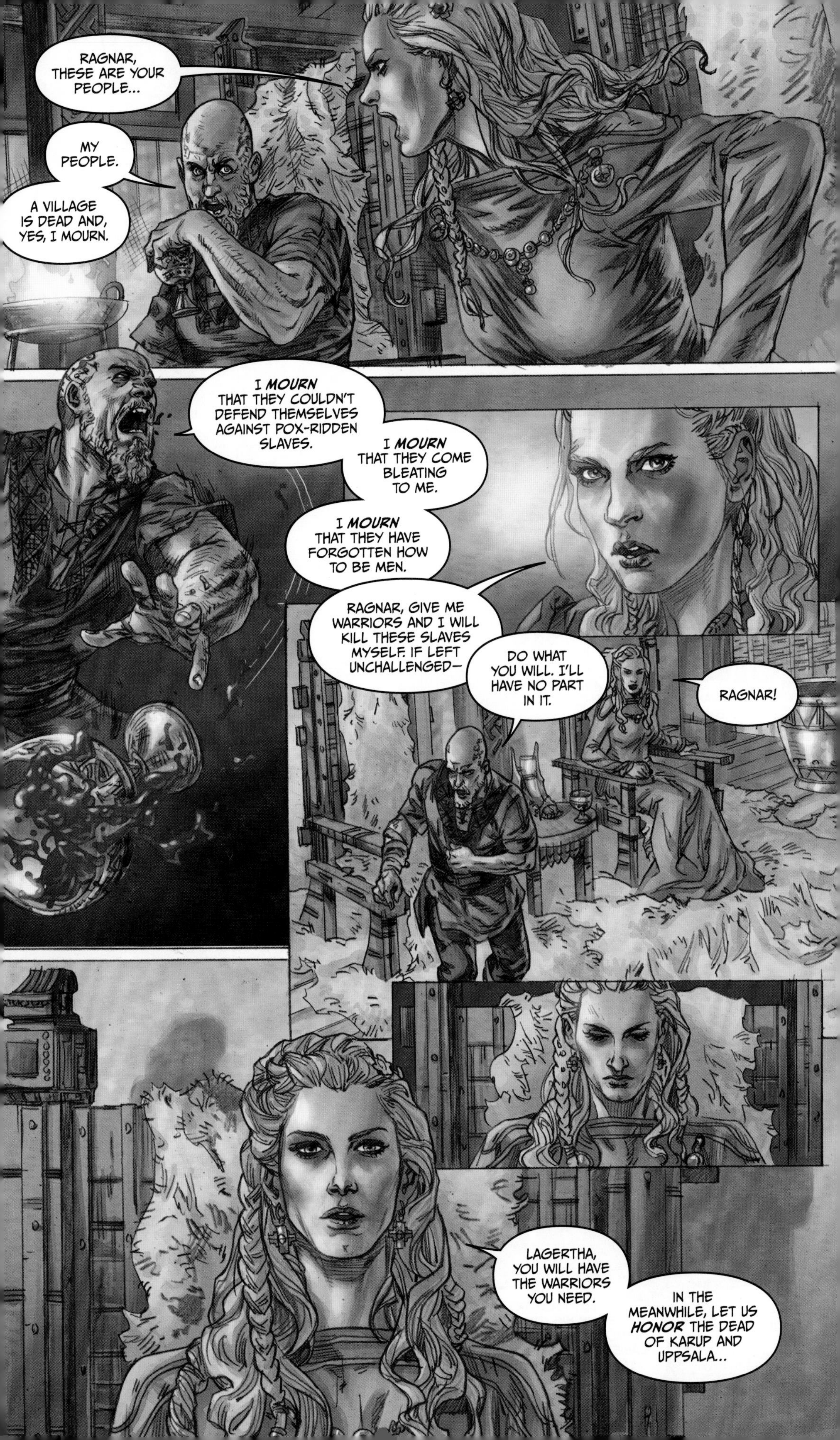
RAGNAR, THESE ARE YOUR PEOPLE...
MY PEOPLE.
A VILLAGE IS DEAD AND, YES, I MOURN.
I *MOURN* THAT THEY COULDN'T DEFEND THEMSELVES AGAINST POX-RIDDEN SLAVES.
I *MOURN* THAT THEY COME BLEATING TO ME.
I *MOURN* THAT THEY HAVE FORGOTTEN HOW TO BE MEN.
RAGNAR, GIVE ME WARRIORS AND I WILL KILL THESE SLAVES MYSELF. IF LEFT UNCHALLENGED—
DO WHAT YOU WILL. I'LL HAVE NO PART IN IT.
RAGNAR!
LAGERTHA, YOU WILL HAVE THE WARRIORS YOU NEED.
IN THE MEANWHILE, LET US *HONOR* THE DEAD OF KARUP AND UPPSALA...

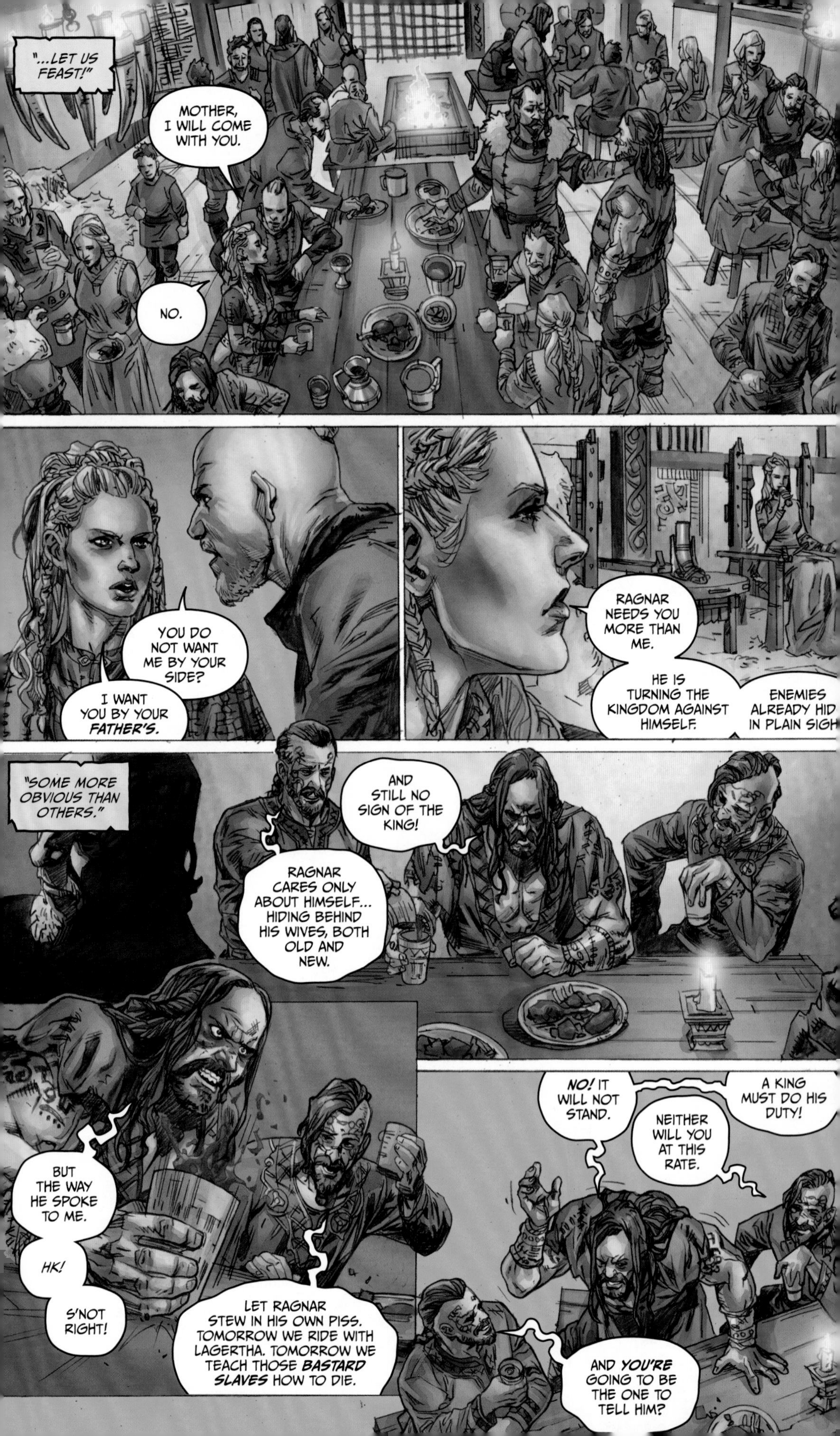
"...LET US FEAST!"
MOTHER, I WILL COME WITH YOU.
NO.
YOU DO NOT WANT ME BY YOUR SIDE?
I WANT YOU BY YOUR FATHER'S.
RAGNAR NEEDS YOU MORE THAN ME.
HE IS TURNING THE KINGDOM AGAINST HIMSELF.
ENEMIES ALREADY HID IN PLAIN SIGH
"SOME MORE OBVIOUS THAN OTHERS."
AND STILL NO SIGN OF THE KING!
RAGNAR CARES ONLY ABOUT HIMSELF... HIDING BEHIND HIS WIVES, BOTH OLD AND NEW.
BUT THE WAY HE SPOKE TO ME.
HK!
S'NOT RIGHT!
LET RAGNAR STEW IN HIS OWN PISS. TOMORROW WE RIDE WITH LAGERTHA. TOMORROW WE TEACH THOSE BASTARD SLAVES HOW TO DIE.
NO! IT WILL NOT STAND.
A KING MUST DO HIS DUTY!
NEITHER WILL YOU AT THIS RATE.
AND YOU'RE GOING TO BE THE ONE TO TELL HIM?

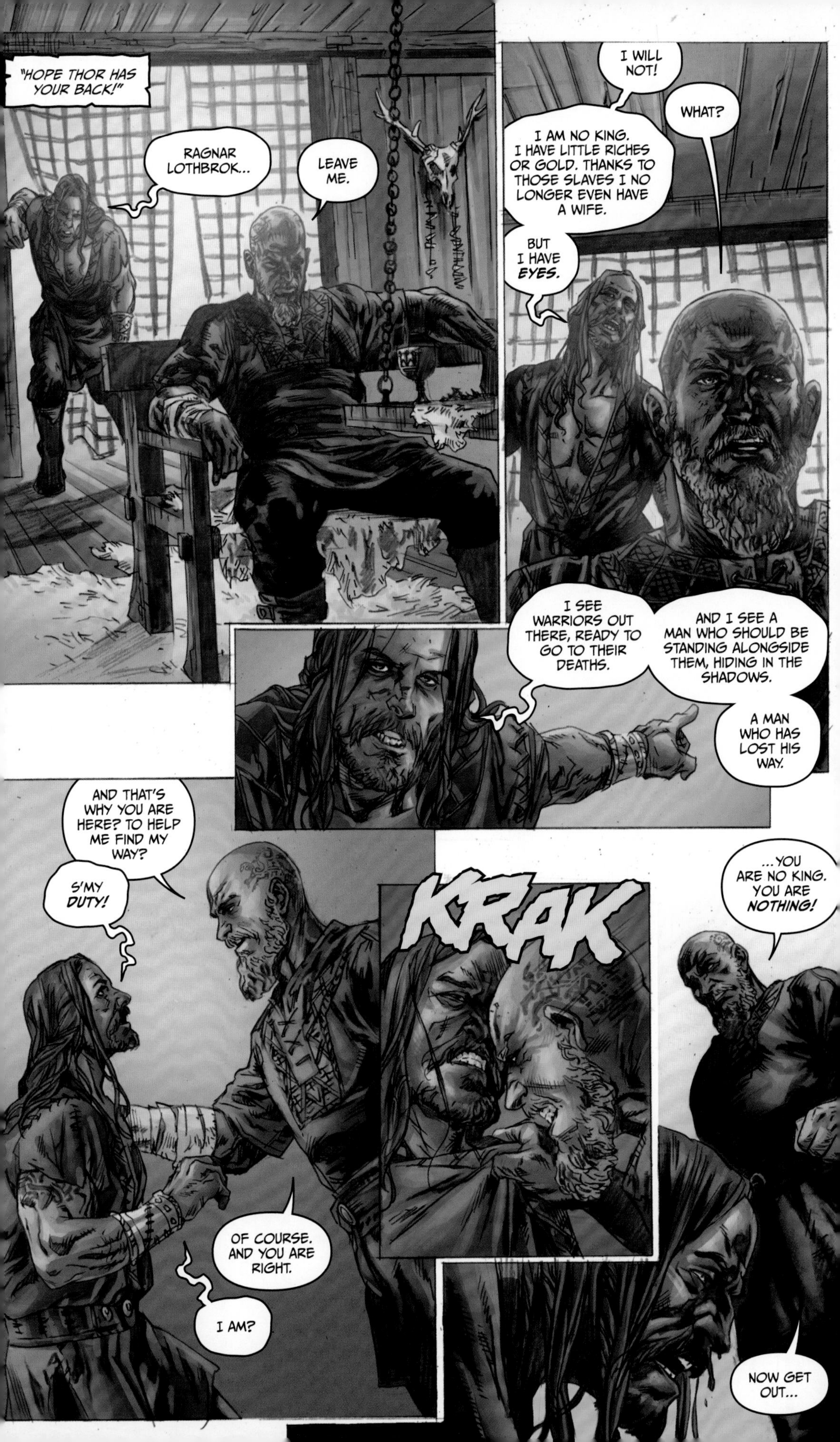
"HOPE THOR HAS YOUR BACK!"
RAGNAR LOTHBROK...
LEAVE ME.
I WILL NOT!
WHAT?
I AM NO KING. I HAVE LITTLE RICHES OR GOLD. THANKS TO THOSE SLAVES I NO LONGER EVEN HAVE A WIFE.
BUT I HAVE EYES.
I SEE WARRIORS OUT THERE, READY TO GO TO THEIR DEATHS.
AND I SEE A MAN WHO SHOULD BE STANDING ALONGSIDE THEM, HIDING IN THE SHADOWS.
A MAN WHO HAS LOST HIS WAY.
AND THAT'S WHY YOU ARE HERE? TO HELP ME FIND MY WAY?
S'MY DUTY!
OF COURSE. AND YOU ARE RIGHT.
I AM?
KRAK
...YOU ARE NO KING. YOU ARE NOTHING!
NOW GET OUT...

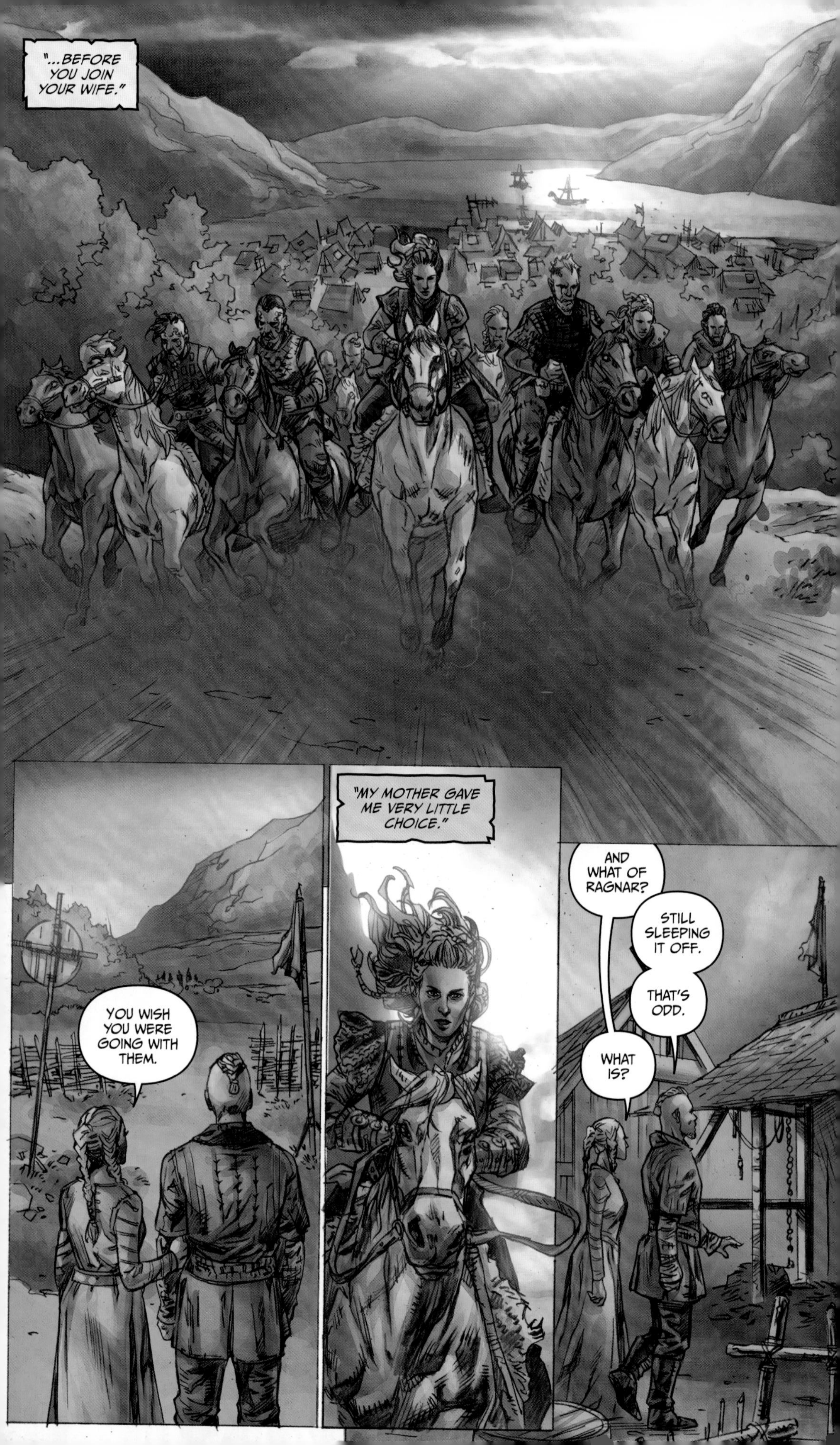
"...BEFORE YOU JOIN YOUR WIFE."
YOU WISH YOU WERE GOING WITH THEM.
"MY MOTHER GAVE ME VERY LITTLE CHOICE."
AND WHAT OF RAGNAR?
STILL SLEEPING IT OFF.
THAT'S ODD.
WHAT IS?

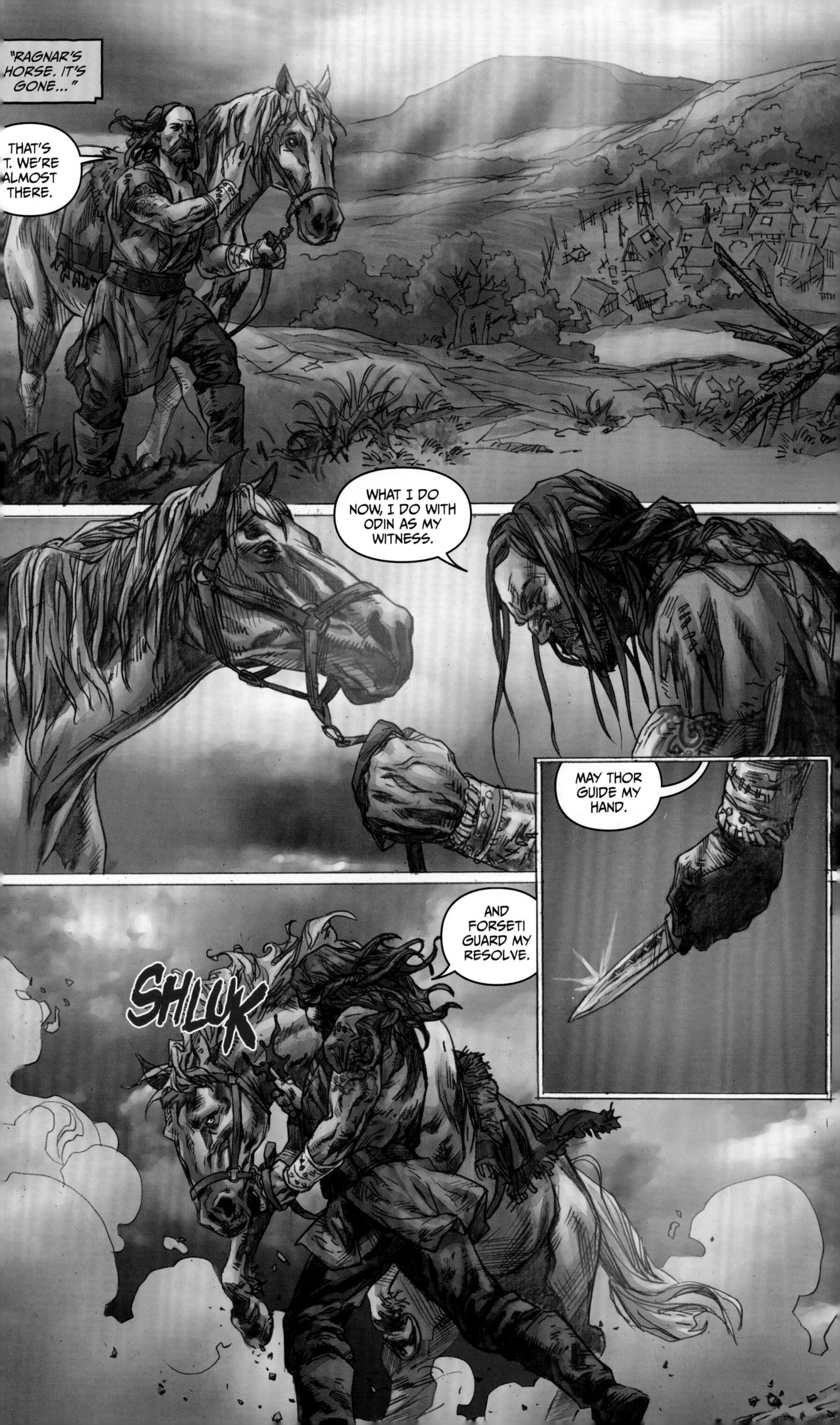
"RAGNAR'S HORSE. IT'S GONE..."
THAT'S T. WE'RE ALMOST THERE.
WHAT I DO NOW, I DO WITH ODIN AS MY WITNESS.
MAY THOR GUIDE MY HAND.
AND FORSETI GUARD MY RESOLVE.
SHLUK

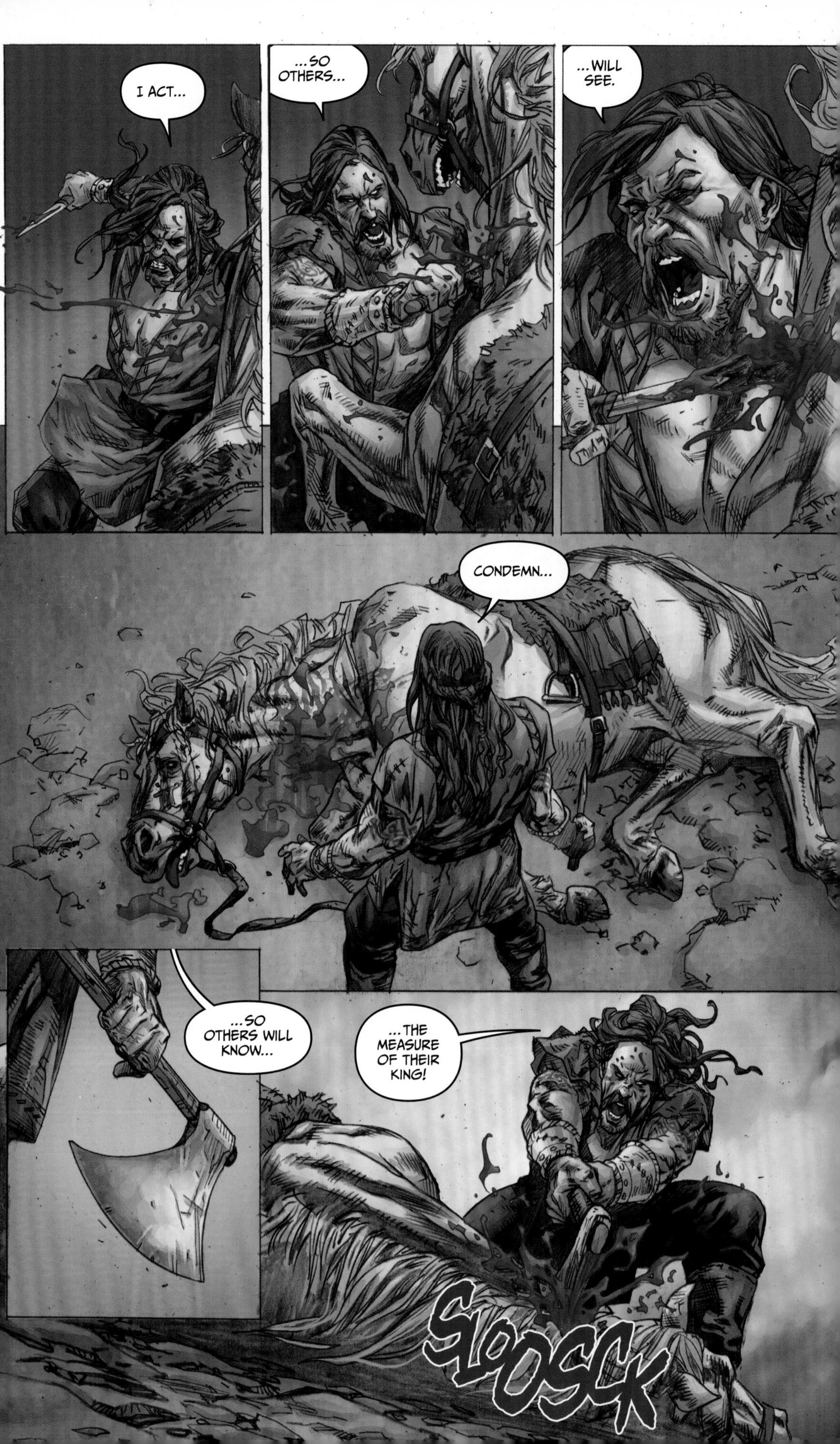
I ACT...
...SO OTHERS...
...WILL SEE.
CONDEMN...
...SO OTHERS WILL KNOW...
...THE MEASURE OF THEIR KING!
SLOOSCK

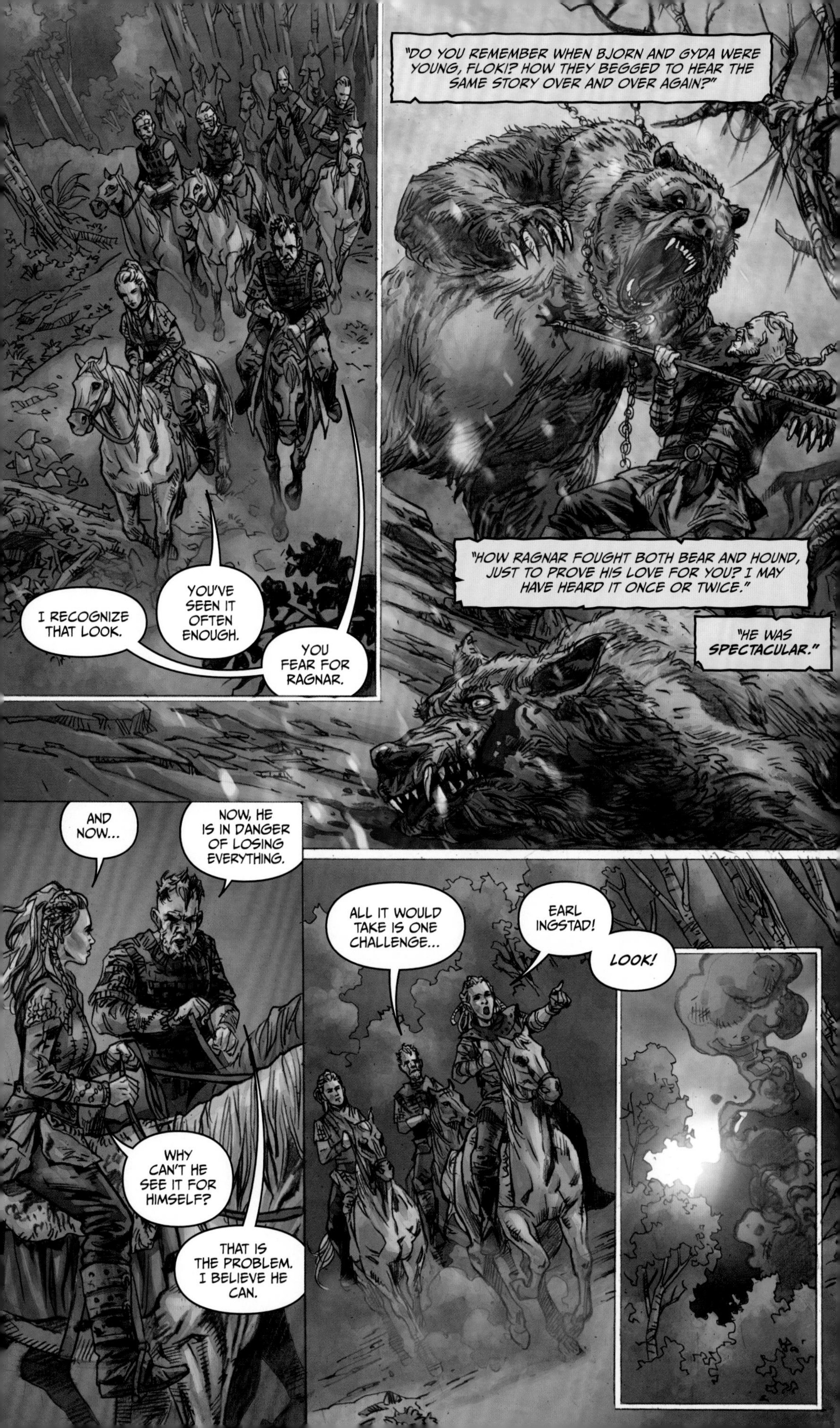
I RECOGNIZE THAT LOOK.
YOU'VE SEEN IT OFTEN ENOUGH.
YOU FEAR FOR RAGNAR.
"DO YOU REMEMBER WHEN BJORN AND GYDA WERE YOUNG, FLOKI? HOW THEY BEGGED TO HEAR THE SAME STORY OVER AND OVER AGAIN?"
"HOW RAGNAR FOUGHT BOTH BEAR AND HOUND, JUST TO PROVE HIS LOVE FOR YOU? I MAY HAVE HEARD IT ONCE OR TWICE."
"HE WAS SPECTACULAR."
AND NOW...
NOW, HE IS IN DANGER OF LOSING EVERYTHING.
WHY CAN'T HE SEE IT FOR HIMSELF?
THAT IS THE PROBLEM. I BELIEVE HE CAN.
ALL IT WOULD TAKE IS ONE CHALLENGE...
EARL INGSTAD!
LOOK!

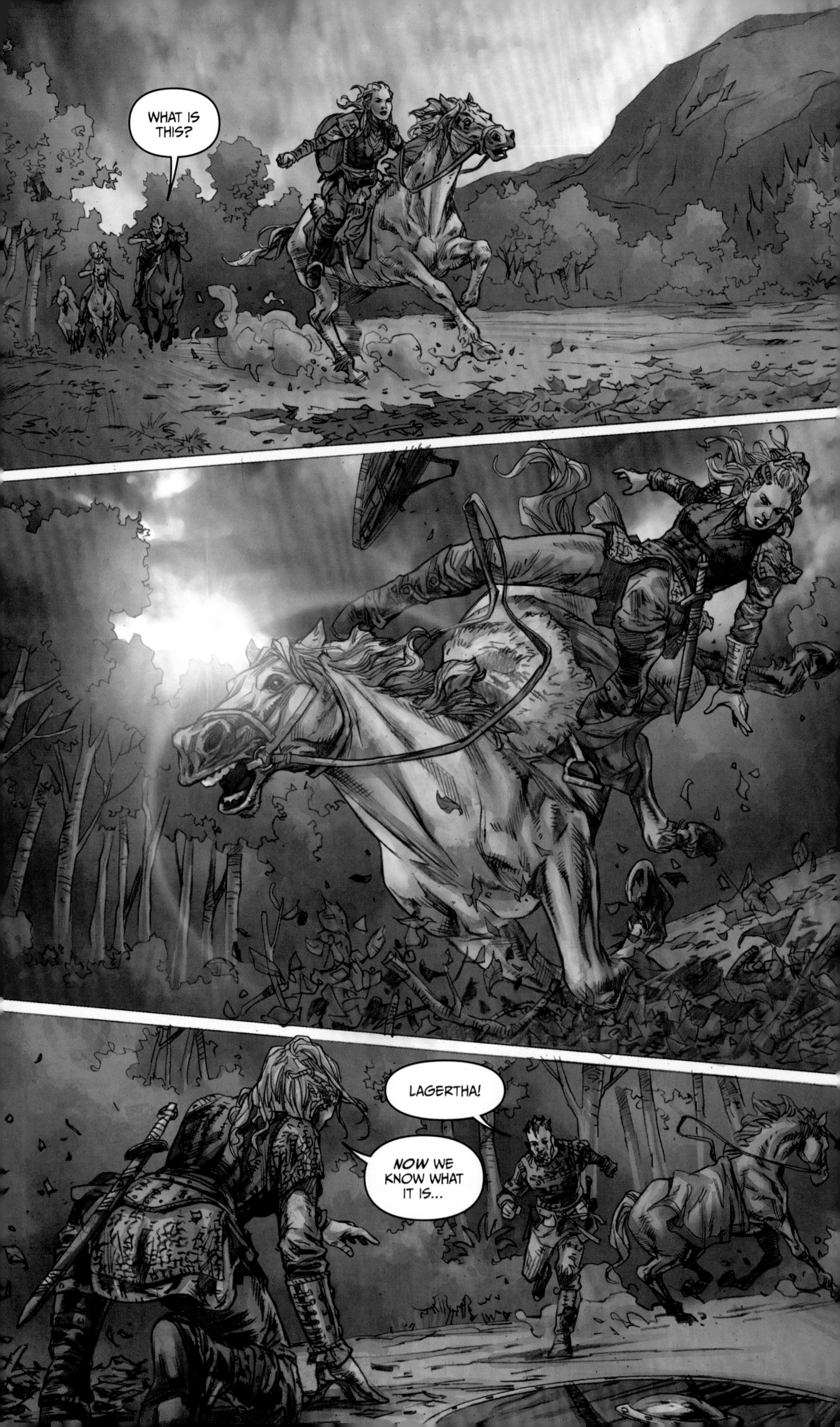
WHAT IS THIS?
LAGERTHA!
NOW WE KNOW WHAT IT IS...

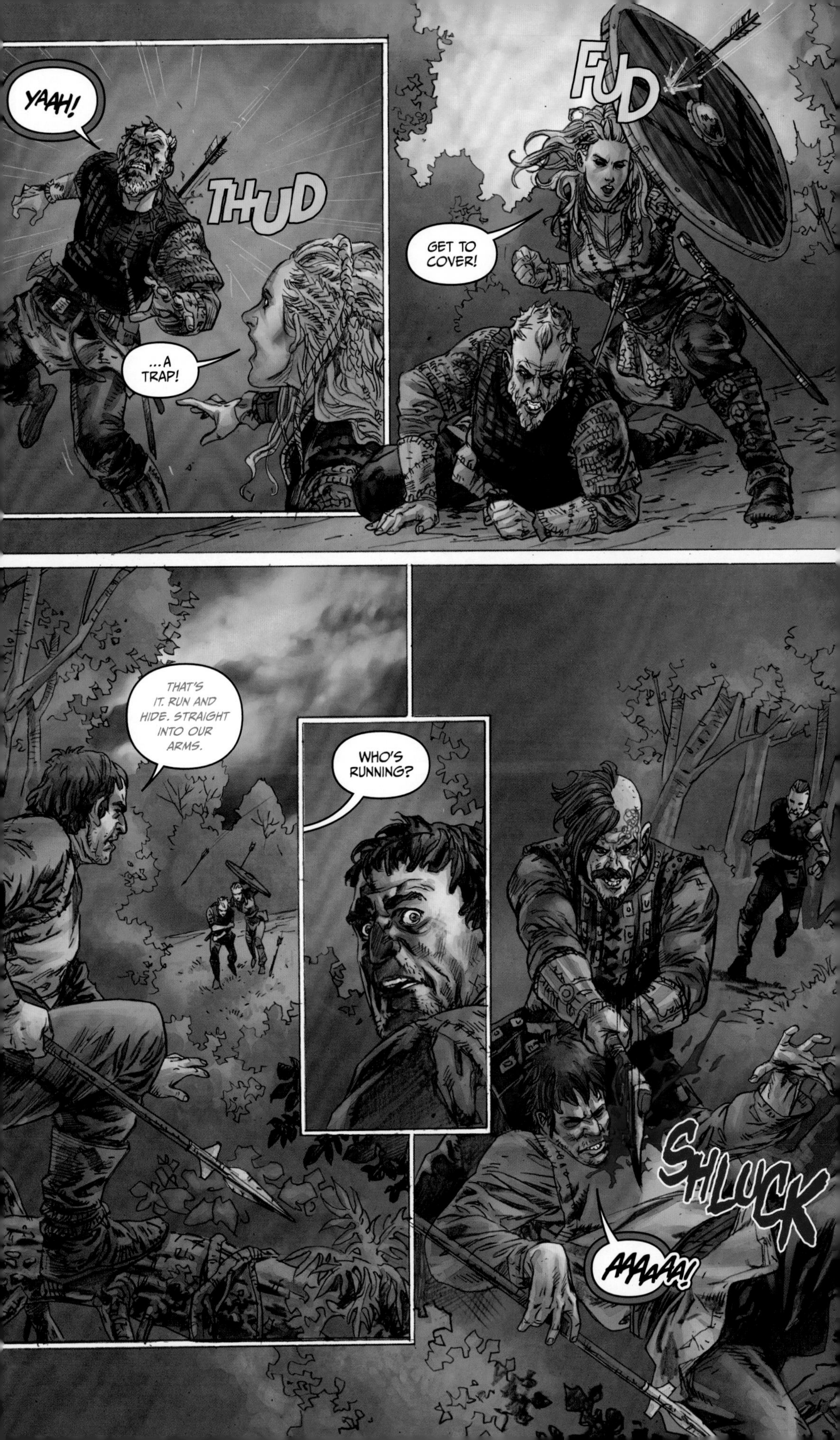
YAAH!
THUD
...A TRAP!
FUD
GET TO COVER!
THAT'S IT. RUN AND HIDE. STRAIGHT INTO OUR ARMS.
WHO'S RUNNING?
SHLUCK
AAAAAA!

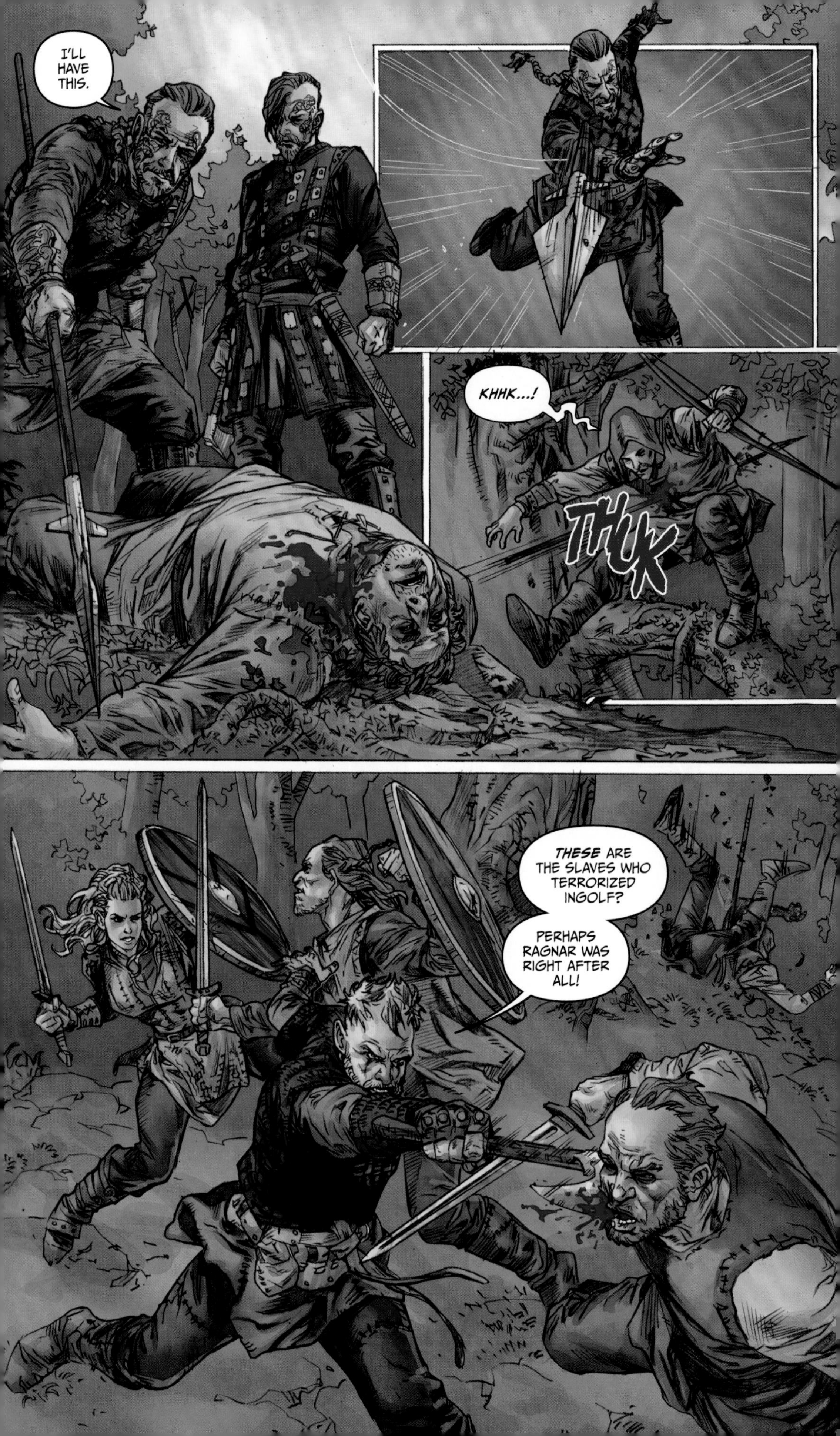

I'LL HAVE THIS.
KHHK...!
THUK
THESE ARE THE SLAVES WHO TERRORIZED INGOLF?
PERHAPS RAGNAR WAS RIGHT AFTER ALL!

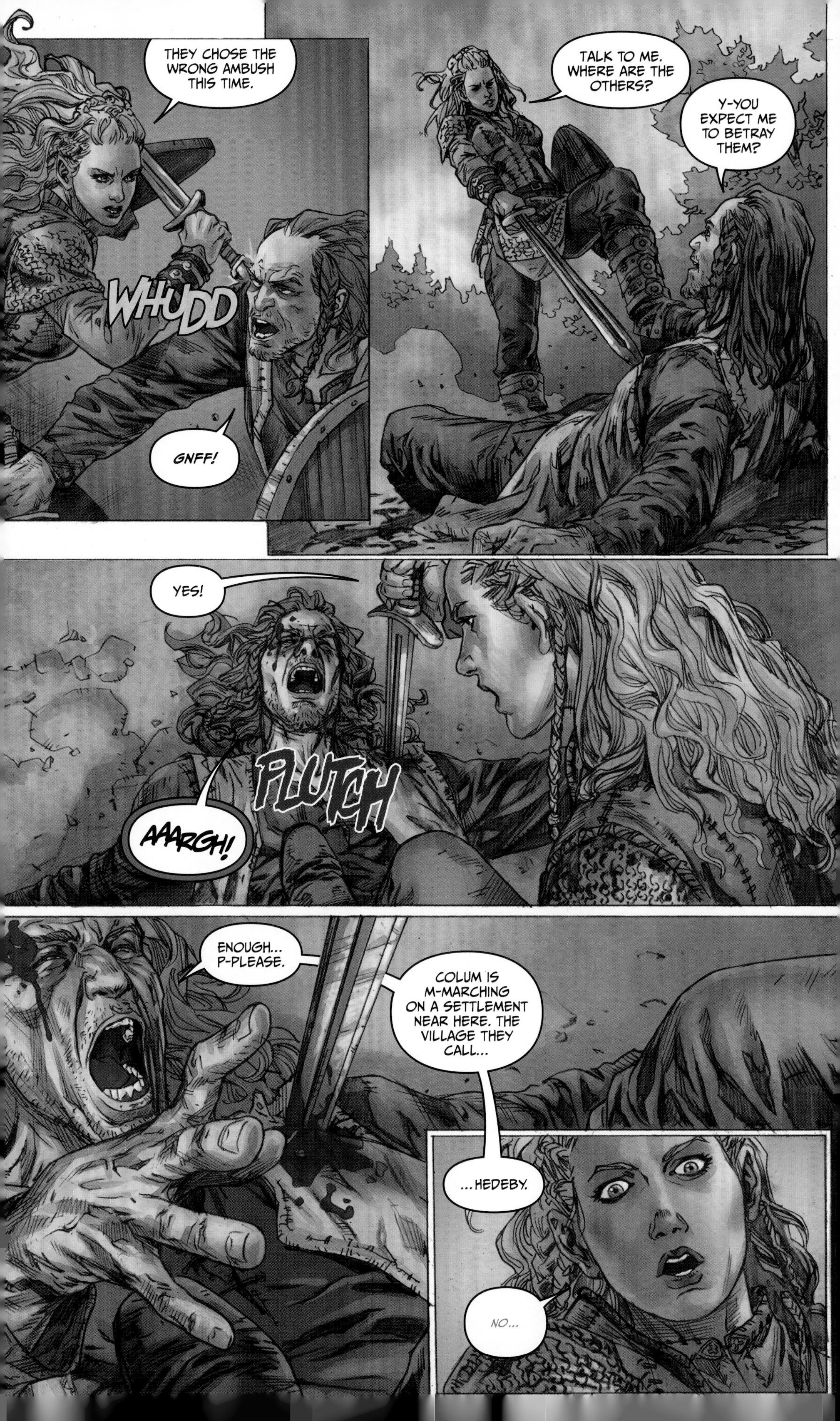
THEY CHOSE THE WRONG AMBUSH THIS TIME.
WHUDD
GNFF!
TALK TO ME. WHERE ARE THE OTHERS?
Y-YOU EXPECT ME TO BETRAY THEM?
YES!
PLUTCH
AAARGH!
ENOUGH... P-PLEASE.
COLUM IS M-MARCHING ON A SETTLEMENT NEAR HERE. THE VILLAGE THEY CALL...
...HEDEBY.
NO...

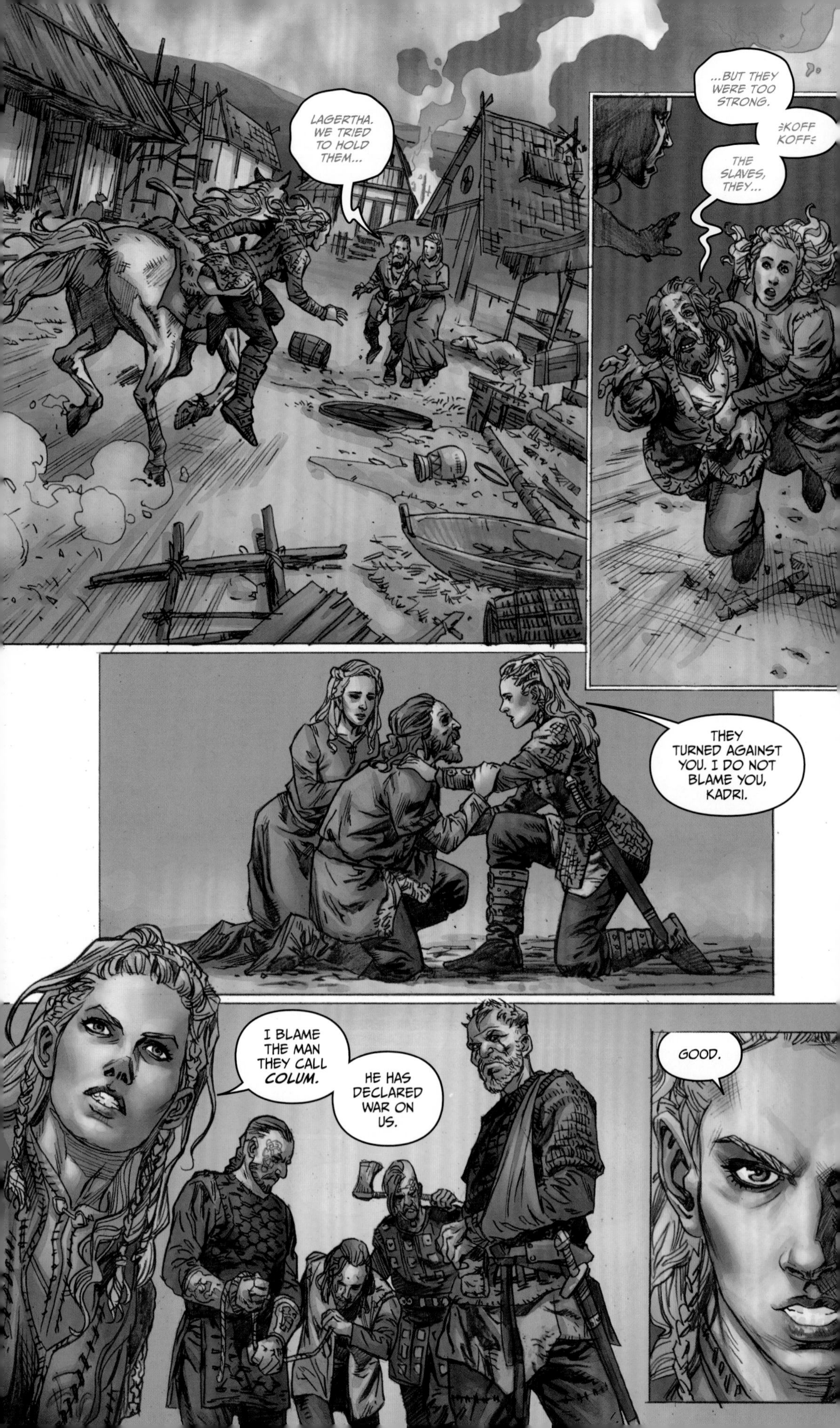
LAGERTHA. WE TRIED TO HOLD THEM...
...BUT THEY WERE TOO STRONG.
KOFF KOFF
THE SLAVES, THEY...
THEY TURNED AGAINST YOU. I DO NOT BLAME YOU, KADRI.
I BLAME THE MAN THEY CALL COLUM.
HE HAS DECLARED WAR ON US.
GOOD.

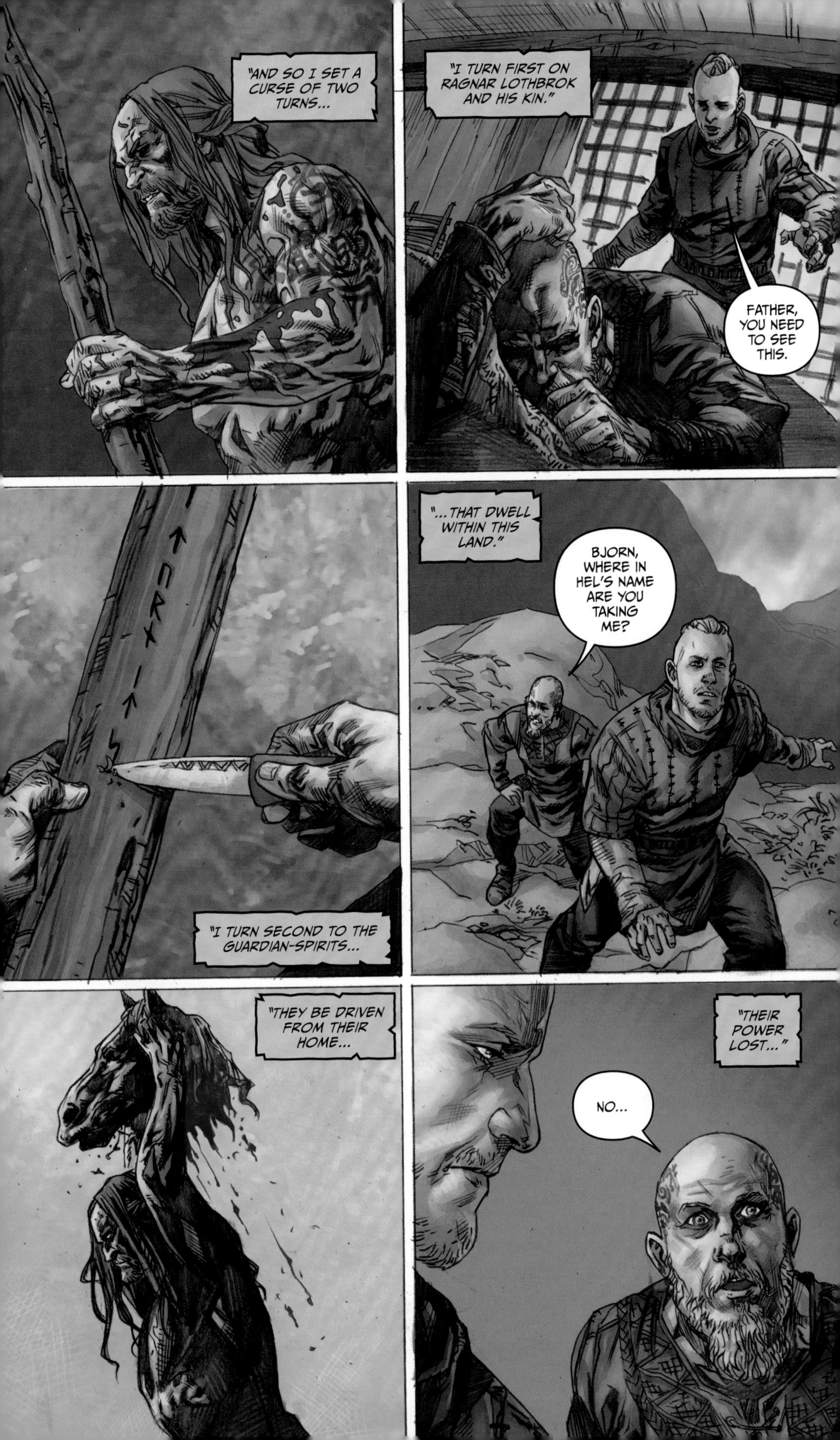
"AND SO I SET A CURSE OF TWO TURNS...
"I TURN FIRST ON RAGNAR LOTHBROK AND HIS KIN."
FATHER, YOU NEED TO SEE THIS.
"I TURN SECOND TO THE GUARDIAN-SPIRITS...
"...THAT DWELL WITHIN THIS LAND."
BJORN, WHERE IN HEL'S NAME ARE YOU TAKING ME?
"THEY BE DRIVEN FROM THEIR HOME...
"THEIR POWER LOST..."
NO...

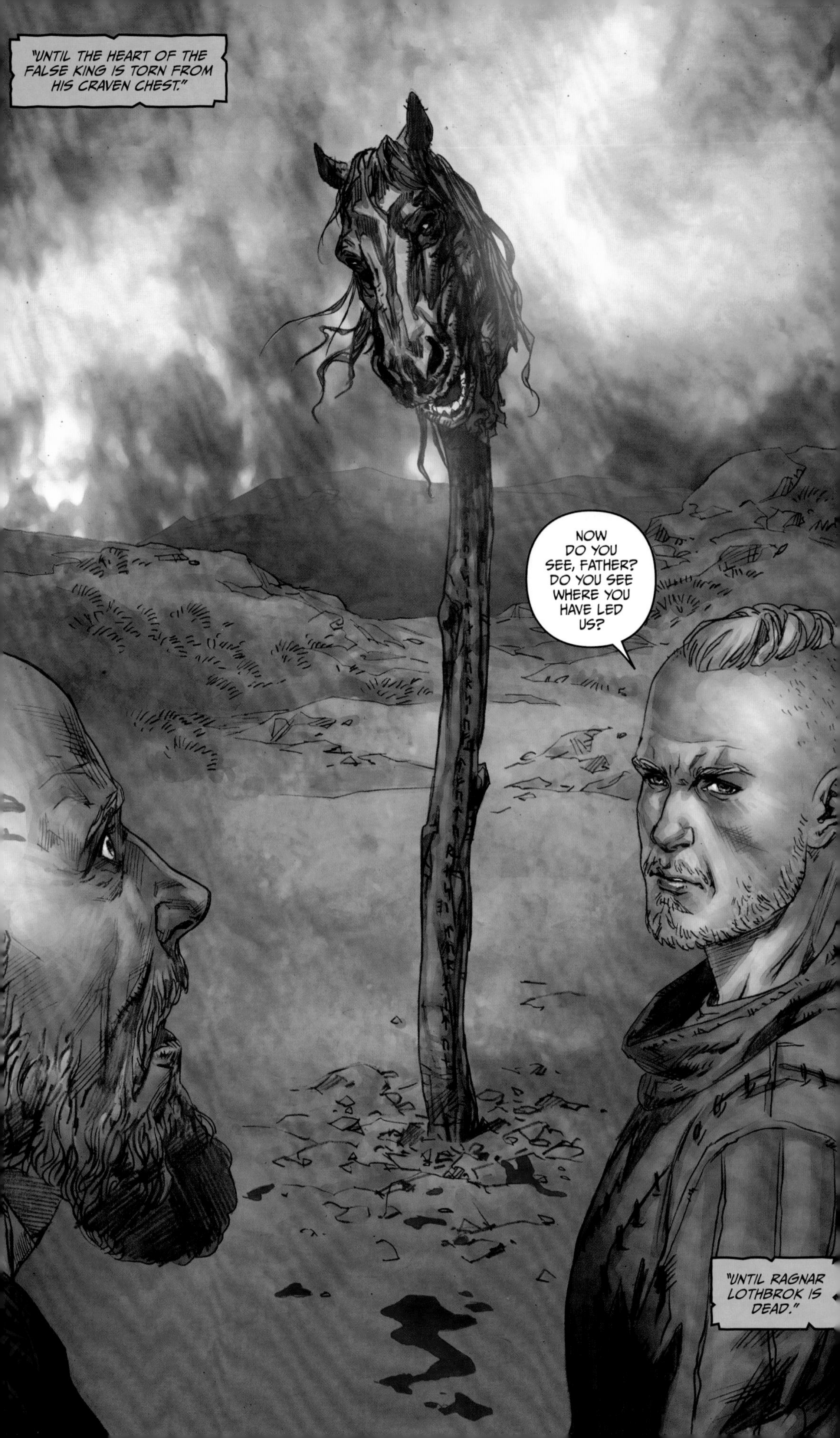
"UNTIL THE HEART OF THE FALSE KING IS TORN FROM HIS CRAVEN CHEST."
NOW DO YOU SEE, FATHER? DO YOU SEE WHERE YOU HAVE LED US?
"UNTIL RAGNAR LOTHBROK IS DEAD."

# CHAPTER 4

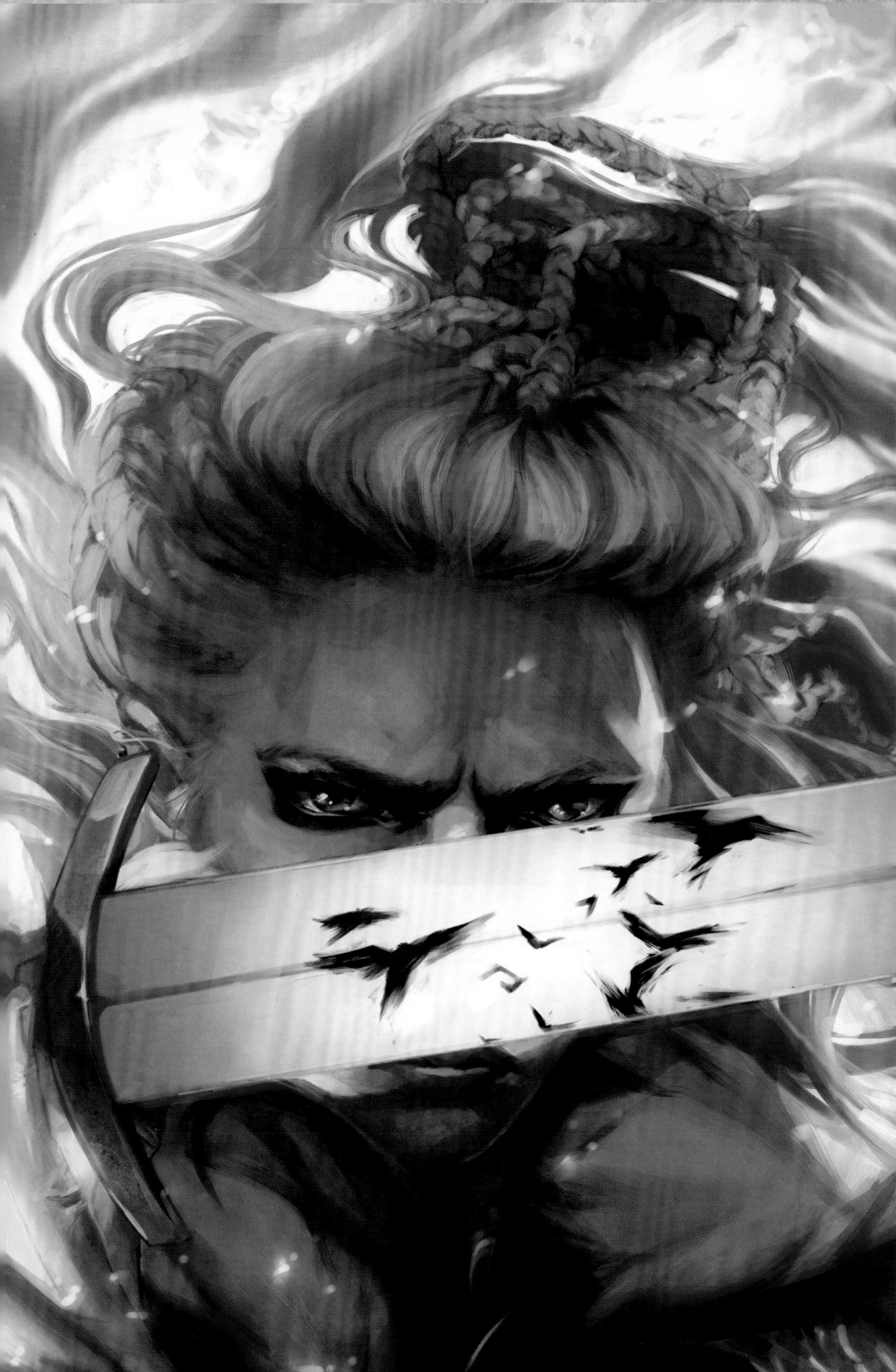

ILLUSTRATION BY VERITY GLASS

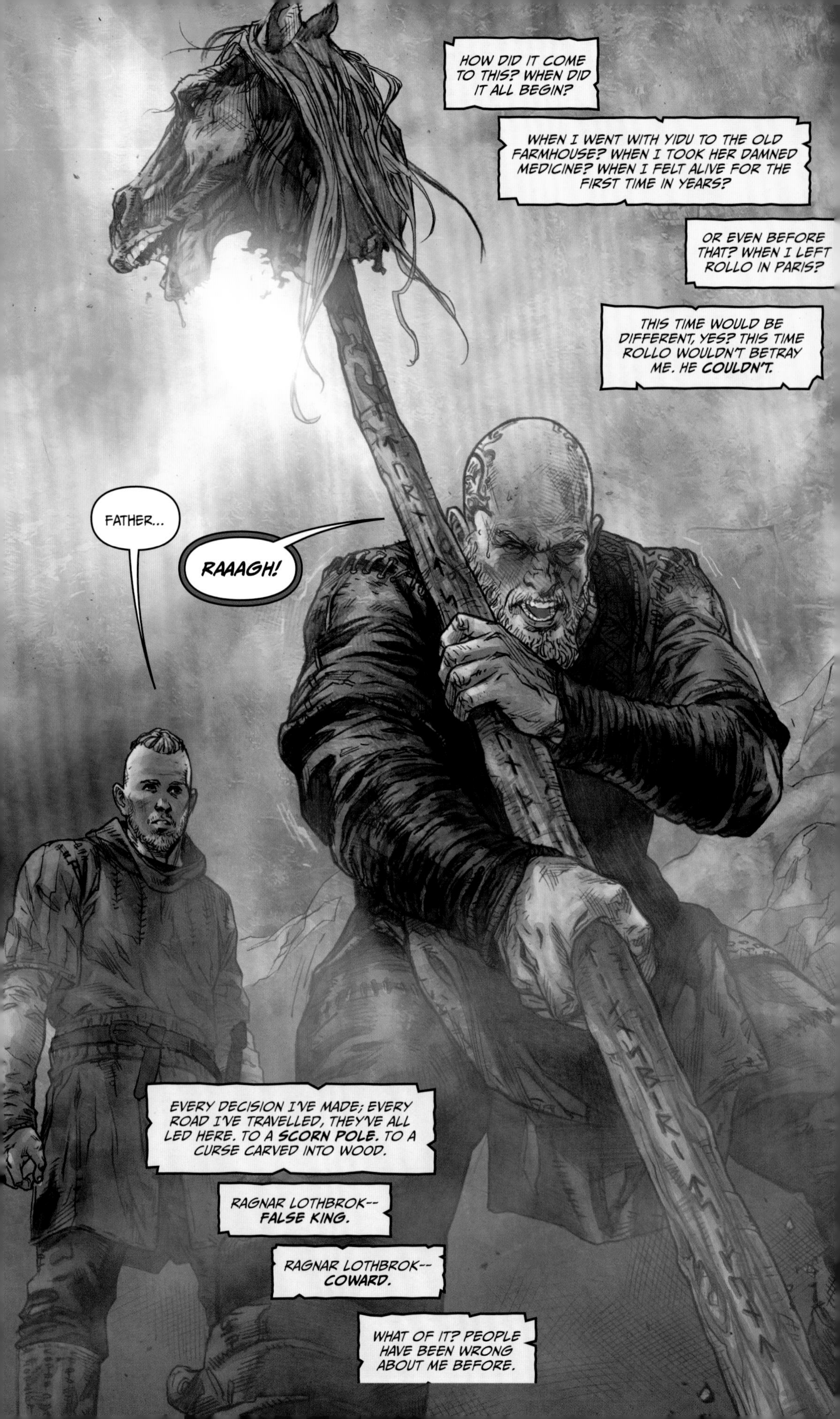
HOW DID IT COME TO THIS? WHEN DID IT ALL BEGIN?
WHEN I WENT WITH YIDU TO THE OLD FARMHOUSE? WHEN I TOOK HER DAMNED MEDICINE? WHEN I FELT ALIVE FOR THE FIRST TIME IN YEARS?
OR EVEN BEFORE THAT? WHEN I LEFT ROLLO IN PARIS?
THIS TIME WOULD BE DIFFERENT, YES? THIS TIME ROLLO WOULDN'T BETRAY ME. HE **COULDN'T.**
FATHER...
**RAAAGH!**
EVERY DECISION I'VE MADE; EVERY ROAD I'VE TRAVELLED, THEY'VE ALL LED HERE. TO A **SCORN POLE.** TO A CURSE CARVED INTO WOOD.
RAGNAR LOTHBROK-- **FALSE KING.**
RAGNAR LOTHBROK-- **COWARD.**
WHAT OF IT? PEOPLE HAVE BEEN WRONG ABOUT ME BEFORE.

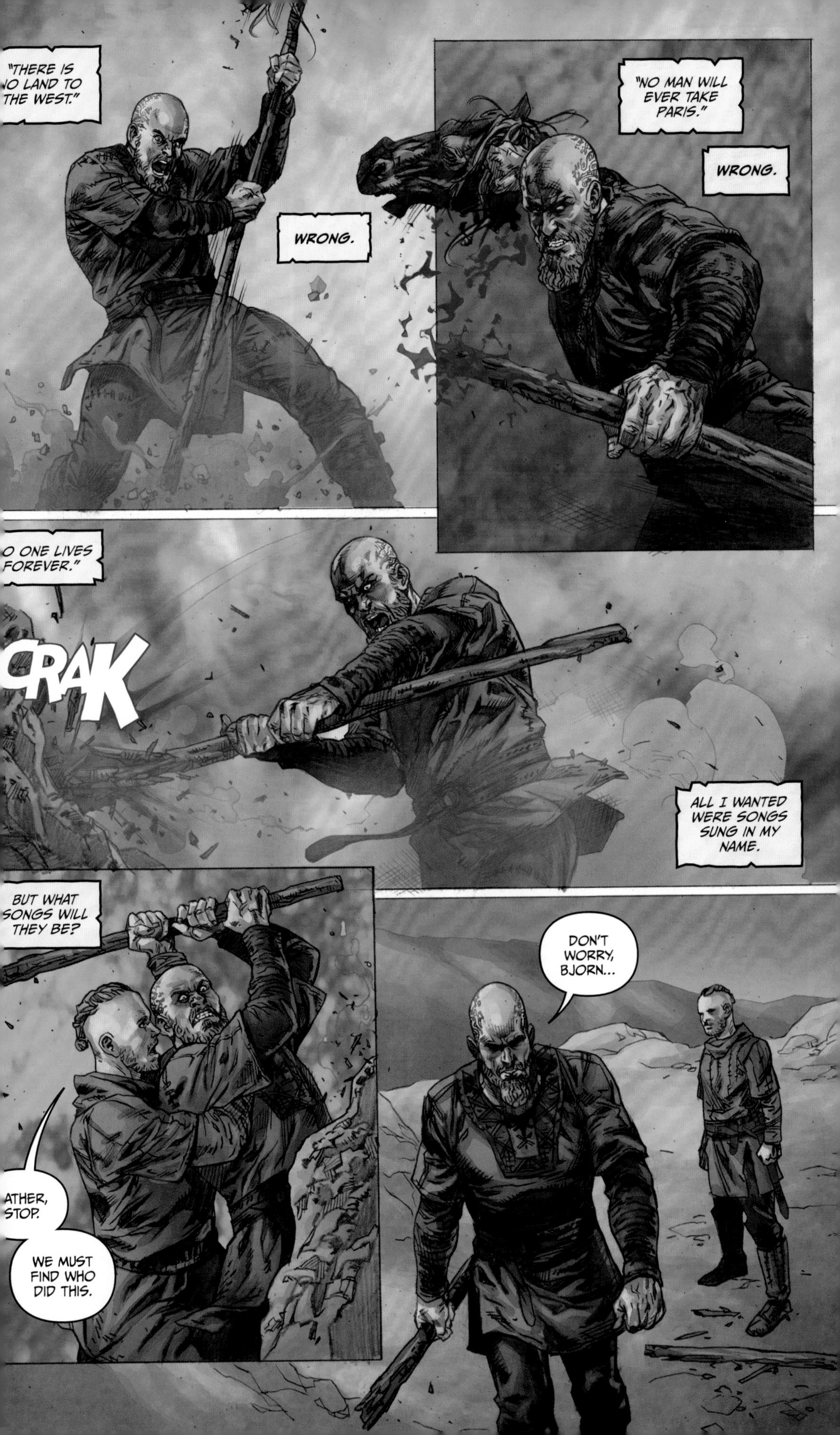
"THERE IS
NO LAND TO
THE WEST."
WRONG.
"NO MAN WILL
EVER TAKE
PARIS."
WRONG.
O ONE LIVES
FOREVER."
CRAK
ALL I WANTED
WERE SONGS
SUNG IN MY
NAME.
BUT WHAT
SONGS WILL
THEY BE?
ATHER,
STOP.
WE MUST
FIND WHO
DID THIS.
DON'T
WORRY,
BJORN...

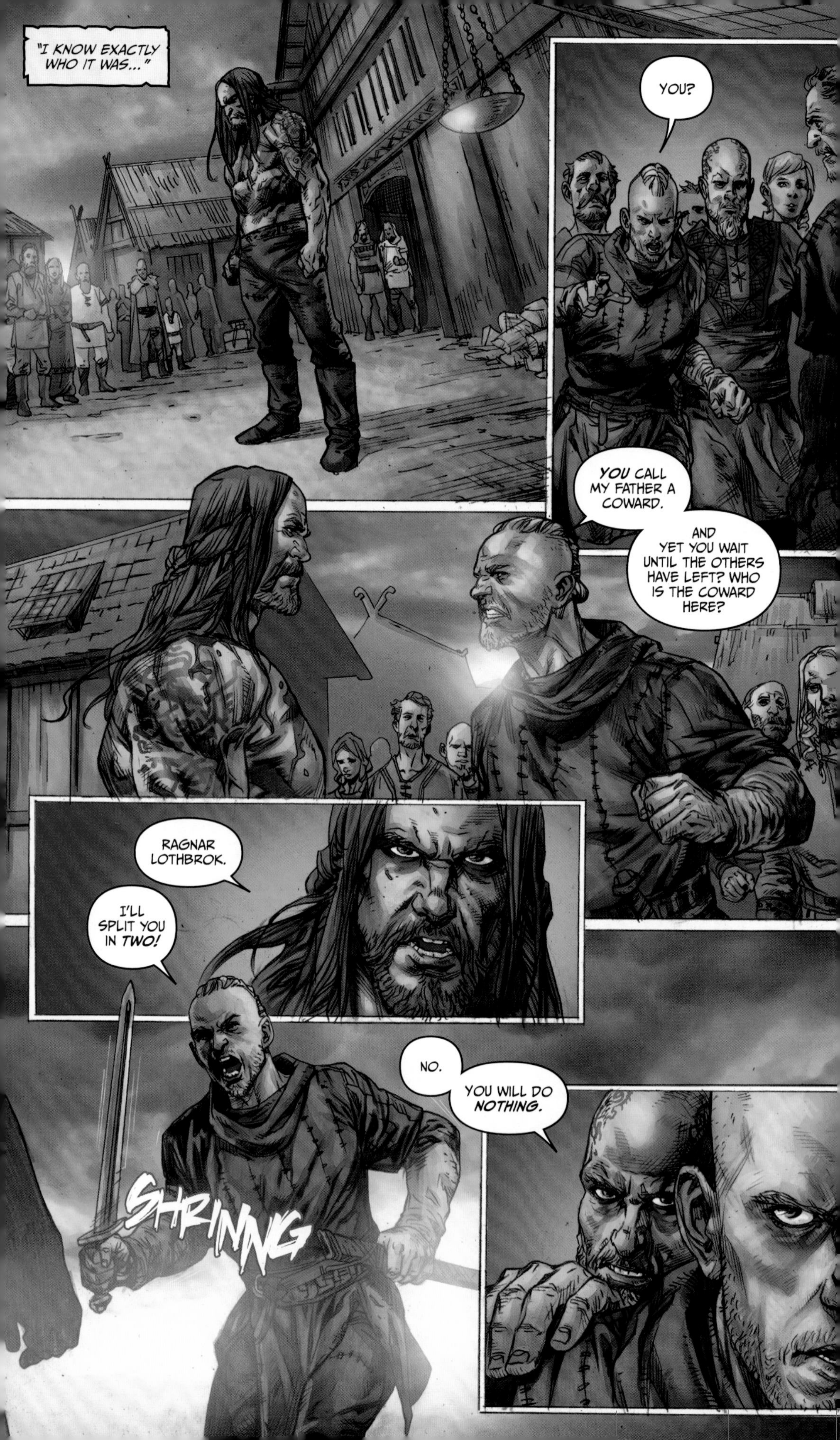
"I KNOW EXACTLY WHO IT WAS..."
YOU?
YOU CALL MY FATHER A COWARD.
AND YET YOU WAIT UNTIL THE OTHERS HAVE LEFT? WHO IS THE COWARD HERE?
RAGNAR LOTHBROK.
I'LL SPLIT YOU IN TWO!
SHRINNG
NO.
YOU WILL DO NOTHING.

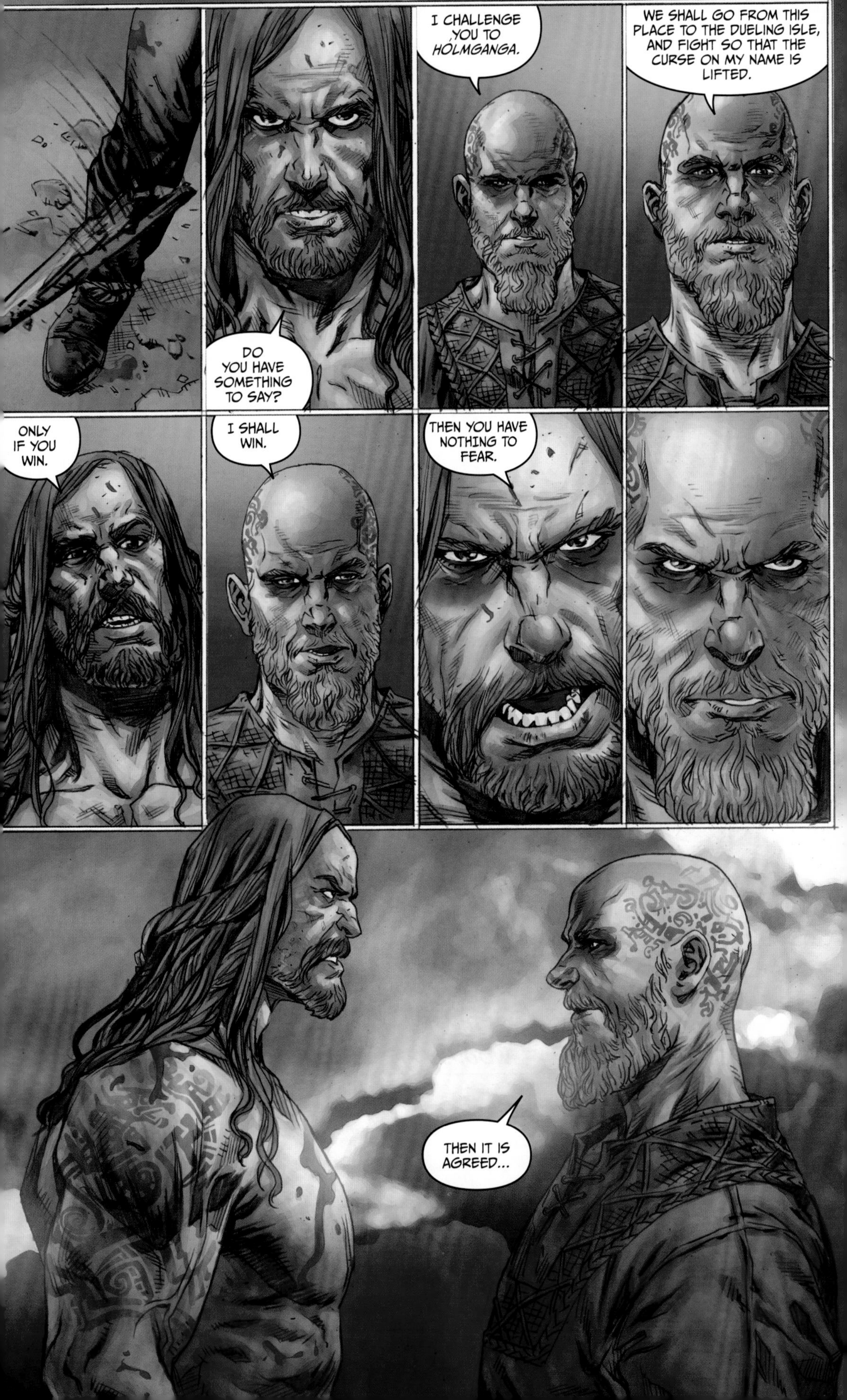
DO YOU HAVE SOMETHING TO SAY?
I CHALLENGE YOU TO HOLMGANGA.
WE SHALL GO FROM THIS PLACE TO THE DUELING ISLE, AND FIGHT SO THAT THE CURSE ON MY NAME IS LIFTED.
ONLY IF YOU WIN.
I SHALL WIN.
THEN YOU HAVE NOTHING TO FEAR.
THEN IT IS AGREED...

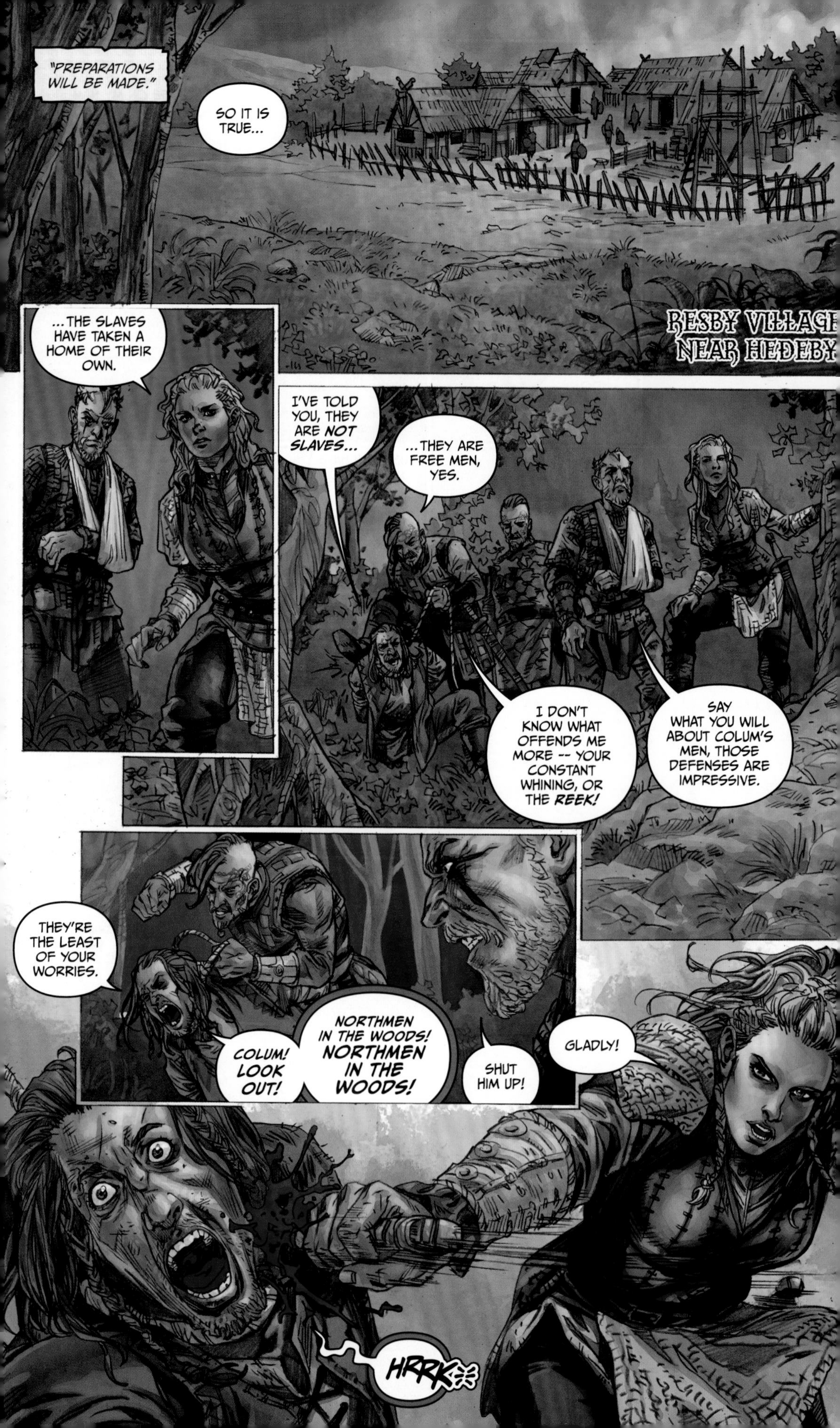

"PREPARATIONS WILL BE MADE."
SO IT IS TRUE...
RESBY VILLAGE NEAR HEDEBY
...THE SLAVES HAVE TAKEN A HOME OF THEIR OWN.
I'VE TOLD YOU, THEY ARE NOT SLAVES...
...THEY ARE FREE MEN, YES.
I DON'T KNOW WHAT OFFENDS ME MORE -- YOUR CONSTANT WHINING, OR THE REEK!
SAY WHAT YOU WILL ABOUT COLUM'S MEN, THOSE DEFENSES ARE IMPRESSIVE.
THEY'RE THE LEAST OF YOUR WORRIES.
COLUM! LOOK OUT!
NORTHMEN IN THE WOODS! NORTHMEN IN THE WOODS!
SHUT HIM UP!
GLADLY!
HRRK

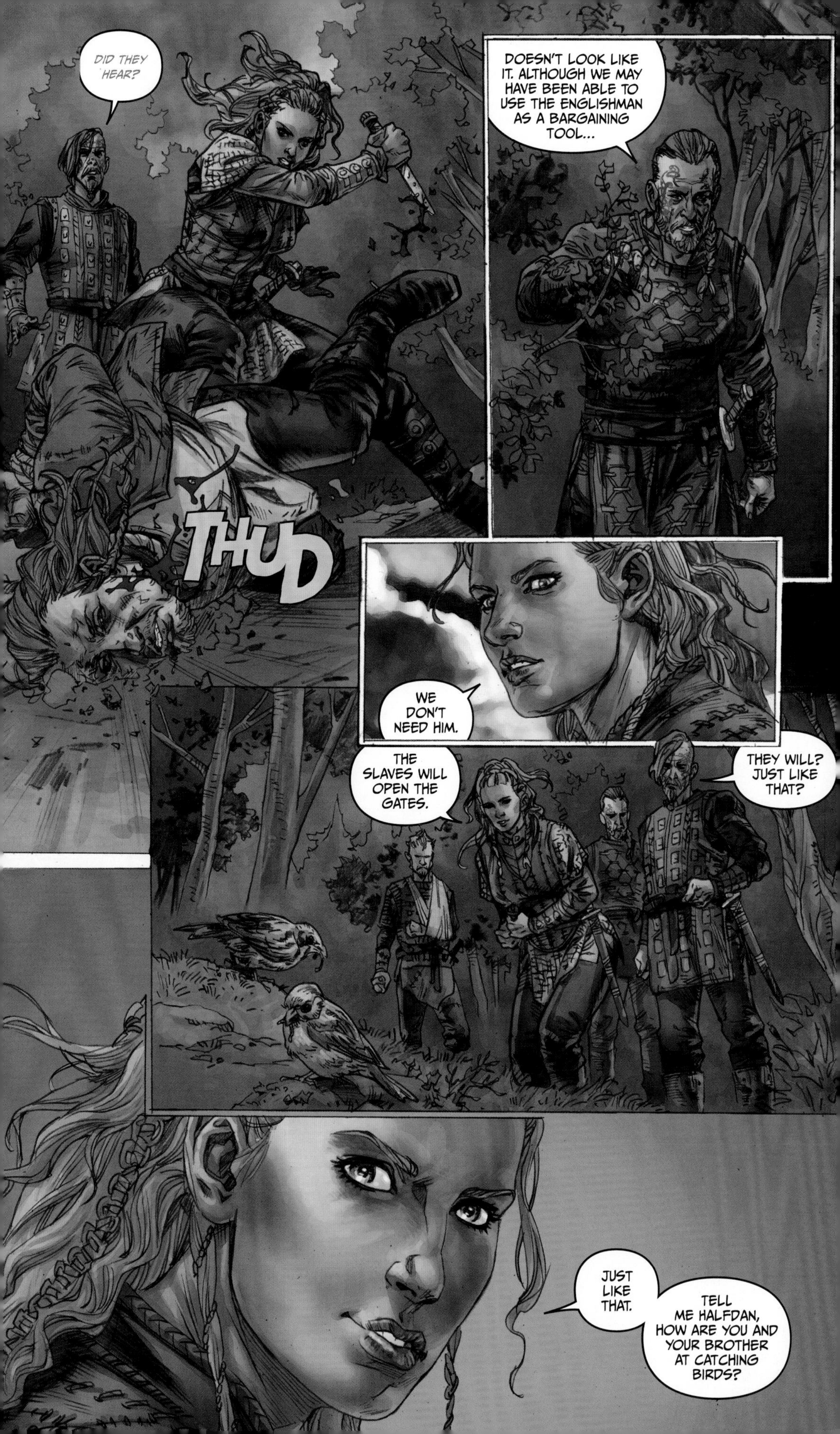
DID THEY HEAR?
DOESN'T LOOK LIKE IT. ALTHOUGH WE MAY HAVE BEEN ABLE TO USE THE ENGLISHMAN AS A BARGAINING TOOL...
THUD
WE DON'T NEED HIM.
THE SLAVES WILL OPEN THE GATES.
THEY WILL? JUST LIKE THAT?
JUST LIKE THAT.
TELL ME HALFDAN, HOW ARE YOU AND YOUR BROTHER AT CATCHING BIRDS?

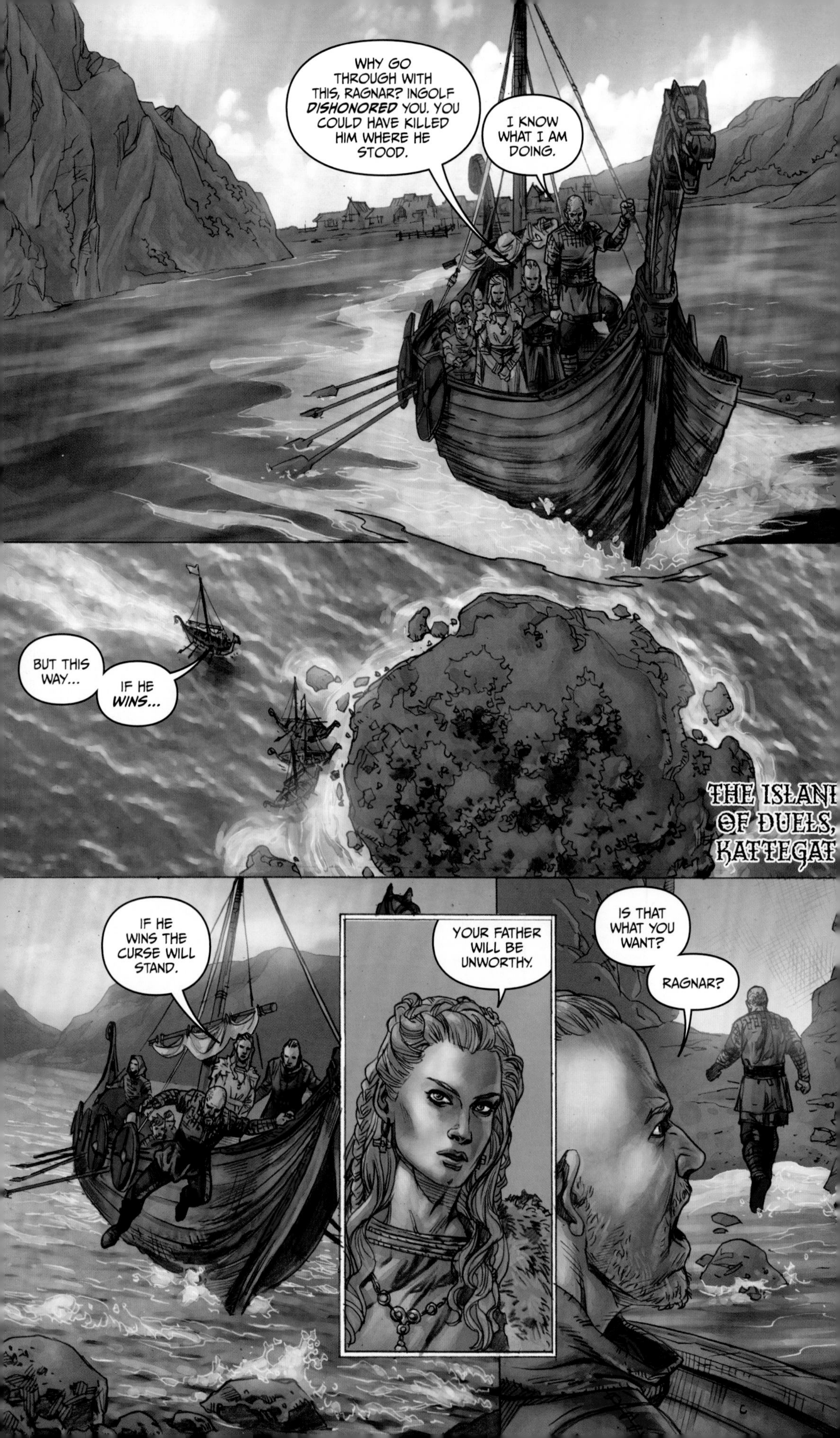
WHY GO THROUGH WITH THIS, RAGNAR? INGOLF DISHONORED YOU. YOU COULD HAVE KILLED HIM WHERE HE STOOD.
I KNOW WHAT I AM DOING.
BUT THIS WAY...
IF HE WINS...
THE ISLAND OF DUELS, KATTEGAT
IF HE WINS THE CURSE WILL STAND.
YOUR FATHER WILL BE UNWORTHY.
IS THAT WHAT YOU WANT?
RAGNAR?

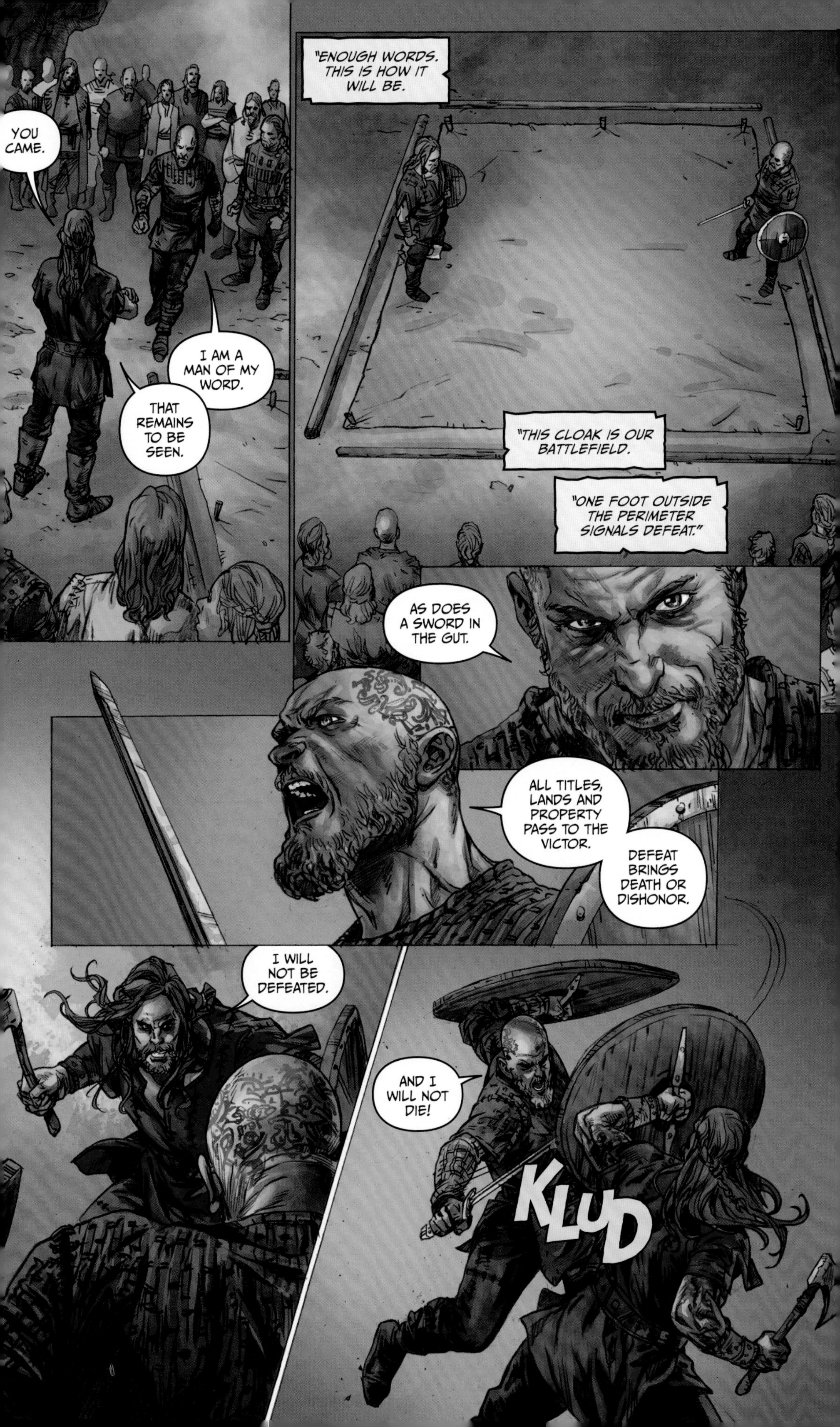
YOU CAME.
I AM A MAN OF MY WORD.
THAT REMAINS TO BE SEEN.
"ENOUGH WORDS. THIS IS HOW IT WILL BE.
"THIS CLOAK IS OUR BATTLEFIELD.
"ONE FOOT OUTSIDE THE PERIMETER SIGNALS DEFEAT."
AS DOES A SWORD IN THE GUT.
ALL TITLES, LANDS AND PROPERTY PASS TO THE VICTOR.
DEFEAT BRINGS DEATH OR DISHONOR.
I WILL NOT BE DEFEATED.
AND I WILL NOT DIE!
KLUD

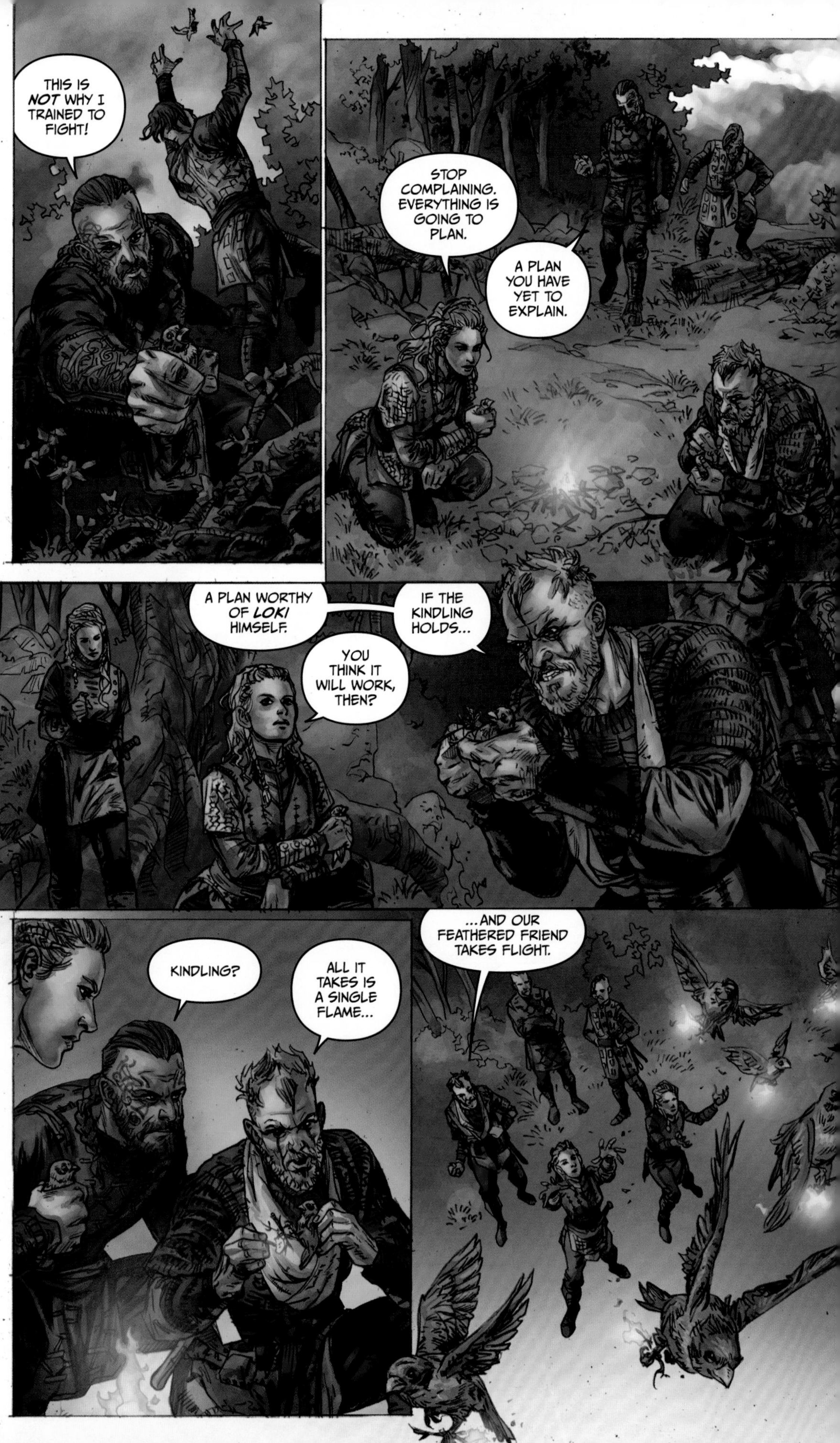
THIS IS NOT WHY I TRAINED TO FIGHT!
STOP COMPLAINING. EVERYTHING IS GOING TO PLAN.
A PLAN YOU HAVE YET TO EXPLAIN.
A PLAN WORTHY OF LOKI HIMSELF.
IF THE KINDLING HOLDS...
YOU THINK IT WILL WORK, THEN?
KINDLING?
ALL IT TAKES IS A SINGLE FLAME...
...AND OUR FEATHERED FRIEND TAKES FLIGHT.

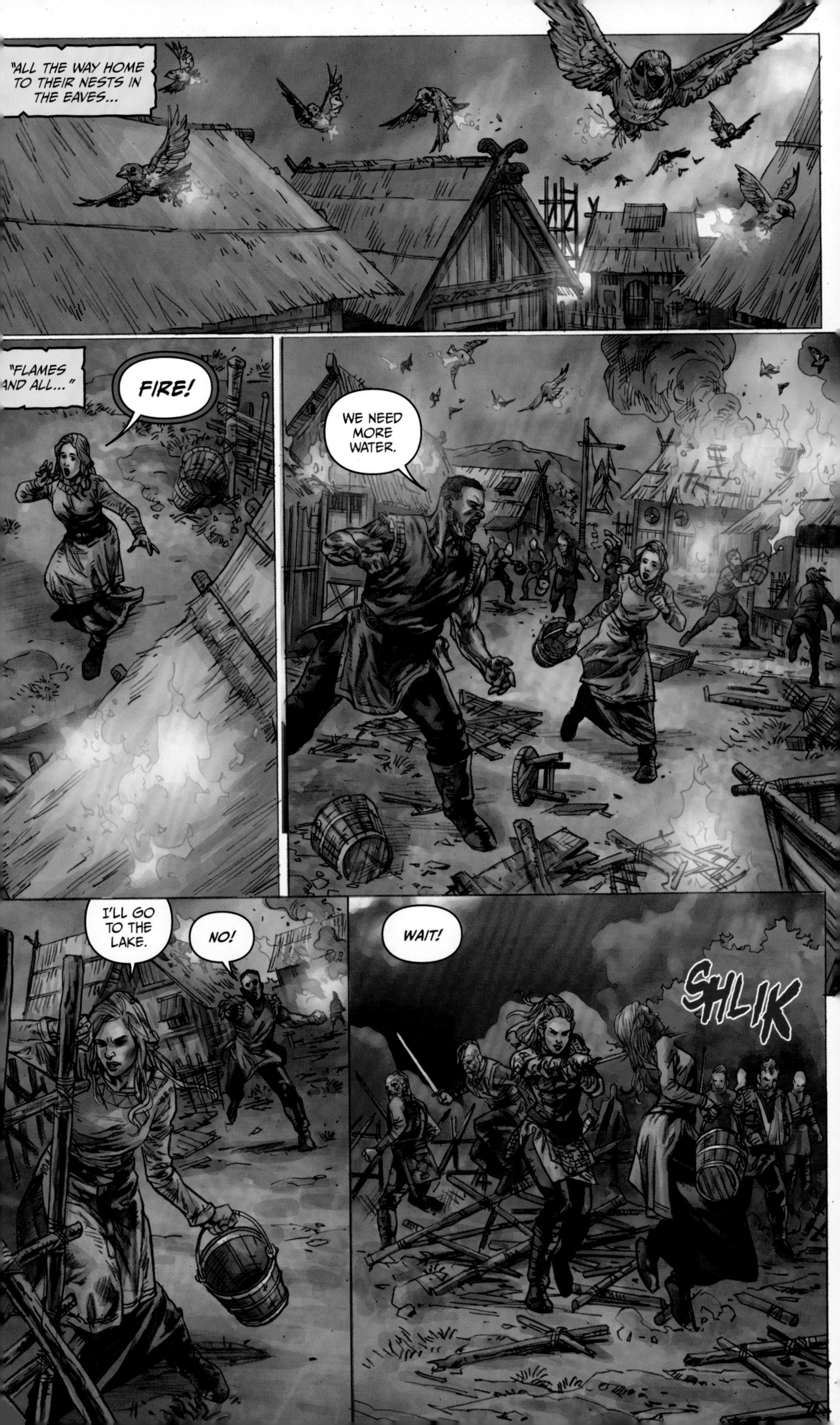
"ALL THE WAY HOME TO THEIR NESTS IN THE EAVES...
"FLAMES AND ALL..."
FIRE!
WE NEED MORE WATER.
I'LL GO TO THE LAKE.
NO!
WAIT!
SHLIK

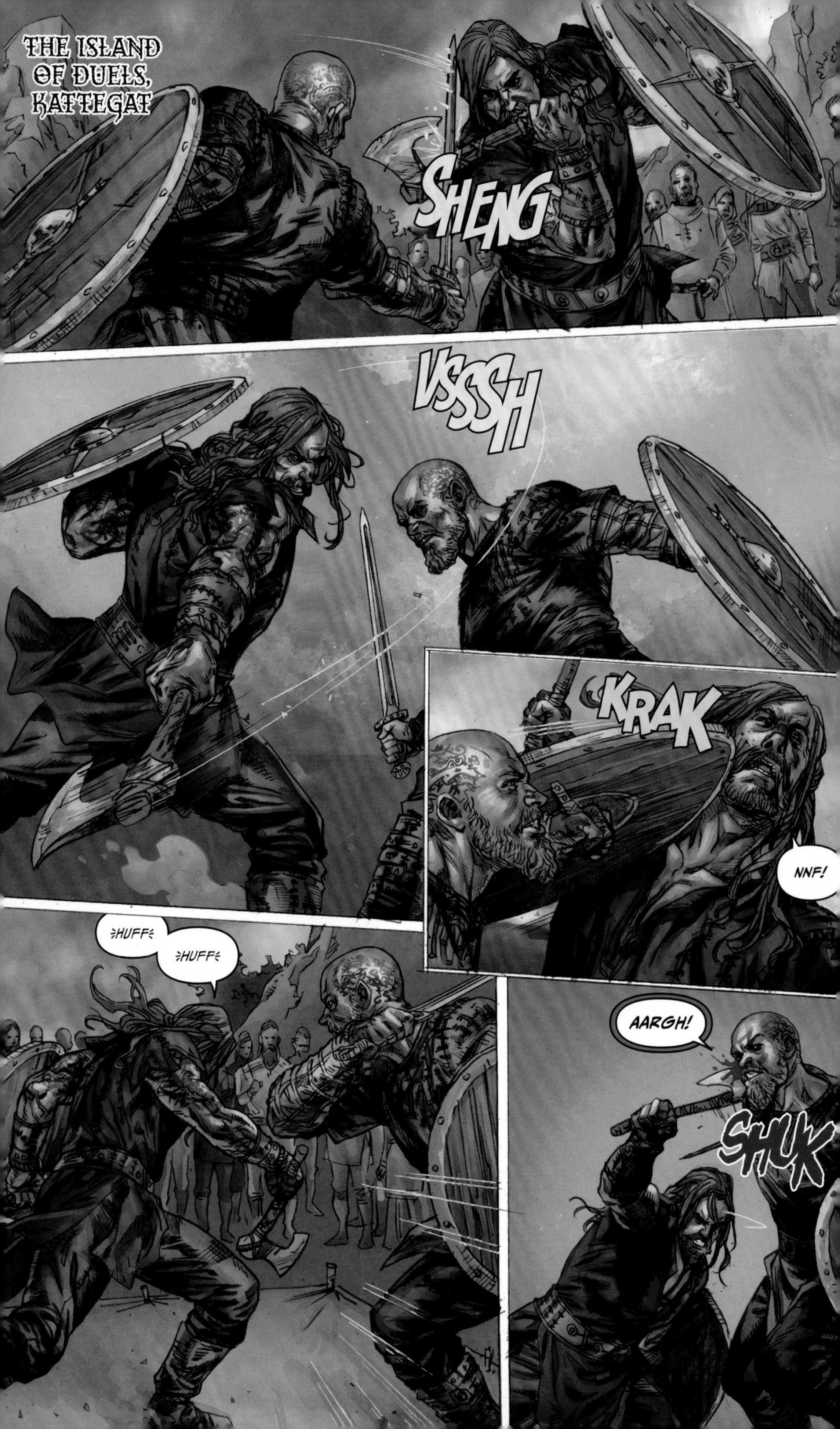
THE ISLAND OF DUELS, KATTEGAT
SHENG
VSSSH
KRAK
NNF!
HUFF
HUFF
AARGH!
SHUK

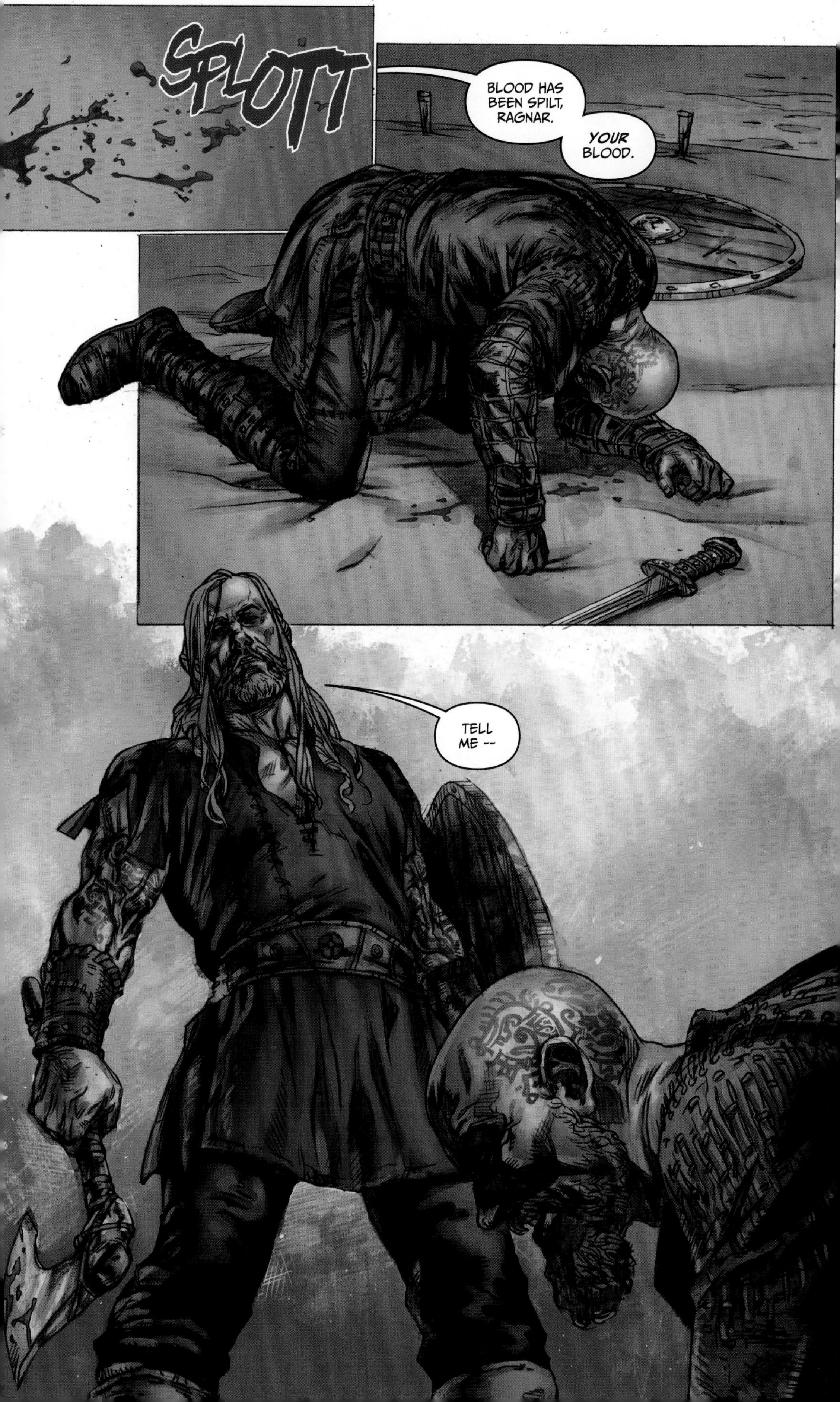
SPLOTT
BLOOD HAS BEEN SPILT, RAGNAR.
YOUR BLOOD.
TELL ME --

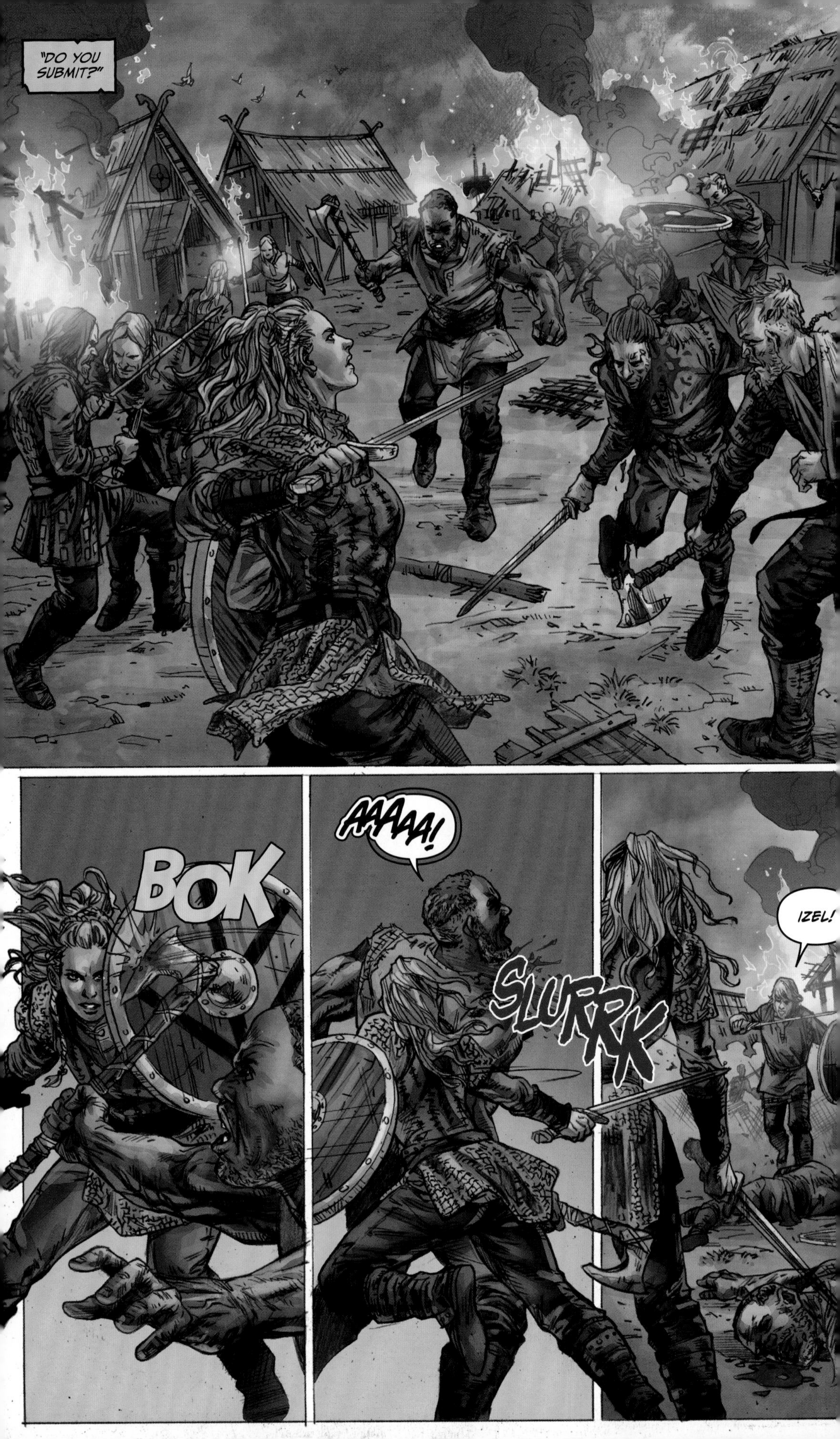
"DO YOU SUBMIT?"
BOK
AAAAAA!
SLURRRK
IZEL!

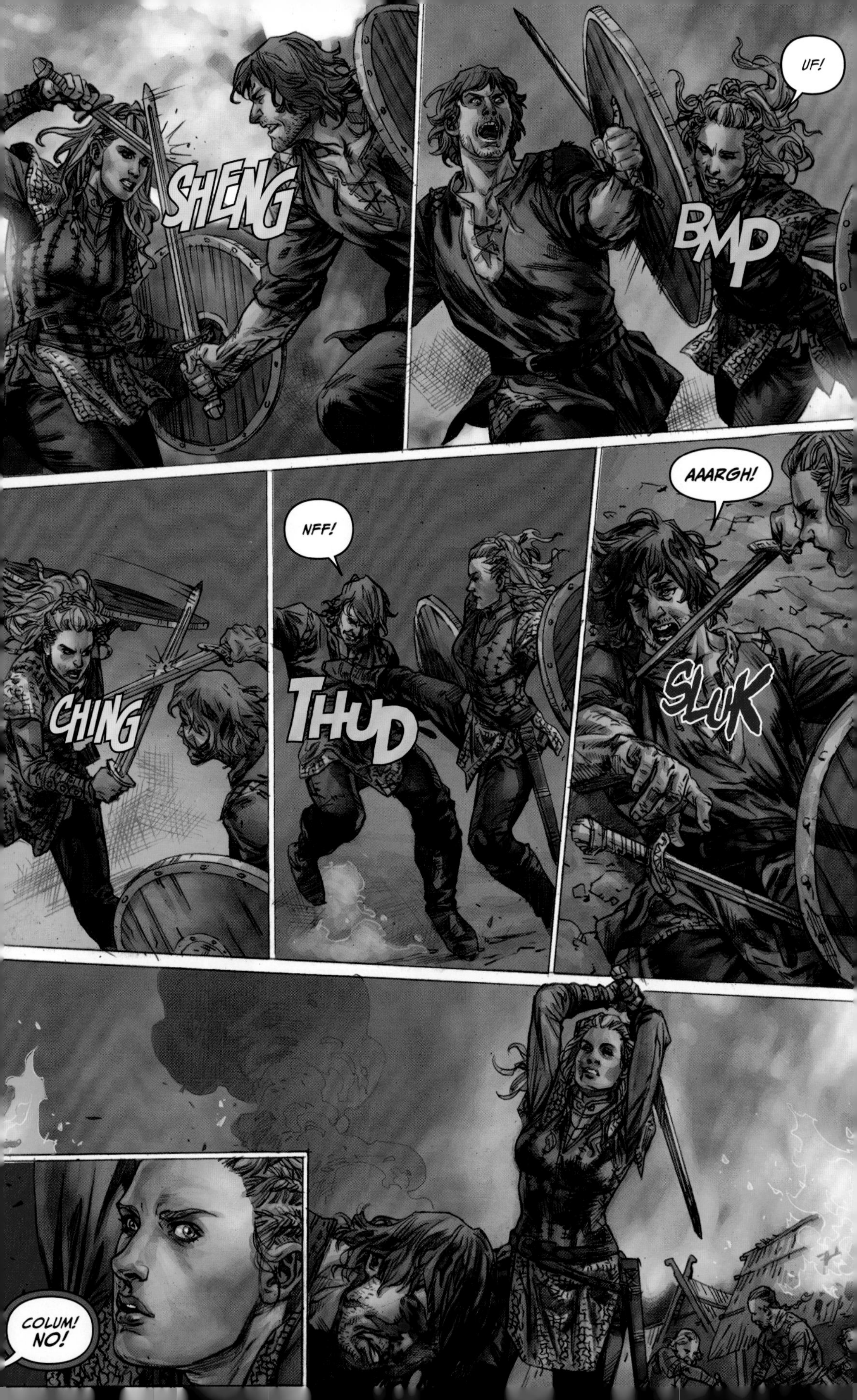
SHENG
UF!
BMP
CHING
NFF!
THUD
AAARGH!
SLUK
COLUM! NO!

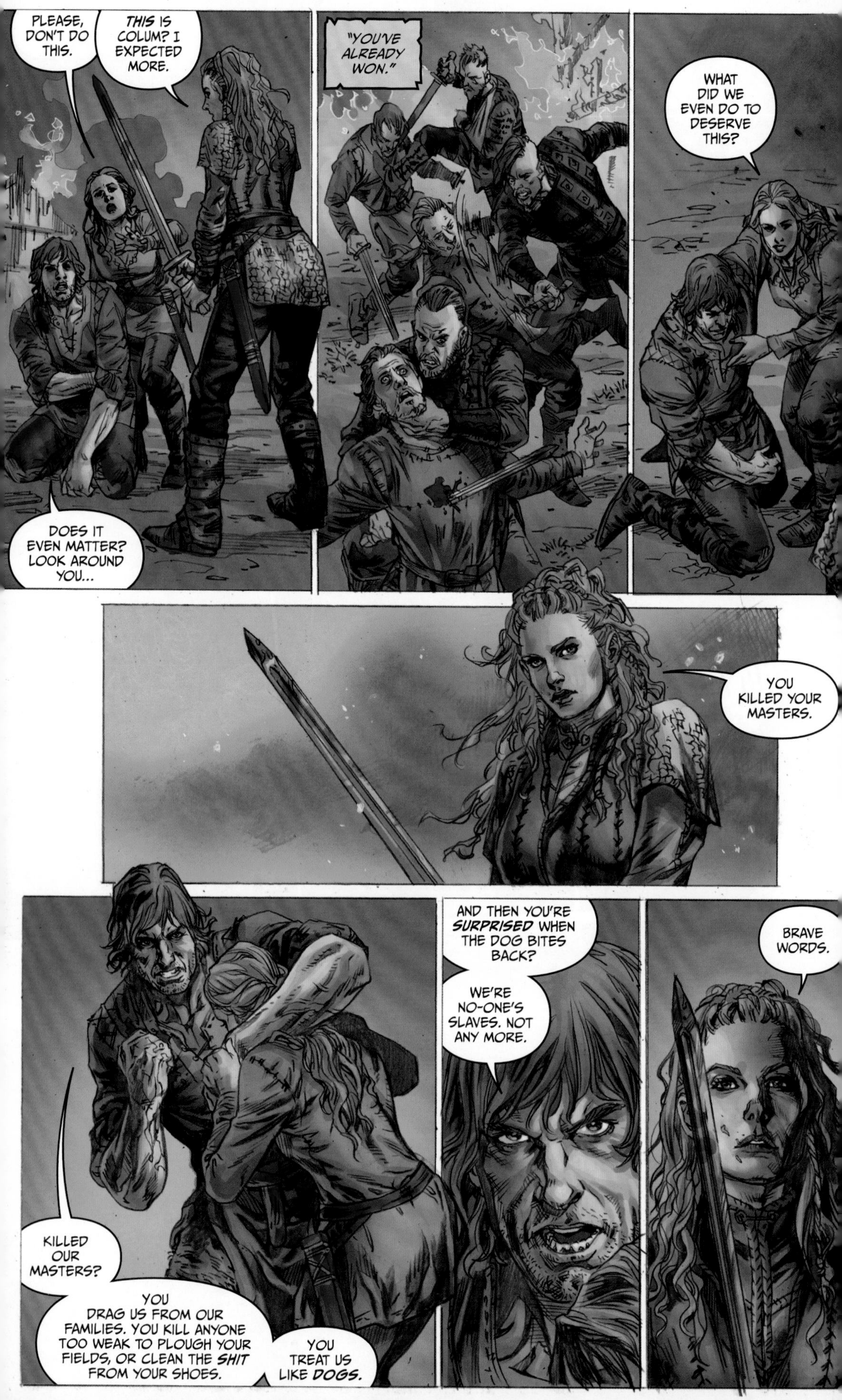
PLEASE, DON'T DO THIS.
THIS IS COLUM? I EXPECTED MORE.
DOES IT EVEN MATTER? LOOK AROUND YOU...
"YOU'VE ALREADY WON."
WHAT DID WE EVEN DO TO DESERVE THIS?
YOU KILLED YOUR MASTERS.
KILLED OUR MASTERS?
YOU DRAG US FROM OUR FAMILIES. YOU KILL ANYONE TOO WEAK TO PLOUGH YOUR FIELDS, OR CLEAN THE SHIT FROM YOUR SHOES.
YOU TREAT US LIKE DOGS.
AND THEN YOU'RE SURPRISED WHEN THE DOG BITES BACK?
WE'RE NO-ONE'S SLAVES. NOT ANY MORE.
BRAVE WORDS.

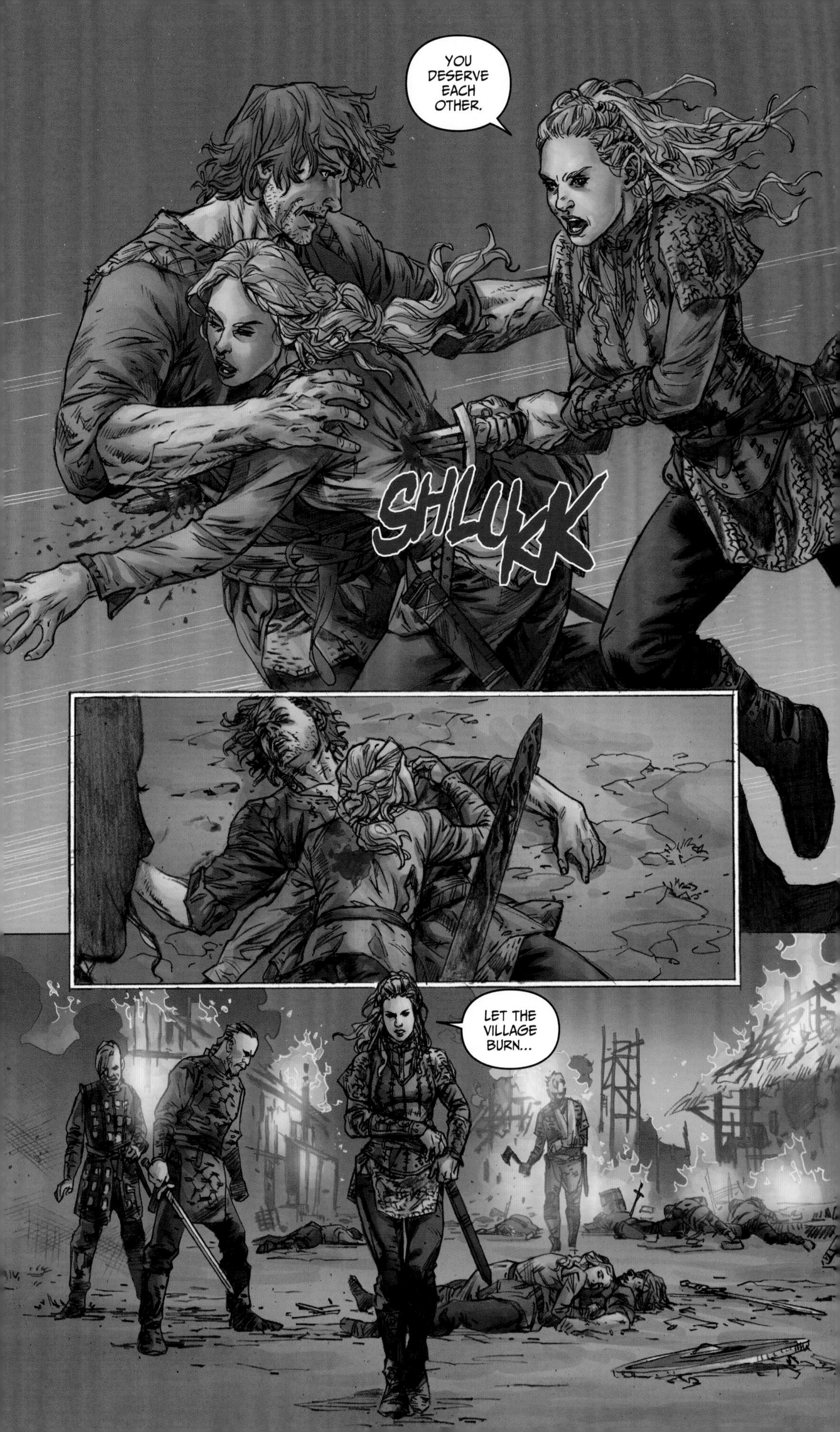
YOU DESERVE EACH OTHER.
SHLUKK
LET THE VILLAGE BURN...

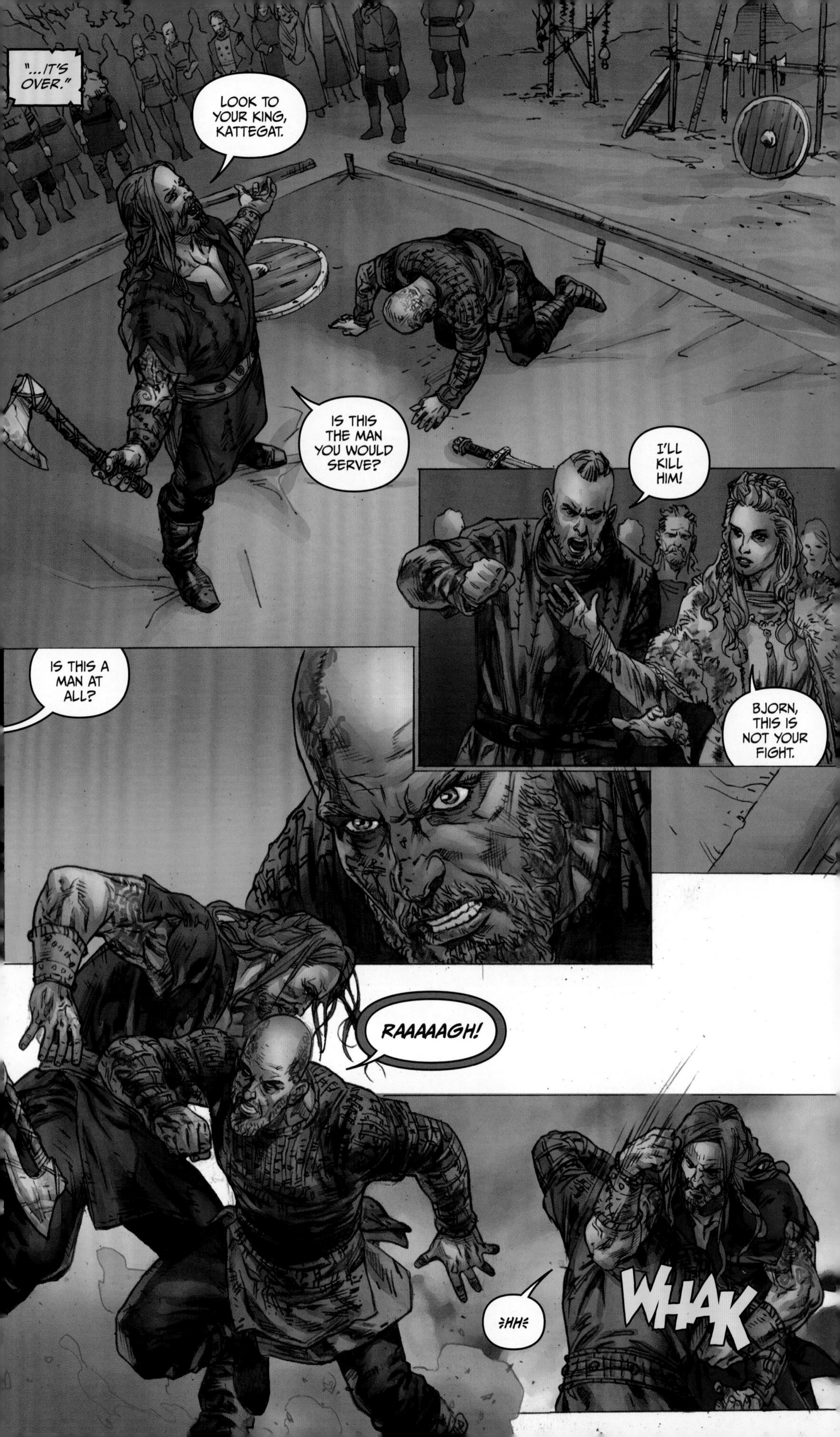
"...IT'S OVER."
LOOK TO YOUR KING, KATTEGAT.
IS THIS THE MAN YOU WOULD SERVE?
I'LL KILL HIM!
BJORN, THIS IS NOT YOUR FIGHT.
IS THIS A MAN AT ALL?
RAAAAAGH!
HH
WHAK

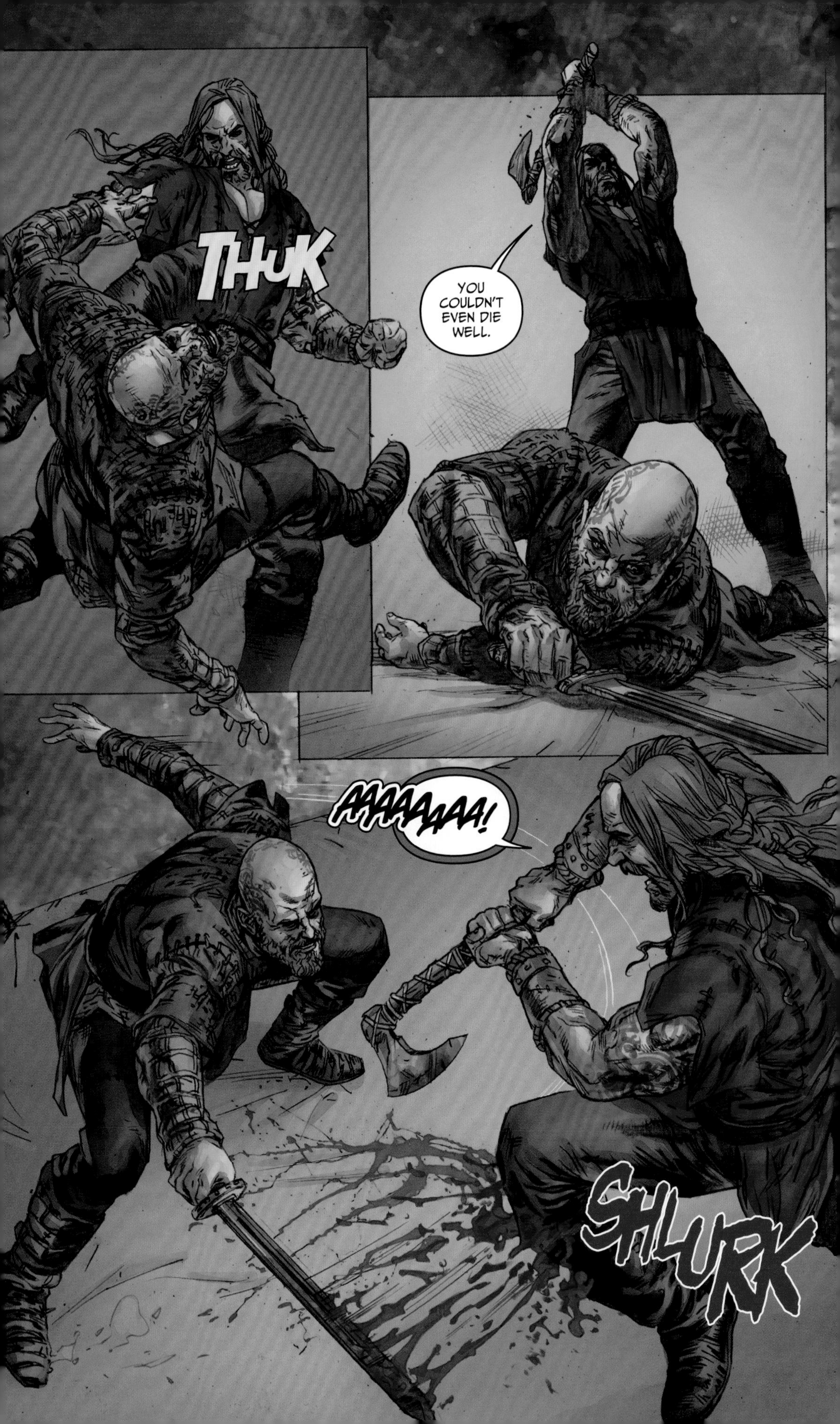
THUK
YOU COULDN'T EVEN DIE WELL.
AAAAAAAA!
SHLURK

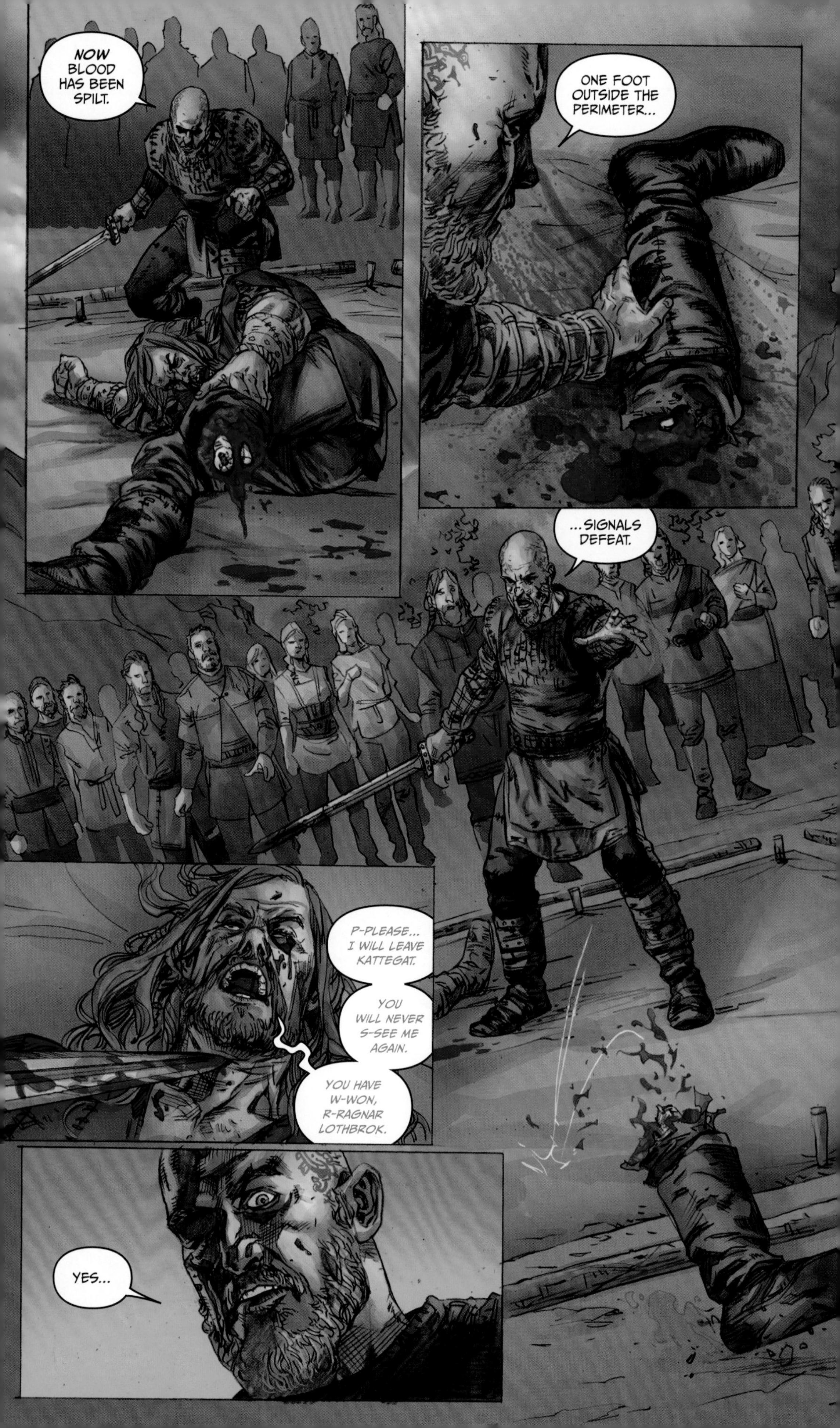
NOW BLOOD HAS BEEN SPILT.
ONE FOOT OUTSIDE THE PERIMETER...
...SIGNALS DEFEAT.
P-PLEASE... I WILL LEAVE KATTEGAT.
YOU WILL NEVER S-SEE ME AGAIN.
YOU HAVE W-WON, R-RAGNAR LOTHBROK.
YES...

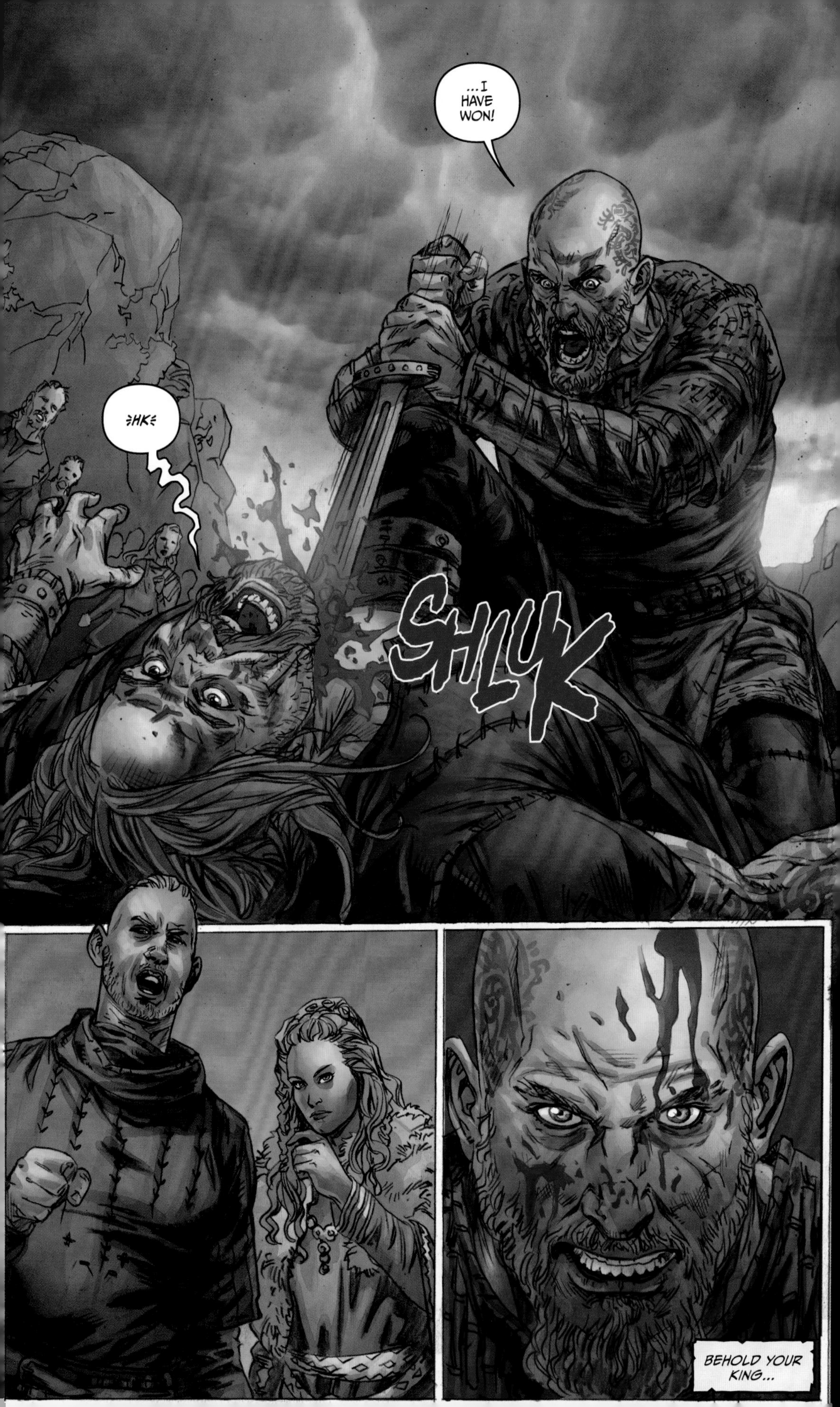
...I HAVE WON!
HK
SHLUK
BEHOLD YOUR KING...

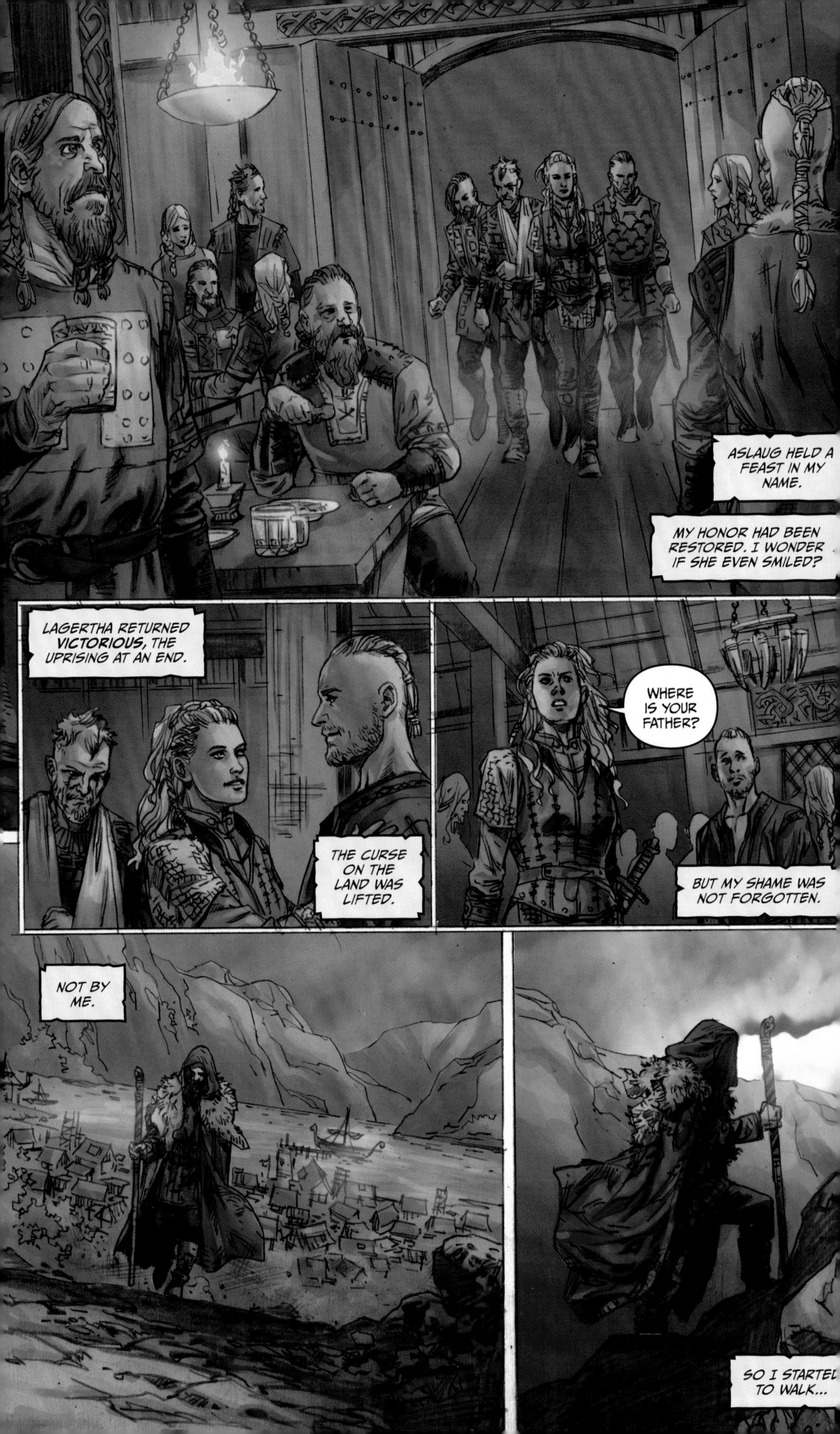
ASLAUG HELD A FEAST IN MY NAME.
MY HONOR HAD BEEN RESTORED. I WONDER IF SHE EVEN SMILED?
LAGERTHA RETURNED VICTORIOUS, THE UPRISING AT AN END.
THE CURSE ON THE LAND WAS LIFTED.
WHERE IS YOUR FATHER?
BUT MY SHAME WAS NOT FORGOTTEN.
NOT BY ME.
SO I STARTED TO WALK...

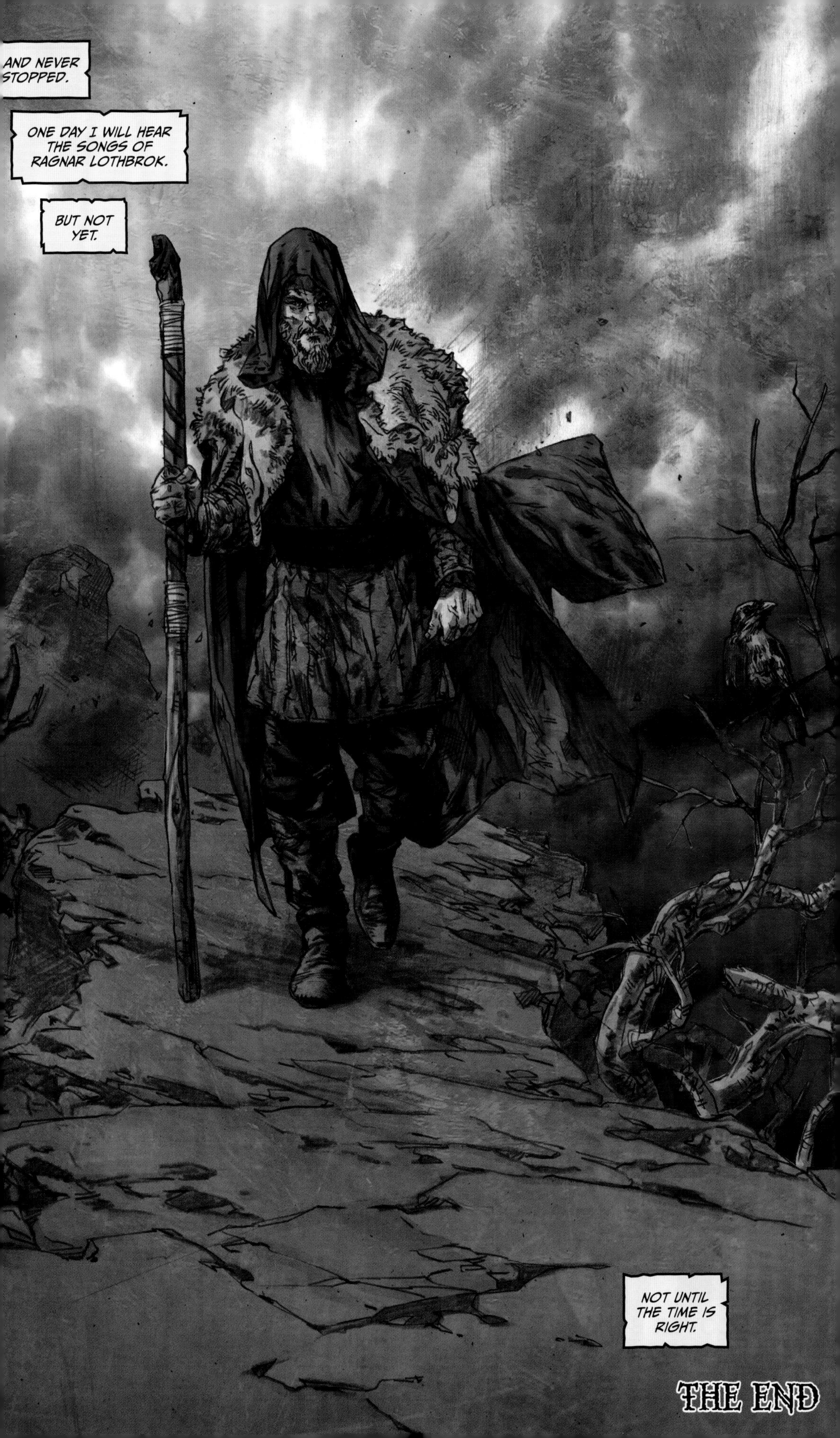
AND NEVER STOPPED.
ONE DAY I WILL HEAR THE SONGS OF RAGNAR LOTHBROK.
BUT NOT YET.
NOT UNTIL THE TIME IS RIGHT.
THE END

# COVER GALLERY

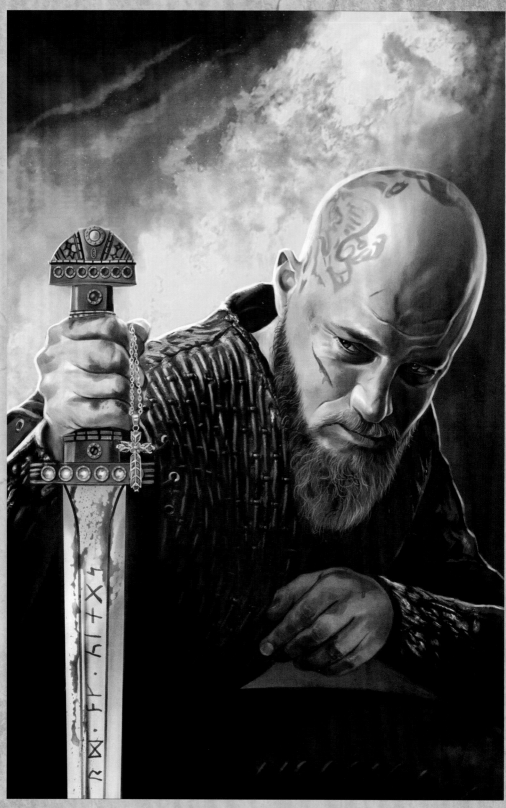

**#1 COVER B
MARK HAMMERMEISTER**

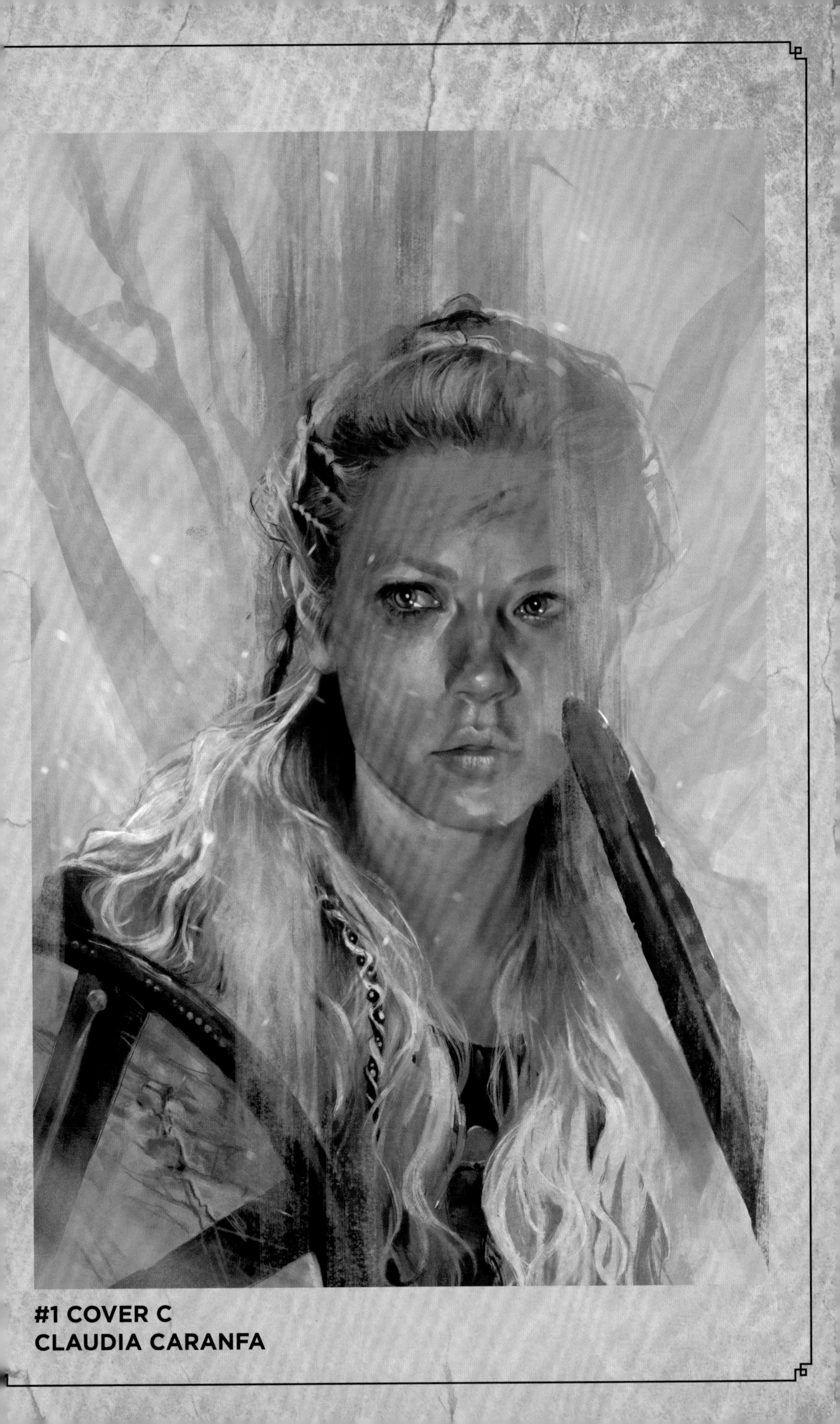

#1 COVER C
CLAUDIA CARANFA

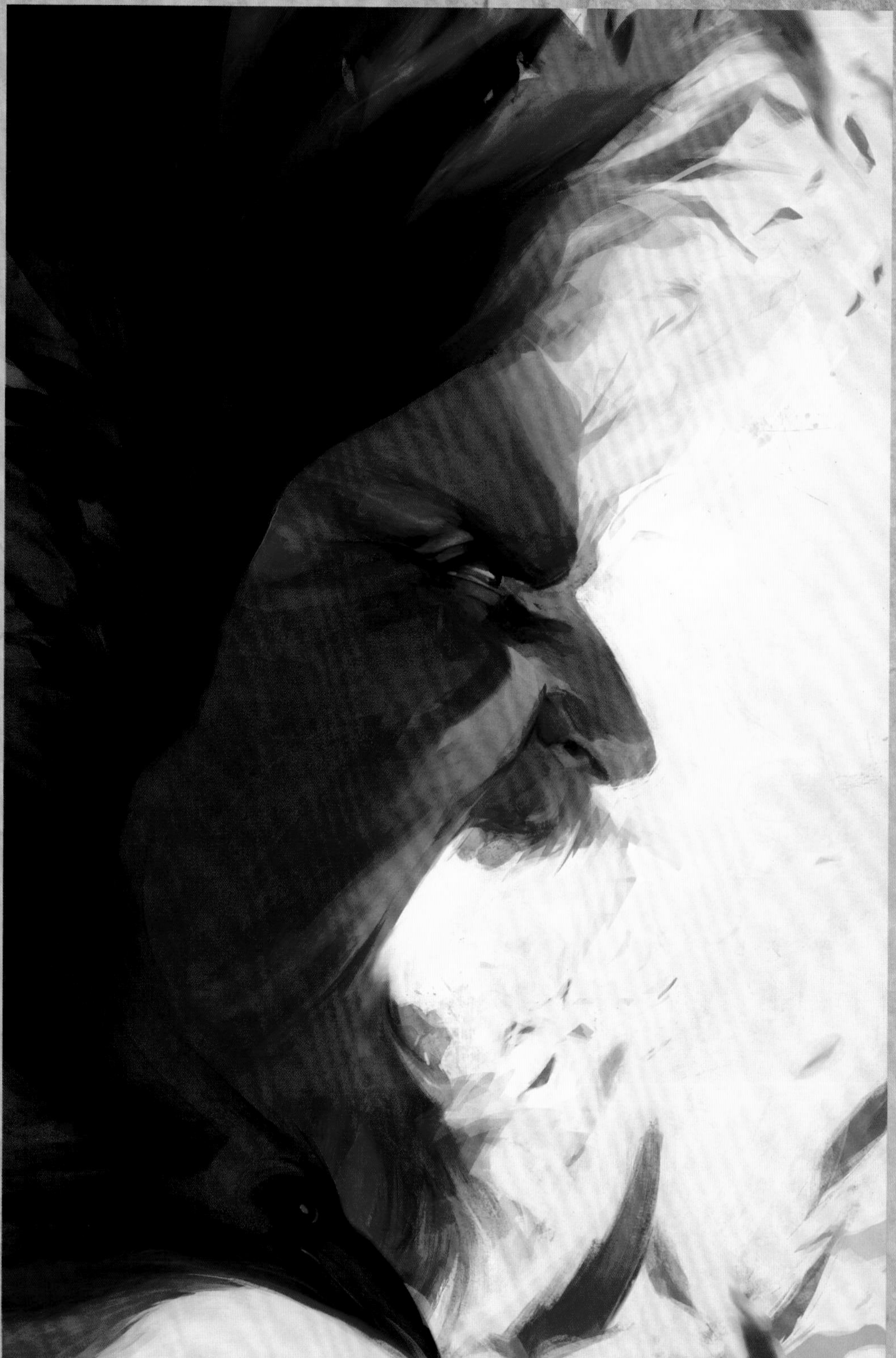

**#1 COVER D**
**VERITY GLASS**

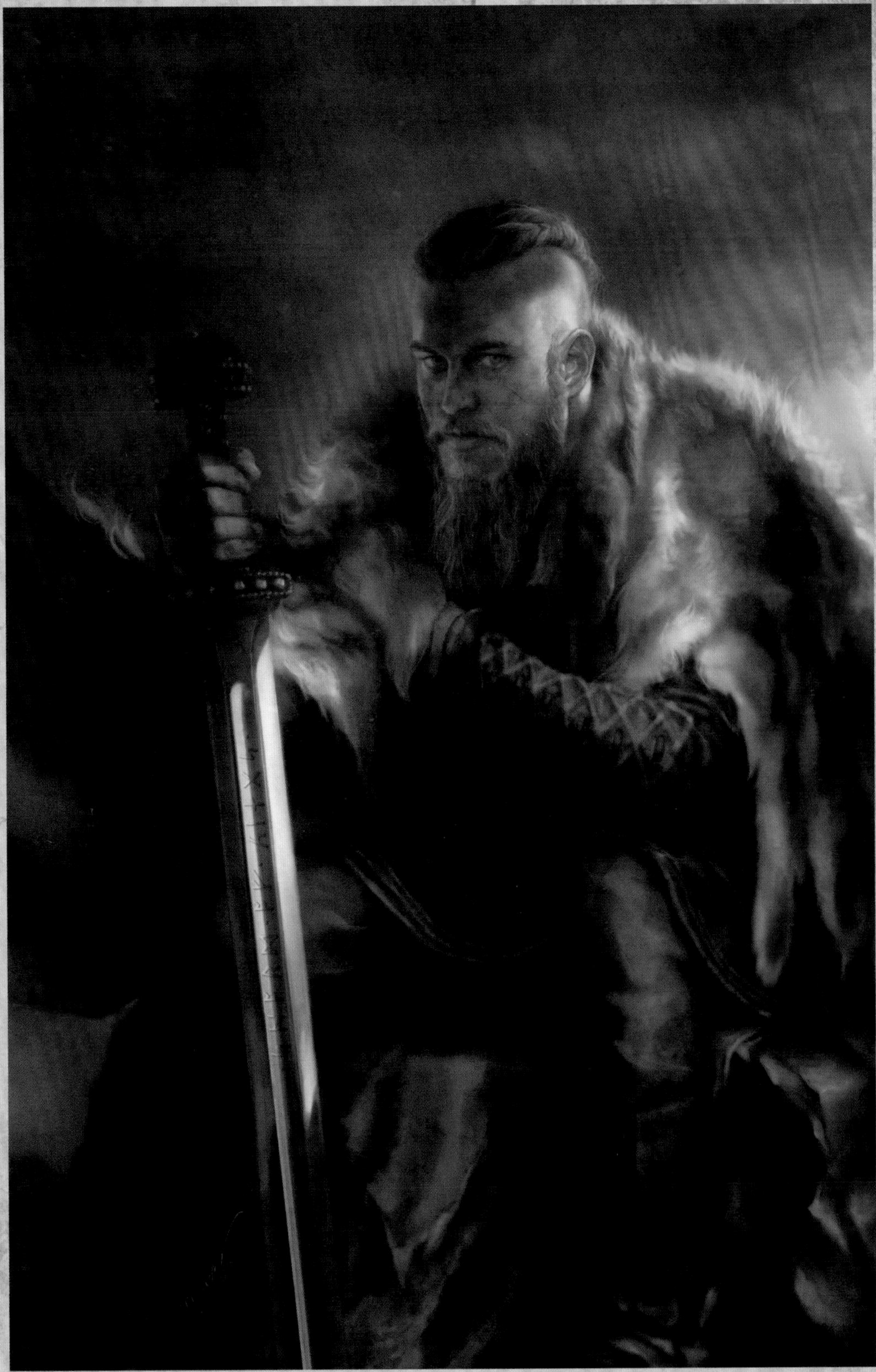

**#1 COVER E**
**JOSH BURNS**

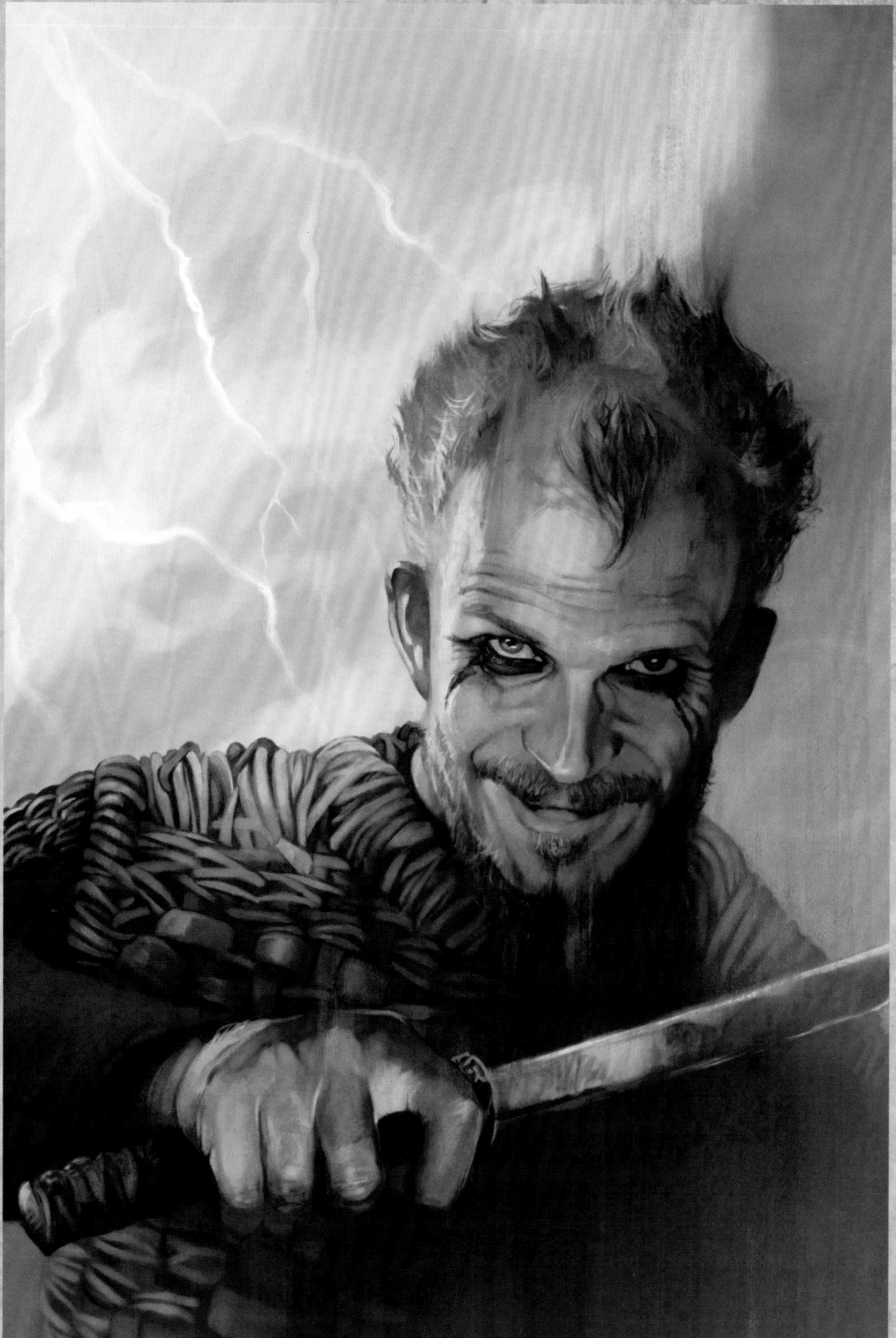
#3 COVER A
CLAUDIA CARANFA

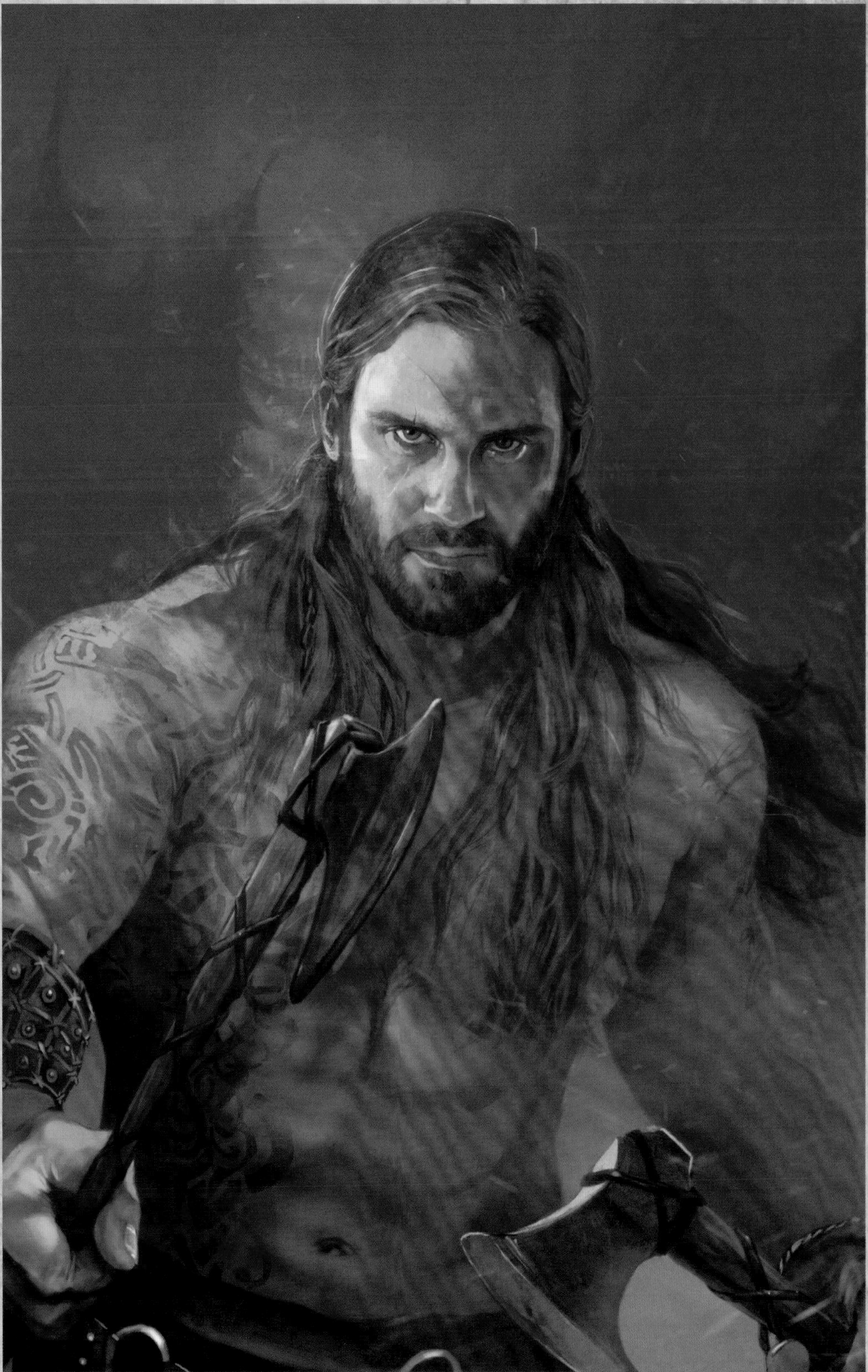

**#4 COVER C**
**CLAUDIA CARANFA**

# CAPTURING THE VIKINGS

**The art on a comic book like *Vikings* starts with the character likenesses, making sure we fully capture the characters you know and love from the screen, from Ragnar and Lagertha to the otherworldly Seer. So as we bring you this collection of *Uprising*, we thought we'd shhowcase these stunning character sketches by our artist Daniel Indro...**

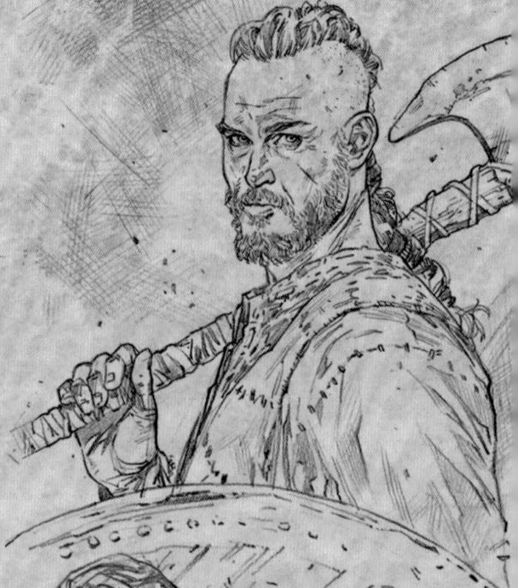

Ragnar

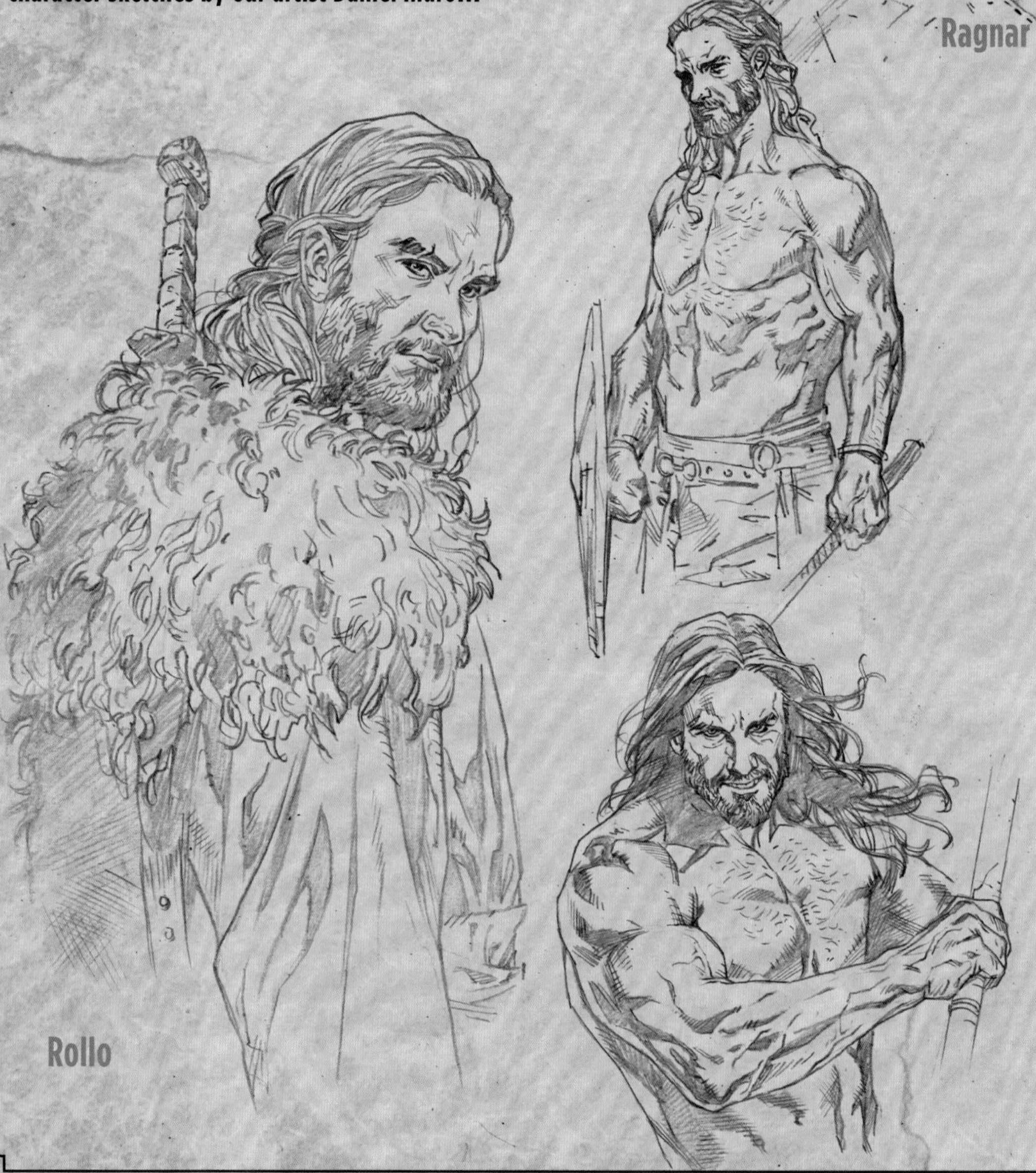

Rollo

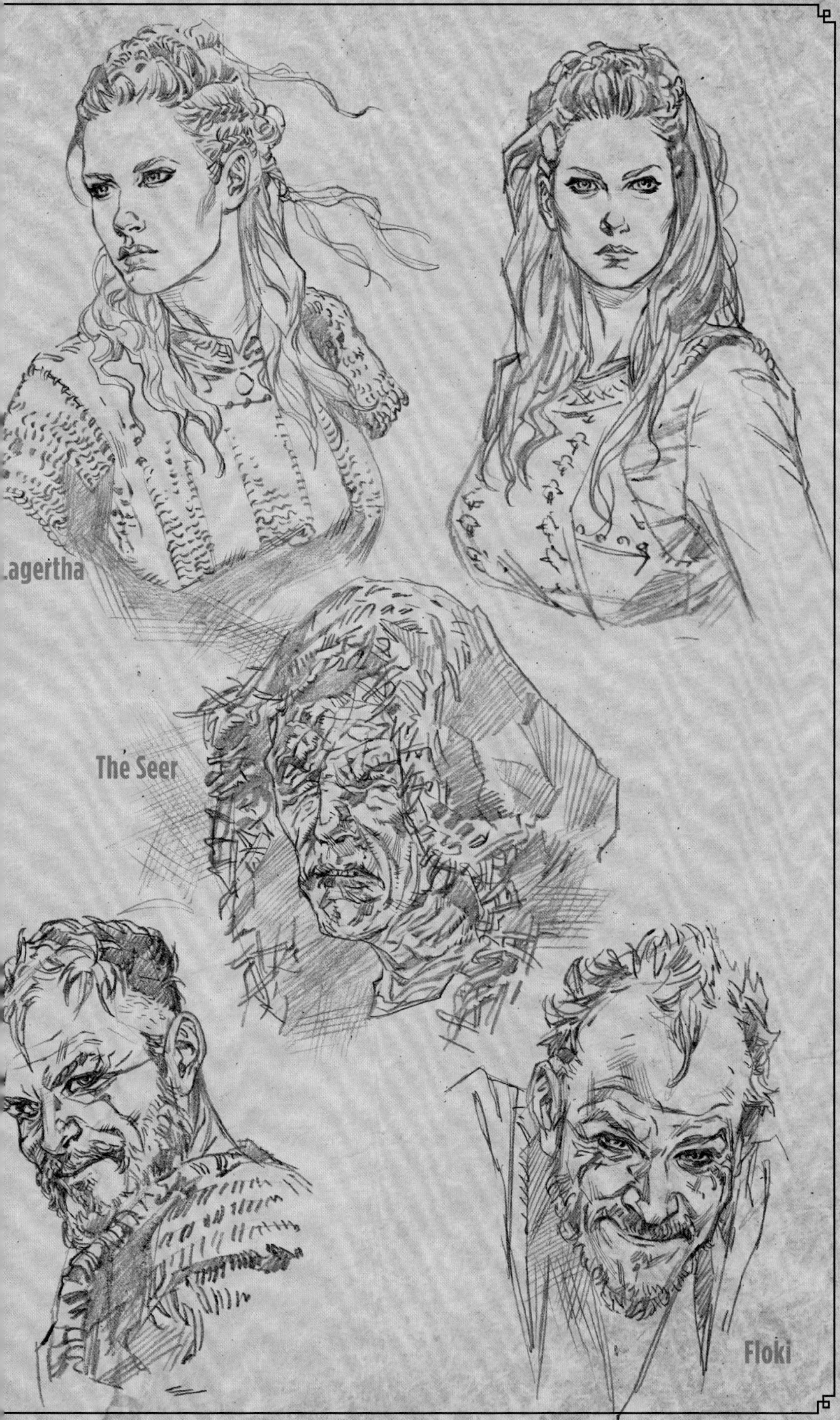
Lagertha
The Seer
Floki

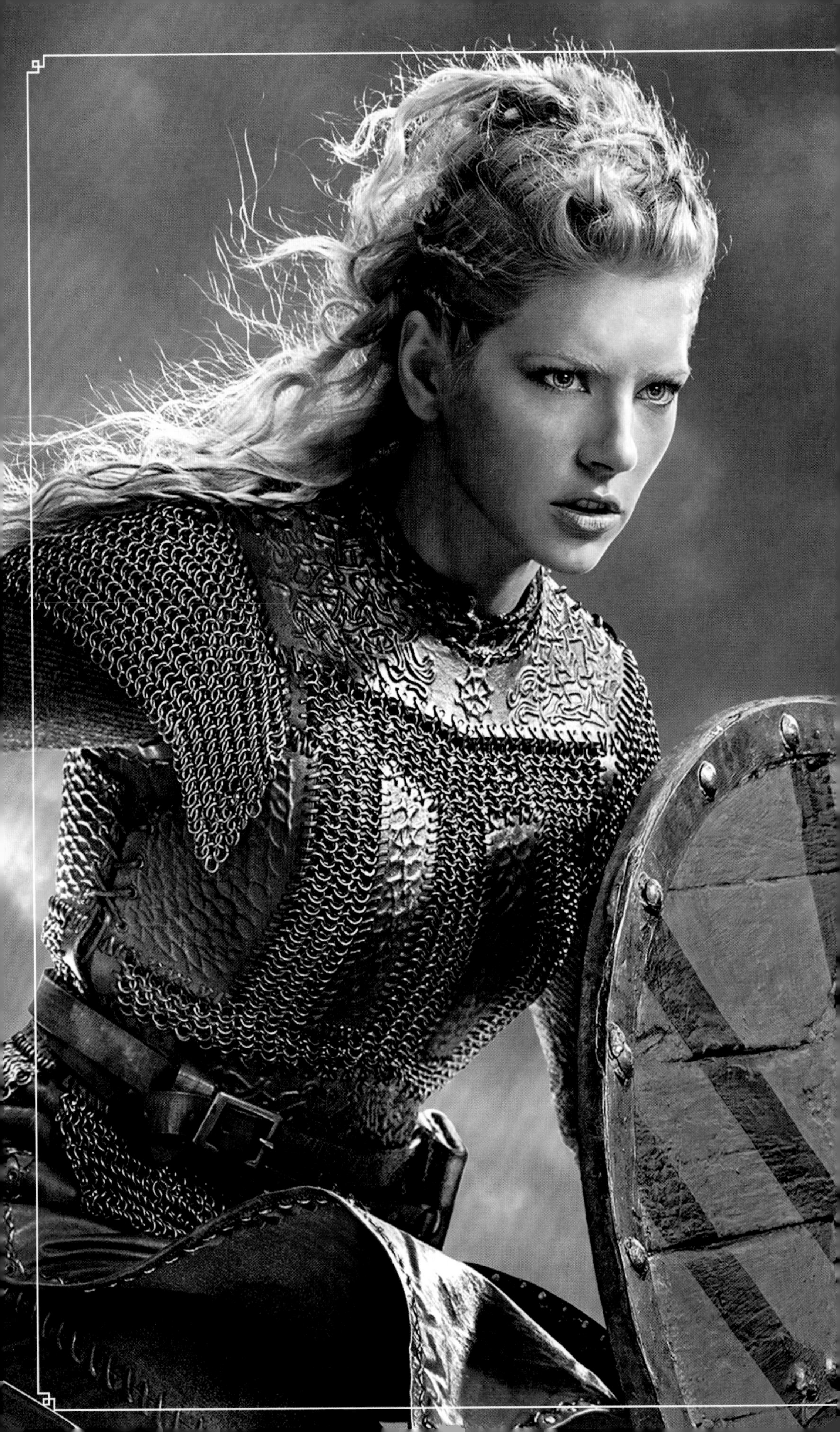

# IN SEARCH OF LAGERTHA

LAGERTHA HAS PROVED TO BE ONE OF *VIKINGS'* MOST POPULAR CHARACTERS, ON BOTH THE SCREEN AND THE COMICS PAGE, A FIERCE AND BEAUTIFUL SHIELD MAIDEN AND EARL WHO CAN HOLD HER OWN AGAINST ANY MAN. BUT DID LAGERTHA EXIST IN REAL LIFE, AND IF SO, WHO WAS THIS WARRIOR WOMAN? CAVAN SCOTT EXPLORES THE WOMAN BEHIND THE LEGEND...

The historical Lagertha is a mystery. Who was this fierce warrior? What was her relationship with legendary Viking Ragnar Lothbrok? And, most importantly, did she really exist at all?

Depending on the translation, we first meet Lathgertha, Ladgerda or Lagertha in the work of the 12th Century Danish chronicler, Saxo Grammaticus. According to his nine-volume *Gesta Danorum* (or *The Deeds of the Danes*), Lagertha's story began when Frø, king of Sweden, killed the Norwegian King Siward, conquering all of Norway in the bargain. To add insult to fatal injury, Frø then proceeded to throw every woman in Siward's family into a brothel.

News of the scandal reached the ears of Siward's grandson, a certain Ragnar Lothbrok. Swearing bloody revenge, Ragnar rode to Norway and clashed with Frø's men. The battle raged, the invaders struggling to gain ground until reinforcements magically arrived, fighting like devils alongside Ragnar. Where had these mysterious warriors come from? No one guessed that Siward's female relatives, understandably annoyed by their ill treatment, had disguised themselves as men in order to join the fight.

The brightest and best of these woman warriors was a young girl called Lagertha. As she charged to the front, her long hair cascaded down her back. Ragnar was stunned. She was a woman? Surely not! According to Saxo, Lagertha fought with "the courage of a man," leading all to marvel at her 'matchless deeds.'

Ragnar instantly fell head over hairy breeches in love.

But the course of true love never runs smoothly. Frø was defeated and Ragnar crowned as king. All he needed was a queen, and none other than Lagertha would do. There was only one snag – Lagertha didn't fancy Ragnar in the slightest.

Never one to admit defeat, Ragnar set off to woo her in typically Viking manner. Lagertha's home was guarded by a bear and great hound. To prove his devotion, Ragnar strangled the ferocious dog with his bare hands, and drove a spear through the bear's heart, killing it with one blow.

Who says romance is dead?

Ragnar's show of strength turned Lagertha's head. She fell into his presumably blood-stained arms and they were wed. Before long, Lagertha gave birth to three children; a son called Fridleif and two daughters whose names are lost in the mists of time.

But there was trouble in paradise. Ragnar never forgave Lagertha for setting her animals on him.

The resentment festered until Ragnar announced that he was divorcing his wife and returning to Denmark. The decision may have also had something to do with the fact that he'd fallen helplessly in lust with Þóra Borgarhjortr, daughter of King Herrauðr of Sweden.

Lagertha remarried, but continued to hold a flame for Ragnar. Years later, she learned that her former husband was fighting a civil war in Denmark. She flew to his side, bringing with her 120 ships. Once again, the battle wasn't going well. Ragnar's son, Siward, had been critically wounded, and all looked lost. That was until Lagertha led her warriors around the back of the enemy and attacked viciously from the rear.

Cue much celebration. Lagertha had saved the day. Again. However, back home, Lagertha's current husband wasn't happy. The pair quarreled on her return, with Lagertha winning the argument, but stabbing him to death with a spearhead she'd secreted in her frock. Her husband dead, Lagertha: "usurped the whole of his name and sovereignty; for this most presumptuous dame thought it pleasanter to rule without her husband than to share the throne with him".

Do you get the feeling that Saxo didn't really like Lagertha?

But did she actually exist? Many scholars believe not. They say that the ultimate shield maiden was a complete fabrication on Saxo's part, in order to show how wild and terrible these heathen women were before they were civilized by good old Christianity. Some claim he took inspiration from a courageous 6th-Century warrior queen called Hlaðgerðr, who helped King Halfdan of the Scylding defeat his enemies with the timely gift of 20 ships.

Others suggest that Lagertha is based upon the goddess Thorgerd, who would bring hailstorms thundering down on her enemies. Like Lagertha, Thorgerd charged into battle with her long hair flowing down her back. Whether she also hid weapons in her gowns is not confirmed.

Whether fact or fiction, Lagertha has proved herself to be a woman to be reckoned with in any of her incarnations, a tradition that continues with her portrayal by Katheryn Winnick on screen in *Vikings*.

# 12 THINGS TO KNOW IF YOU'RE A VIKING SLAVE!

## WORDS: CAVAN SCOTT

IF YOU'RE READING THIS, YOU PROBABLY FIND VIKINGS INHERENTLY COOL. HOWEVER, NOT EVERY ASPECT OF VIKING LIFE CAN BE CELEBRATED. LET'S FACE IT, VIKING RAIDERS REGULARLY MURDERED, PILLAGED AND RAPED. THEY ALSO CAPTURED SLAVES. LOTS OF THEM. ACCORDING TO THE MEDIEVAL ANNALS OF ULSTER, 3,000 LOCALS WERE CAPTURED DURING A SINGLE RAID AROUND 900AD. THERE'S NO DOUBT ABOUT IT – SLAVERY WAS BIG BUSINESS. BUT WHAT COULD YOU EXPECT IF YOU WERE A VIKING SLAVE? THE ANSWER IS, NOT A LOT!

1. As a slave, you'd have little in the way of rights. Your masters could treat you like dirt, kill you, sacrifice you to the gods (usually by burning), or sexually abuse you, and no-one would come to your aid.

2. Sometimes other Vikings would also try to have sex with you. They'd try to keep it quiet though. If they were caught in the act without having asked permission, they'd have to pay a fine for the unauthorized use of someone else's property. Likewise, if they killed you without asking your master first, they'd also have to pay your full market value.

3. As well as helping around the home, slaves were required to help work the land, or to create textiles. Growing Viking fleets led to a huge demand for woolen sails, so slaves were tasked with weaving huge swathes of cloth.

Male thralls were also used to cut timber, build the longboats and even to row the boats to further raids.

4. You wouldn't eat as well as your masters. A slave's diet consisted largely of fish, while their owners feasted on meat and dairy.

5. If you died in service, your body would probably be left for the dogs or birds to eat. Waste not, want not.

6. If you became too old or infirm to work, you'd most likely be put out of your misery. After all, why would your master bother to look after a sick slave?

7. Any child of a female slave would automatically become the property of her master. He'd probably be the child's father anyway.

8. Slaves were sometimes expected to fight on behalf of their master. They could be forced to serve in local militia, or even ordered to fight to settle blood feuds.

9. You might not end up enthralled to a Viking family at all. Vikings sold slaves in the thousands. The biggest markets were the Greek, Moorish or Saracen territories, where literate young monks would often be castrated to become teachers or administrators.

Traders also took special care of female slaves – an attractive girl slave could fetch three times the price of a healthy male.

10. Slaves wore heavy iron neck rings on the way to market. Some masters even insisted that their thralls wore them at home too.

11. Even your master's death wasn't a cause for celebration. You'd probably be killed too. On the Isle of Man, female slaves were bludgeoned to death and cremated with animals.

Their remains were then placed in their master's tomb to serve him in death as they did in life.

12. There was a chance – a very small chance – that as a slave you could be freed for loyal service. Freed men and women became a part of society, sometimes even going on further raids themselves. However, if as a freed man you died without an heir, your former master could legally claim your property as his own.

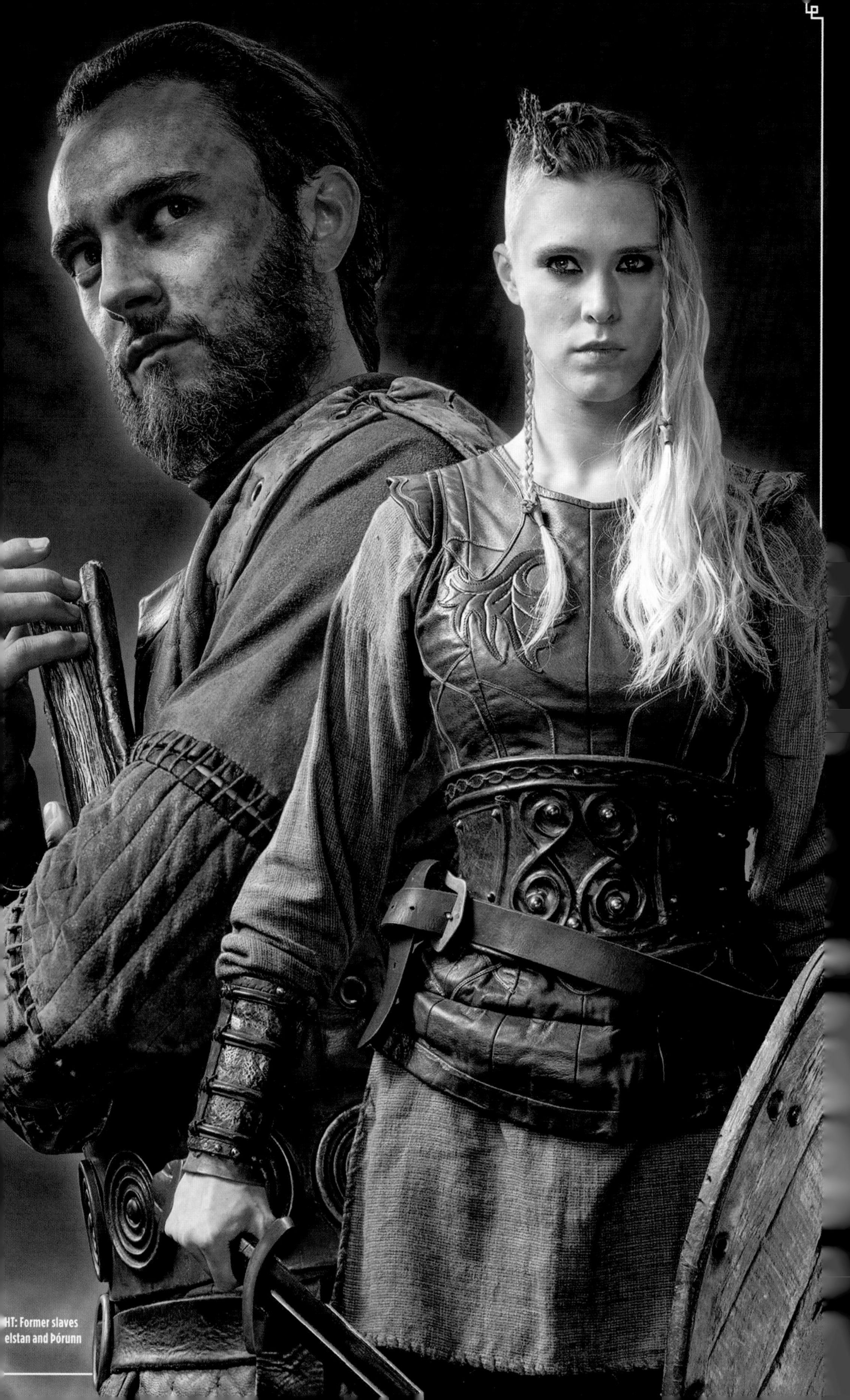

HT: Former slaves
elstan and Þórunn

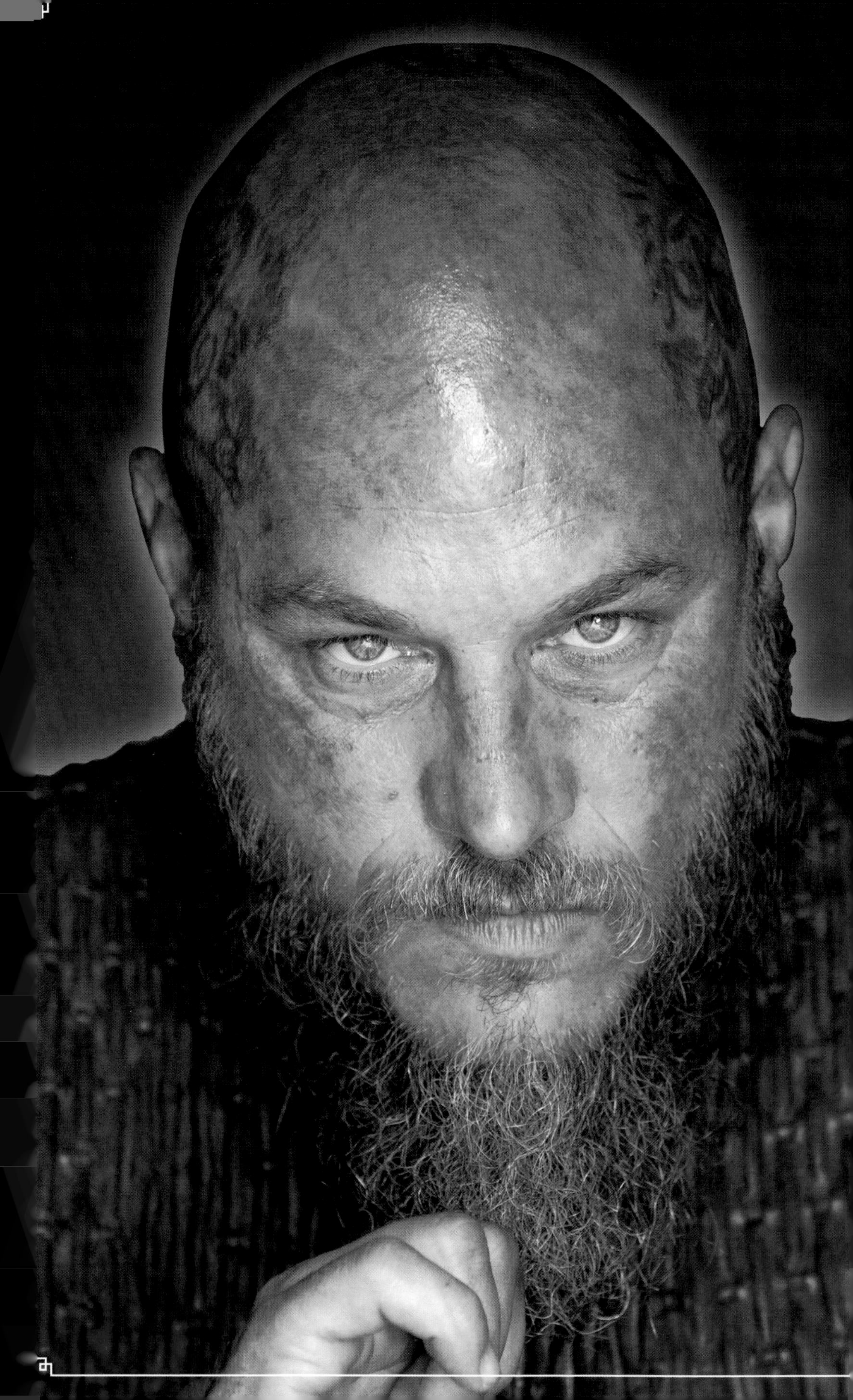

# A MATTER OF HONOR

CAVAN SCOTT ON BLOOD FEUDS, DUELS, VIKING HONOR AND HOW SCORN POLES ARE STILL BEING RAISED IN SCANDINAVIA IN THE 21ST CENTURY...

Insulting a Viking's honor was a risky business. In a society where bravery, strength and fair play were revered, being publicly shamed could bring dire consequences.

If you were insulted, you had to respond as quickly as possible. Having your honor called into question was as shameful as being caught fleeing from battle.

Of course, you could simply kill the person who had insulted you. However, this was classed as manslaughter. You would be expected to pay compensation to their grieving family, and if you didn't, you risked triggering a blood feud that could last for generations.

The legal way of defending your honor was to challenge the person who had dared insult you to an *hólmganga*. This was a duel, fought on an uninhabited island.

The *hólmganga* operated under strict rules. A cloak or ox hide was pegged out on the ground, usually no larger than eight-feet square. This was your battlefield. Step off the cloak during the fight and you would be named a *níðingr* - a nobody - and could face exile from the village.

You were allowed three shields, in case your first broke, and could fight with spears, sword or axes. If you were wounded in battle, you could buy yourself out of the duel. However, if you were killed, your property would automatically go to your opponent. Deaths during *hólmganga* were not classed as manslaughter. There was no compensation to pay, and the dead man's family couldn't slaughter one of your own kin in retaliation. The loser was officially dishonored... forever.

The practice of *hólmganga* was so widespread that it even proved to be a profitable enterprise for some travelers. They would wander from town to town, searching for the weediest-looking men they could find. They would then insult the weakling, safe in the knowledge that the disgruntled local would have no choice but to call a *hólmganga* to protect their honor. Once the traveler had wiped the floor with their victim, he would collect his winnings and continue happily on their way, looking for the next poor specimen to insult.

The worst insult of all was the *níðstöng*, or scorn-pole. The process was simple. First, you carved a curse into a nine-foot staff, then thrust the pole into the ground outside the gates of your enemy's town or outside their particular house.

Now came the gruesome bit. You would decapitate a horse, ideally your enemy's own horse. There was no need to ask their permission first. The head (whch was often skinned) was placed on top of the pole, and pointed towards your enemy's door. If this was too gruesome for you, then you could use an animal's skull instead, although if you couldn't stand the sight of blood, you frankly had no right to call yourself a Viking!

The horse's head served two purposes. First of all, it was thought to scare away any spirits that protected your enemy's land in hope that their harvest would fail. The second was less spiritual. Anyone who saw the pole would know that your enemy was either as stupid or cowardly as the slaughtered animal – or in most cases, probably both. They would be a laughing stock of the community until they could restore their honor or died.

While the most famous account of a *níðstöng* dates back to 1200AD and the Egil saga, scorn-poles are still being used in the modern day. On December 21, 2006, Icelandic newspaper *Fréttablaðið* reported that a farmer from Bíldudalur had raised a *níðstöng* against his neighbor, complete with a skinned calf's head. The feud between the two men started when Oskar Björnsson ran over Þorvaldur Stefansson's puppy in his eight-ton tractor. Stefansson insisted that Björnsson had targeted the dog on purpose, and raised the pole, declaring that he wouldn't rest until Björnsson was either outlawed or dead.

In the 21st Century, of course, the dispute wasn't resolved by a *hólmganga*. Instead, Björnsson went straight to the local police!

# VIKINGS™
## UPRISING

## CREATOR BIOS

### CAVAN SCOTT

Award-winning author Cavan Scott is the writer of *Vikings: Godhead* and *Vikings: Uprising, Torchwood,* and *Doctor Who: The Ninth Doctor* for Titan Comics. He also writes the bestselling *Star Wars: Adventures in Wild Space* book series. Find him at www.cavanscott.com

### DANIEL INDRO

Daniel Indro is an Indonesian comic book artist whose work includes *Vikings: Uprising, Doctor Who: The Tenth Doctor* and *Doctor Who: The Twelfth Doctor* and *Warhammer 40,000: Will of Iron*, all for Titan Comics.

### KEVIN ENHART

Kevin Enhart is a French writer, artist and colorist, living in France with his love, his kids, his crazy cats and his invisble friend, who seldom leaves his side. After working with several artists and small publishers, he allied with Titan Comics for *Puss in Boots*, before coloring over the amazing work of Daniel Indro on *Vikings*. Besides preparing his creator-owned series, he has since excelled on coloring *Warhammer 40,000* and Kim Newman's *Anno Dracula*.